AF521283

STRATEGIC MATERIALS

A Resource Challenge for India

STRATEGIC MATERIALS

A Resource Challenge for India

Ajey Lele
Parveen Bhardwaj

idsa
INSTITUTE FOR DEFENCE STUDIES & ANALYSES
NEW DELHI

PENTAGON PRESS

Strategic Materials: A Resource Challenge for India

Ajey Lele and Parveen Bhardwaj

First Published in 2014

Copyright © Institute for Defence Studies and Analyses, New Delhi

ISBN 978-81-8274-786-9

All rights reserved. No part of this publication may be reproduced, stored in a retrieval system, or transmitted, in any form or by any means, electronic, mechanical, photocopying, recording, or otherwise, without first obtaining written permission of the copyright owner.

Disclaimer: The views expressed in this book are those of the authors and do not necessarily reflect those of the Institute for Defence Studies and Analyses, or the Government of India.

Published by
PENTAGON PRESS
206, Peacock Lane, Shahpur Jat,
New Delhi-110049
Phones: 011-64706243, 26491568
Telefax: 011-26490600
email: rajan@pentagonpress.in
website: www.pentagonpress.in

In association with
Institute for Defence Studies and Analyses
No. 1, Development Enclave,
New Delhi-110010
Phone: +91-11-26717983
Website: www.idsa.in

Printed at Aegean Offset Printers, Greater Noida, U.P.

Contents

APPENDICES

Acknowledgements

We would like to thank Dr Arvind Gupta, Director General IDSA for encouraging us to undertake this work. We would also like to thank Mr Vivek Kaushik, Ms Nidhi Pant, Mr Vivek Dhankar, Ms Asha Malik, Mr Sudhanshu Sharma, Mr Shyam Hari and Mr Mukesh Jha for all the assistance provided to bring out this work. The contents of this manuscript reflect our personal views.

Ajey Lele

Parveen Bhardwaj

List of Figures and Tables

Figures

Tables

The Thought

The March 26, 2011 issue of the *Wall Street Journal* published a report pointing out that the car manufacturing giants like Ford Motor Co, Volkswagen, BMW, Toyota, etc. were facing problems due to the non-availability of the material Xirallic, which is used in metallic paints required for glistening and shimmering the car appearance. The sole producer of the pigment—a Japanese company located at the east coast of Japan—suffered significantly because of the March 11, 2011 tsunami and the subsequent release of nuclear radiation from the Fukushima nuclear plant.

The Japanese plant was the only one feeding global demands. Therefore, as production there crashed, the car manufacturers were not able to offer many colours in the 2011 range, due to shortage of Xirallic. This subsequently resulted in forcing them to make wholesale changes across the board: brochures, dealer inventories, press photographs, touch-up paint kits, model codes and so on.

The industry nevertheless tried to find a solution to this problem. A new plant was opened in some other state. Also, many makers switched to alternative pigments, due to the supply issues. Over a period of time, the Onahama plant in Japan too restarted production.[1] However, such an incidence triggers various questions. First, is overdependence on a single source correct? Second, will the alternative materials always be available? Third, in case of non-availability of the alternative material, wouldn't a company having monopoly manipulate the market? Fourth, can the possibilities of creating artificial shortages (including industrial rivalry) be ruled out even though the Xirallic short supply resulted because of a natural disaster?

The important question that ultimately follows is: what would happen if suddenly the supply of an important material required for the production of medical or military equipment gets discontinued? Based on this single incidence, we can visualise the ramifications. In short, any brake in supply chain of critical materials would possibly lead to disastrous consequences.

It is important for the states (or non-states) to have a plan to address the issues in this regard. They need to appreciate the requirements of the materials which could be critical in nature for their industries including important strategic industries. Every state has a certain amount of dependency on foreign sources in respect of procurement of technology, hardware and software required to cater for their strategic industry needs. On occasions, industrial houses do have technologies and expertise available with them to run their industrial complex, but are dependent on various other agencies both within and outside the country for the procurement of raw material. Such material comes from the nature and is sold to the industry either in the natural or processed form. Mostly, strategic and critical materials are found either beneath the earth or under the sea. Obviously, owing to the inherent composition of the 'mother earth', such materials are not available within the geographical boundaries of every state. Hence, states depend on other natural resources rich states for the procurement of such materials.

Various materials can be found in nature either in pure or composite forms. Minerals are the substances which are naturally formed in the earth and have specific chemical structure and composition and are found stable at room temperatures. On various occasions, in the literature, the terminologies 'strategic materials' and 'strategic minerals' are used interchangeably. This could be probably because there is hardly any difference between them, particularly, since the word 'strategic' has been prefixed to both 'materials' and 'minerals'.

This study attempts an analysis of strategic materials/minerals in the Indian context. Here, the purpose is to study the availability, requirement, utility and deficiency of strategic materials. Also, an attempt has been made to identify the deficiencies and discover the dependence on other states. This is a constricted study which essentially revolves around appreciating the possible requirements of few major strategic sectors of technologies in respect of strategic materials/minerals.

The basic limitation of this study arises from the limited availability of the (specific) data in general. Also, in the Indian context, there is no detailed information available to realise the nature of critical materials supply chain. More importantly, strategic industry leaders are not ready to discuss the actual requirements of the strategic materials and demand and supply patterns for their industries for obvious reasons. Hence, this study attempts more of a macro-level analysis based on various approximations.

The purpose behind undertaking this study is to identify the vulnerabilities (if any) of the strategic industry and suggest a possible way forward. The intention over here is not to get into any specificity, but to attempt to understand the bigger picture. The work is entirely based on the information available in the open sources. It is important to note that the process for the successful management of a state's strategic material needs would involve a multi-disciplinary effort and require the contribution from various government agencies, including science and technology, defence, commerce and foreign affairs. The recommendations at the end of this work take into account this fact.

NOTE

1. http://www.richardaucock.com/xirallic-what-is-it/#sthash.8rabN3f5.dpuf (Accessed November 12, 2011).

1

Introduction

Since time immemorial states have been fighting wars amongst each other for various reasons. One of the reasons has been to gain control of natural resources. It has been observed that the survival of a nation rests upon continued access to and use of natural resources. Access to water is essential for everything: from the maintenance of a healthy population to agricultural production and industrial development. Food, mineral deposits, forestry resources and oil deposits provide a socioeconomic basis for the development of a state. The crucial significance of various natural resources thus ensures that threats to these resources become much politicised, sparking controversy, and at times even leads to intrastate or interstate conflicts.[1]

Control over natural resources has been one of the key determinants of wars in the past. An early study of causes of modern wars points out that during 1878–1918, 14 of the 20 major wars had significant economic causes, often related to conflicts over resources. The rise of industrialism has led to the struggle for raw materials. There have been cases like the desire of Chile to secure a share in the nitrate trade. Chile was up in arms against Bolivia and Peru for the control of guano mineral deposits (War of the Pacific, 1879–1884).[2] In recent times, the best example, in respect of conflicts over resources, is the 1990 Gulf War. The United States (US) had justified fighting this war by claiming that it was in tune with the Carter Doctrine.[3] All this essentially indicates that 'management' of resources is a difficult art, and 'mismanagement' could even lead to a war. Interestingly, particular types of resources are required not only for undertaking the socio-economic development of a nation but also for keeping its war-waging potential intact. For the development and manufacture of various types of military hardware, different types of natural materials are used as raw materials.

Over the years, technologies have dictated the war-fighting doctrines of various nation-states. Both the World Wars demonstrated the importance of the transportation facilities and enormous quantities of equipment of all kinds required to fight a war and also sustain waroperations. The experience brought forth, as no human experience had ever done before, the value of minerals and of the metals derived from them. Steel, copper, lead, zinc, coal, petroleum and the common mineral products and many others little known or appreciated before, such as tungsten, chromium, manganese, etc., all were in unprecedented demand to keep the war-fighting formations operational.[4] In every quarter of the world, there was a scramble for supplies. This forced the states to develop domestic mineral resources and take measures to import these materials and, possibly, acquire control of foreign supplies. In the 21st century, the war-fighting requirements of states should have shown a change with the passage of time; however, the fundamental doctrine still remain the same. Developments in technology have been a key to various changes in warfare tactics, and that has led to increased dependence on strategic materials.

However, it important to note that materials of various kinds have always been of great significance for human society as a whole, and not just for militaristic reasons. In fact, since ancient times, materials have already remained central to human progress. An archaeological system called 'Three-Age System' depicts the advancements of societies. The three-age system[5] is a periodisation of human prehistory into three consecutive time periods, named for their respective tool-making technologies:

- The Stone Age
- The Bronze Age
- The Iron Age

This system could be viewed as the most apt system towards describing the progression of human society. It is important to appreciate that 'materials' have always been central towards depicting the progress of human society since prehistoric times. Steel Age could also become part of such system to depict the progression from the prehistoric to the present era.

This book focuses more on strategic materials, and hence the history of materials discussed in the earlier paras is from the point of view of warfare. Materials as such are the key elements for any form of industry. Strategic materials are vital mainly for the Military Industrial Complexes for nation-states. No singular definition of strategic materials is possible because of the diversity in respect of usage, necessity, production and procurement of such materials. This term gets used under particular circumstances and is also governed by political and geographical parameters. A 'material' which could be of strategic relevance for one state need not necessarily be so for another state. Hence, it is important to put the notion of strategic materials into a broad context.

Essentially, the word strategic has a direct connotation with the military. However, in the 21st century world, it has gained a wider sense. In any long-term plan in the different fields of life—from social aspects to business interests to defence planning—the word strategic gets used copiously. Hence, various considered frameworks of planning are found being employed in various aspects of policymaking and schematising as Corporate Strategy, Social Strategy, Defence Strategy, etc.

The term materials is viewed as an all-encompassing word. It includes solids, liquids or even gases. Usually, the word material is synonymous with matter which broadly means a physical substance like water, sand, wood, rubber, coal, air, etc. Various kinds of materials are required to make or build any form of apparatus, structure, equipment, product, etc. Broadly, most of the materials usually discussed are solid in nature. At the same time, it needs to be emphasised that oil and gas are also called 'materials' at places.

When the word 'strategic' gets prefixed to the word 'materials', then the scope of subtext gets narrower. There may not be real consensus on the exact ambit of strategic materials; however, its direct as well as circuitous association with the military becomes obvious.

The subject 'materials' is more of a multidisciplinary theme, and hence could have different classifications based on the approach of analysis. Traditionally, the three major classes of materials are metals (e.g., steel), polymers (e.g., cloth) and ceramics (e.g., pottery). These classes usually have different sources, characteristics and applications.[6] Also, materials could be classified as minerals, organics or advanced materials.[7] Form the point of view of industry, minerals are viewed as the most important components of materials. In literature, the mineral materials have mostly been referred simply as minerals or materials. Various publications available on strategic materials, critical materials or strategic minerals have also been essentially debating similar issues. This book also uses the terminologies 'strategic materials' and 'strategic minerals' interchangeably. For the sake of clarity, in this book, the words 'mineral' and 'material' imply the same.

Probably, the first attempt to define strategic materials was made by the US Army and Navy Munitions Board following World War I. Two classifications were identified: strategic materials and critical materials. Strategic materials were distinguished by their essentiality to the national defence, their high degree of important reliance in wartime and the need for strict conservation and distribution control. Critical materials were considered less essential and more available domestically, requiring some degree of conservation.[8] Post-1994, the US agencies have stopped using the terminology critical materials, and identified them as either those materials being essential in war or those that would require prior provisioning or stockpiling. In general, the terminology critical materials has been rarely used in the literature.

Broadly, strategic materials could be defined[9] as the material:

- needed to supply the military, industrial and essential civilian needs of a state during a national emergency
- the material not found or produced in sufficient quantities to meet such needs of the state.

In general, strategic materials are viewed as key resources that transcend individual industries in their application.[10] These materials are obtained from several primary sources mainly by the extraction of natural minerals. They are made usable by processing them further, and in certain cases, they are mixed together to create a new material. It is difficult to have a universal definition of strategic materials. This is because these materials are required for the strategic industry, and every state could have a different perception regarding the definition of strategic industry. Also, the nature of the military hardware used by each country varies based its individual threat perceptions. The availability of the materials with a particular state either in natural form or otherwise also defines its criticality for that state. Hence, individual states have their own outlook regarding the materials that are strategic to them.

There are diverse materials available in nature. It is essential for every nation to device a comprehensive and coordinated policy first to identify the most important strategic materials for them. The basic problem arises from the lack of sufficient and exact knowledge about the end-user materials requirements for strategic industry both in the short- and long-term. It is important to note that any assessment about the nature of strategic materials needs would involve contributions from many people belonging to different branches of science and engineering besides the planners, lawyers and policymakers. To develop a holistic understanding of the subject, it is important to engage soil scientists, geologists, mining engineers, chemists, environmental and climate scientists, defence scientists and planners and economists.

The entire gamut of the management of strategic material involves various complex issues. The state agencies involved in this business require monitoring the adequacy of resources and reserves and keeping a check on production capacity and actual production cycle. They need to identify various constraints on production like potential bottlenecks, disruption scenarios, local cost structures, levels of political mortality, taxes and tariffs, incentives for further processing, markets for raw and processed products, competition from other producing countries, technological development impacting both supply and demand for materials. To undertake long-term planning, they need to factor in issues like the potential impact of embargoes, cartels, stockpiles and monopolies of particular states or agencies. Moreover, government policies, laws and regulations would affect the availability, reliability, and cost of producing materials.

Strategic materials in their natural form are not evenly distributed all across the globe. There are few regions in the world which are resources reach regions. However, it would not be correct to conclude that only the presence or absence of natural resources within a state makes that state prosperous. On the one hand, there are reach and developed states without abundant natural resources. On the other hand, there are poor, third world states in possession of abundant natural resources. Further, the industrial revolution during the 19th century played a major role in exploiting weak states with natural resources. Nevertheless, over a period of time, industrialised states have mostly been successful in 'managing' the materials to cater for their needs.

Particularly, states from the regions like Asia, Africa and Latin America are in the possession of abundant natural resources; however, for many years, industrial development has taken place outside these regions. This unequal distribution of natural resources continues to exist. Various international economic and trade policies have been covertly designed to suit the requirements of the big states. Also, there exists possibility that big states do undertake their stockpile planning by factoring the geopolitical realities in mind and would be building on their strategic materials reserves. It is also possible that each country could develop its own approach to address this issue mainly based on its needs for materials. It is important to appreciate that all materials could have some kind of strategic utility from industry perspective. However, amongst various known materials only a limited few (may be 20–25 in number) are viewed to have actual utility for the defence industry. Naturally, based on scale of use (military and non-military needs), level of import dependence and economic implications, individual states would take their own decisions on stockpile goals. This list of 20/25 types of materials could change based on the changes in the manufacturing processes and advent of new technologies.

Many strategic materials require substantial amount of energy for their processing. This may be in the form of electricity, coal, oil or gas depending on the type of processing or the location. The availability and the cost of energy can be critical to many mining and mineral producing ventures.[11] Also, at times the availability of water is important closer to the mining/processing site. States which are able to manage the resources and technologies for the purposes of mining and processing always stand to gain. In very many cases, it has been observed that the states that physically own the mines actually end up in engaging the developed states for the purposes of managing those mines.

The military industrial complex of a state is expected to make a significant contribution towards maintaining the security and defence of a state. In the present era, it would be incorrect to link only the organisations producing the guns, ships, missiles, aircraft and tanks as net contributors towards developing security infrastructure. Some industries could be directly supporting the security architecture, while some industries could be producing the dual-use technology. For example, the industries associated with information and communication technology (ICT) and agencies dealing with satellite technologies play an important role in various aspects of nation development including defence. More importantly, in the 21st century, the idea of security has expanded significantly, and its focus has widened from military security to energy security to environmental security. This change in sensitivities in regard to identifying what security means to a state in the present era also impacts the consideration about categorisation and identification of materials which are strategic for nation-states.

For the purpose of this book, essentially, the areas of the strategic interests for a nation-state have been acknowledged (obviously, with an India bias), and then subsequently a board identification has been done in respect of the materials required for such industries of strategic importance. Roughly, the materials required for strategic industries are viewed as strategic materials. Also, it is important to factor in the availability factor of such materials. There could be a case when a particular material required for a strategic industry is abundantly available with the geographic limits of the state, and the state has got the (affordable) wherewithal to extract and process this material. Under such circumstances that particular material may not fall under the category of 'strategic' for that state.

In addition, the materials identified as strategic are based on literature survey, availability factor and discussions with the experts. Few states have officially identified the materials which they consider strategic or the industries which they view as strategic. Such information also allows making a judgment for classification of the materials.

Aerospace industry is one of the most vital industries from the defence and economic standpoints. This sector also includes many industries related to electronics and sensor devolvement sectors. Avionics is at the heart of any aerospace industry. Air power for any nation-state constitutes aircraft and helicopters available on the inventory of defence forces and the air assets with the civilian sector (put in use during national emergencies). Moreover, satellite technologies are essentially dual-use technologies with both civilian and military utility. Aerospace sector also deals with manufacture of robotic technologies like unmanned aerial vehicles (UAVs) of different kinds. The 'space' constituent of this sector mainly constitutes rockets, satellites, radars, sensors, etc. As a whole, the aerospace industry is a strategic industry. This industrial sector is one of the largest consumers of a variety of materials, including many which are considered strategic.

Various materials used in defence industry are obviously viewed as strategic materials. This industrial sector involves two main components: one dealing with the production of military platforms like ships, tanks, missiles, etc. (a major component of aerospace industry is viewed as defence industry), and the other dealing with the manufacture of fighting equipment like guns, various types of weapons, ammunition, etc. Also, allied industries are involved in making items required for the usage of soldier like batteries, tents, uniforms, shoes, etc. Such items are available in the commercial domain too; however, the requirements of armed forces are of a specific nature because they operate in harsh and unfriendly terrain and weather conditions. Depending on the nature of warfare (mountain warfare, desert warfare, amphibious operations, etc.), the requirements of weapon systems as well as personal clothing differ. Hence, even a specific type of leather could be of strategic importance to a state.

Strategic significance of nuclear industry is obvious. Heavy metals such uranium, thorium, radium, plutonium and lithium are sources of nuclear energy. Uranium is the most important among these metals. The main ores of uranium are pitchblende, uranite, samarskite and thorianite. All over the world, there are some important geographical areas of uranium deposits. As compared to uranium, the geographical distribution of thorium is much more restricted. Main ores of thorium are monazite, allanite and thorianite.

Beryllium (obtained from beryl, which is found in association with feldspar and mica in pegmatites), zirnium (found in zircon in beach sands) and ilimenite (foll in the concentrated form in the beach sands) are other important nuclear minerals.[12] Broadly, nuclear power is generated mainly using uranium, which is a metal mined in various parts of the world. It is important to note that some military ships and submarines operate on nuclear power. For the production of nuclear weapons (bombs), uranium or plutonium is used. All this indicates that the nuclear policies (energy or military) of the country are heavily dependent on the availability of various kinds of materials. Apart from such materials required to perform the core functions, there are various other hardware requirements in respect of running a nuclear reactor and remaining in the state of readiness for demonstrating the capability to launch a nuclear attack.

Since the Second World War, the nuclear politics is found dominating the global security discourse, and any investment even in the nuclear energy sector also gets heavily scrutinised in respect of intent, nature of programme and the sources from which the materials required for the production of energy are procured. Nuclear material is the most controlled entity in the world and is controlled by a global nuclear regime. There are various rules, regulations and legal mechanisms concerning production, processing, use, reprocessing, control, safety standards, etc. in regard to such materials. The International Atomic Energy Agency (IAEA) is an international organisation responsible to promote the peaceful use of nuclear energy and controls nuclear materials. In general, the management of nuclear materials is a peculiar subject having varying geopolitical and technical subthemes. This book avoids debating the 'core' materials required for the nuclear sector. This is because such materials could be considered as a special category of materials, and they require a different approach for assessment. However, the materials that play an important role in the other hardware requirements in connection with the nuclear energy and nuclear weapons industry are discussed here.

Energy/Green technologies are fast emerging as the technologies of the modern era. Energy is essential to human civilisation, and the production of energy is dependent on a range of technologies, which, in turn, depend on a multitude of materials. Serious scarcities of any of these materials would limit our choices in the production and use of energy.[13] The increasing relevance and necessity of the energy and green technologies from the socioeconomic perspective makes this technology strategically important. Obviously, the materials needed to sustain this technology assume greater significance and could be described as strategic materials.

Particularly, post 1991, the Gulf War and the subsequent military conflicts have ended up making many states in the world conscious about the importance of strategic materials. Presently, the world is witnessing a rising phenomenon called Resource Nationalism. This form of nationalism depicts the tendency of people and governments to assert control over natural resources located within their territory. It has been observed that states hosting large reserves of natural resources try to secure greater economic benefit from their exploitation or leverage political gain through restricting supplies. Such an approach has operational and financial implications and also could lead to instability for the global markets. This issue is gaining importance particularly in the states which are poor and have problems regarding governance.[14] The general public perception in such states is that natural resource companies (both state owned and private) exploit the local population and the excavation sites for profits.

For any strategic industry, selecting the proper materials for a structural component is critical to engineering design. Materials selection is governed by many factors, some of which are in opposition. The principal selection factors include the service requirements and design life of the product; the availability of candidate materials and the appropriate data on application-specific properties for them; the company's *make* or *buy* decision for the system components; the customer preferences and, most importantly, the total life-cycle cost. Hence, it is important to have the current materials-property data, knowledge of factors such as materials options and life-cycle costs and available materials for a design based on experience derived from previous product developments.[15]

Against this backdrop, this book undertakes primary investigation of strategic materials with specific reference to India. It is understood that every state has different approaches towards its economic, foreign and strategic properties. Broadly, the scope of this work is restricted to studying the importance of strategic materials/minerals. No specific assessment has been carried out about the individual materials/minerals policies of the states and that of the status of materials/minerals industry.

The book has two overarching themes. First, it presents an overview of strategic minerals in general, and second, it undertakes India as a case study. Some of the chapters are informative in nature to set the tone for further analysis.

Majority of data collected and used for this work (the Indian context) is gathered from publications, annual reports, policy documents, and bilateral agreements, etc. of the following agencies:

- India's department of Mines
- Indian Geological Survey
- Ministries of Defence, External Affairs and Commerce
- Defence Research and Development Organisation (DRDO)
- Indian Space Research Organisation (ISRO)
- Depart of Atomic Energy (DAE)
- Indian Rare Earth's Limited
- Official reports, newspaper reports, research papers on various related issues, etc.

The data consists of:

- Production cycle
- Exports/imports statistics
- Supply/demands details
- Information on Stockpiles/reserves

Due care has been taken for the identification of strategic materials. A group of materials has been identified as strategic, and no order of precedence among this group has been identified. The work also presents a brief on the new materials and their possible utility. Appendices provide relevant information in respect of rules and regulations formulated by the Government of India.

NOTES

1. Ashley Hamilton, "Resource Wars and the Politics of Abundance and Scarcity", *Dialogue*, 1 (3), 2003, pp. 27–38.
2. Daron Acemoglu, et al., "A Dynamic Theory of Resource Wars", *The Quarterly Journal of Economics*, Oxford University Press, 2012, 127(1), pp.283–331.
3. The Carter Doctrine was a policy proclaimed by the US President in his State of the Union Address on January 23, 1980, which stated that the US would use military force if necessary to defend its national interests in the Persian Gulf region. The doctrine was a response to the threat posed by the Soviet troops in Afghanistan to the free movement of Middle East oil.
4. H. Foster Bain, "World Mineral Production and Control", *Foreign Affairs*, 11 (4), July 1933, pp. 706–710.
5. Princeton University, "Three-age system", at http://www.princeton.edu/~achaney/tmve/wiki100k/docs/Three-age_system.html (Accessed September 2, 2013).
6. University of Wisconsin Oshkosh, "Classification of Materials", at http://www.uwosh.edu/faculty_staff/mihalick/materials/CHAPTER1.pdf (Accessed July 9, 2013).
   It may also be noted that for structuring this chapter the authors have also used two hearings before the US subcommittee on Science, Technology and Space and the subcommittee on Energy and Mineral Resources, Serial No. 97–44 (Jun 24, 1981) and Publication No. 97–14 (Apr 1,7 and 9, 1981), US Government Printing Office, Washington, 1981.
7. Homeland Security Digital Library (HSDL), "Strategic Materials", at http://www.hsdl.org/?view&did=1794 (Accessed July 9, 2013).
8. Kenneth A. Kessel, *Strategic Minerals: U.S. Alternatives*, National Defence University Press, Washington, DC, 1990, pp. 13–14.
9. Rae Weston, *Strategic Materials*, Rowman & Allanheld, New Jersey, 1984, p. 1.

10. Homeland Security Digital Library (HSDL), No. 7.
11. W.C.J. van Rensburg (Sred), *Strategic Materials*, 1, Prentice-Hall, New Jersey, 1986, p. 5.
12. "Minerals Knowledge: Nuclear Minerals", at http://mineralsknowledge.blogspot.in/2009/11/ nuclear-minerals.html (Accessed July 14, 2013).
13. University of Augsburg, "Materials critical to the energy industry: An introduction", at http:/ /www.bp.com/liveassets/bp_internet/globalbp/STAGING/global_assets/e_s_assets/ e_s_assets_2010/downloads_pdfs/Materials_March2012.pdf (Accessed July 14, 2013).
14. Maplecroft, "New Products and Analysis", at http://maplecroft.com/about/news/ resource_nationalism_index_2012.html.
    The European, "Kirchner Joins the Resource Wars", at http://www.theeuropean-magazine.com/ 381-hammond-joseph/682-global-resource-nationalism (Accessed September 10, 2013).
15. *Computer-aided Materials Selection during Structural Design*, Committee on Application of Expert Systems to Materials Selection During Structural Design, Commission on Engineering and Technical Systems, National Research Council, National Academies Press, p. 1, at http:/ /www.nap.edu/catalog/4829.html (Accessed January 1, 2014).

2

Strategic Materials: An Overview

Mineral Chemistry

Mineralogy is probably the oldest branch of material science, and is also considered the oldest branch of geology. For several centuries, mineralogy dealt with materials that appear in nature as minerals, and it still continues to provide inspiration to material chemists in the synthesis of new materials.[1] Various minerals have been used as materials ever since the earliest days of mankind. Early usages were certainly restricted to the minerals as found in nature, or at best as primitively processed species. However, this situation did not last for too long, and various changes were observed with the beginning of the era of pre-industrial processes like ore smelting or sintering of ceramics, thereby extending the application fields of representatives of the mineral kingdom. A more or less smooth evolution over centuries driven by the great inventions of chemistry and physics has allowed a gradual development of technology, and continues to do so.[2]

Broadly, minerals are identified as naturally occurring, crystalline solid substances, of inorganic origin, with specific (but not necessarily fixed) chemical compositions.

In the above definition, to be crystalline indicates that the atoms within a solid are arranged in a geometric pattern that is unique to that mineral. Any change in this structure in any way results in the creation of a new mineral. Additionally, substances formed from the other phases of matter, namely liquid and gas, are not minerals. For that reason, ice from a glacier is a mineral, while liquid water, steam, and ice cubes are not. The minerals are of inorganic origin means they are not organic compounds such as amino acids, peptides or enzymes.[3] Most importantly, each mineral has a unique chemical composition. It is, therefore, possible to write a unique chemical formula for any mineral.[4]

Largely, minerals can form under a variety of conditions, such as:[5]

- During the cooling of molten materials (steel, from lavas, igneous rocks)
- During the evaporation of liquids (salt, sugar)
- The cooling of liquids (saturated solution)
- At high temperatures and pressures new crystals may grow in solid materials (diamonds from coal, metamorphism)

No matter what process is involved, a particular mineral cannot form unless the chemical ingredients necessary to make the mineral are present. Thus, the most common minerals have a chemical composition made of the common elements found in their environment.

Various types of minerals are classified into different groups based on their chemical composition. These groups are as follows:

- Elements (carbon [diamond], sulphur, zinc, gold, etc.)
- Halides (element and halogens, such as chlorine, bromine or iodine; one example is table salt [sodium chloride])
- Oxides (element and oxygen, e.g., hematite [iron oxide])
- Sulphides (element and sulphur, e.g., pyrite [iron sulphide], galena [lead sulphide])
- Elements and complex ions (ion not just a single charged atom); common examples are:
    a) Carbonates (CO_3^{2-}) (calcite, egg shells)
    b) Sulphates (SO_4^{2-}) (gypsum)
    c) Silicates (SiO_4^{4-}) (feldspar, quartz)

Most observable minerals occur is the Earth's crust. The Earth's crust is made up of about 95 per cent igneous and metamorphic rocks, 4 per cent shale, 0.75 per cent sandstone, and 0.25 per cent limestone. Table 2.1 provides information in regards to the approximate weight fractions of elements in the crust.

Table 2.1 indicates that oxygen is the most abundant element. Elements from oxygen to magnesium make up 98.5 per cent of the crust and are called 'major' elements. The elements that make up the remaining 1.5 per cent are called the minor elements (abundance some tenth of a per cent) and the trace elements (abundance measured in parts per million [ppm]). In general, it is concluded that there are more than 3,000 known minerals known till date and about 20 are very common and only nine of these constitute 95 per cent of the crust.

Table 2.1: Composition of the Continental Crust

Element	Approximate percentage by weight
Oxygen (O)	46.6
Silicon (Si)	27.7
Aluminium (Al)	8.1
Iron (Fe)	5.0
Calcium (Ca)	3.6
Sodium (Na)	2.8
Potassium (K)	2.6
Magnesium (Mg)	2.1
All other	1.5
Total	100

Source: *Mineralogy* by Prof. Stephen A. Nelson, Tulane University.

Historically, it has been observed that minerals do contribute to the affluence and influence of nation-states. States do trade in various materials/minerals for economic and strategic purposes. It is important to note that the relevance of minerals is dynamic in nature. It depends on various factors, and the importance of these factors could also change over time. Following are the materials which have wider utility in various industrial sectors:

Important Materials

- Alumina
- Aluminium
- Antimony
- Arsenic
- Asbestos
- Barytes
- Bauxite
- Bentonite
- Beryl
- Bismuth
- Borates
- Bromine
- Cadmium
- Chromium
- Coal
- Cobalt
- Copper
- Manganese
- Mercury
- Mica
- Molybdenum
- Natural gas
- Natural sodium carbonate
- Nephelinesyenite
- Nickel
- Niobium
- Perlite
- Petroleum
- Phosphates
- Platinum
- Potash
- Pyrites
- Rare earths
- Salt

- Diamond
- Diatomite
- Feldspar
- Ferro alloys
- Fluorspar
- Fuller's earth
- Germanium
- Gold
- Graphite
- Gypsum
- Iodine
- Iron ore
- Iron and steel
- Kaolin
- Lead
- Lithium
- Magnesite
- Magnesium
- Fluorite
- Selenium
- Silicon
- Sillimanite
- Silver
- Strontium
- Sulphur
- Talc
- Tantalum
- Tellurium
- Tin
- Titanium
- Tungsten
- Uranium
- Vanadium
- Vermiculite
- Wollastonite
- Zinc
- Zirconium

The following is a smaller list of key materials having strategic utility:

Vital Strategic Minerals

- Antimony
- Borates
- Chromium
- Cobalt
- Copper
- Diamond
- Germanium
- Lithium
- Molybdenum
- Nickel
- Rare earths
- Silver
- Titanium
- Tungsten
- Vanadium
- Zinc

Elucidating Strategic Minerals

In this section, the characteristics and usage of the above-mentioned vital strategic materials have been discussed.[6]

Antimony

'Antimony' is derived from the Greek word *anti monos* which means 'never found alone'.[7] Antimony is a silvery, white, brittle, crystalline solid that exhibits poor conductivity of electricity and heat. It's the member of group V element of the periodic table with atomic number of 51.[8] Antimony is a chalcophile, occurring with sulphur and the heavy metals copper, lead and silver.

Uses

During the First World War, antimony was used as alloying material for lead to produce munitions that capable of armour plate penetration.[9] It is mainly used in photographic material, electroplating cosmetic, plastics and textile industries. Antimony is extensively used worldwide to harden and increase the mechanical strength of lead; hence, it has applicability in the battery industry. It is used in glass production as a decolourising agent mainly for optical glass production used for cameras, photocopiers, binoculars and spectacles, and in fluorescent light glass tubing. Antimony as antimony trioxide is most commonly used as a synergist to improve the performance flame retardants; hence it is used in making aircraft overhead and seat covers.[10] Another wide usage is in semiconductors for making infrared detectors and diodes which have multiple defence applications. Presently, the scientific community is working towards the development of 'Phase-change' Random Access Memory (PRAM) chips which can process data faster. Many such developments are likely to increase the demand of this mineral. Antimony semiconductors also have possible usage in aircraft night vision systems.

Figure 2.1 represents typical worldwide distribution of antimony.

Figure 2.1: Typical Antinomy Usage Across the World

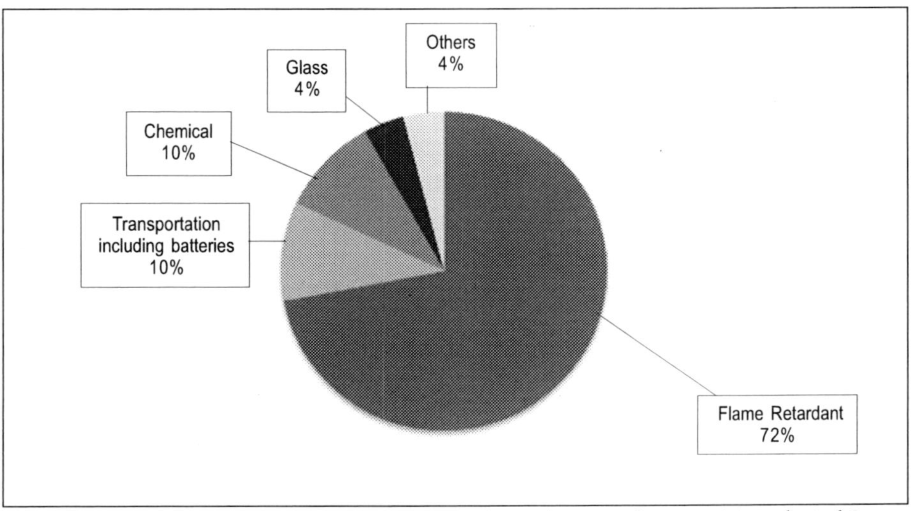

Source: Compiled from the metallurgy of antimony by Corby G. Anderson MIT, Geological Survey of America, Department of Natural Resources & Energy, and Fredericton, New Brunswick, Canada.

World Production and Reserve

Antimony has been produced from ores in over 15 countries (see Table 2.2). China is the leading producer accounting 90 per cent of world production,[11] and 95 per cent of world production and reserve together with South Africa, Bolivia and Russia.

Table 2.2: Antimony World Mine Production and Reserves (data in metric tons)

Countries	Production	Reserve
China	150,000	950,000
South Africa	5,000	27,000
Bolivia	4,000	310,000
Russia (recoverable)	33,000	350,000
Tajikistan	2,000	50,000
Others	13,1000	150,000
World Total	180,000	1,800,000

Source: U.S. Geological Survey, Mineral Commodity Summaries, January 2013.

Mineral Processing[12]

In China, manual processes have been adopted for antimony production. This is possible because of the cheap and sufficient labour availability. Although, some processing is also being done by processing units, but hand separation is still popular. These methods include primarily conventional crushing and grinding followed by combined gravity concentration and flotation. In the first stage, the ore is manually separated on the feeder belt and then sent to another unit where crushing takes place. In the second stage, after the material is crushed to 150 mm in size, it enters the heavy medium separator where the gangue (or a portion of it) is discarded, and the material is ground to 10mm. The third stage provides the final ore by going through a series of conjunctions. During this process, the heavy product is sent to the grinding section where it is prepared for flotation. Bulk flotation is performed with natural pH[13] on the ore ground to 60 per cent. Overall 33 per cent of the ore is treated by hand sorting, 7 per cent by heavy media separation and 60 per cent by flotation.

Substitutes

Combination of tin, calcium, copper, selenium, cadmium, strontium and sulphur could be possible substitutes. To a certain extent antinomy could be replaced by organic compounds or hydrated aluminium oxide in flame retardants.

Recycling

Recycling of antimony from flame retardant material is practically impossible; hence it cannot be recovered. Most secondary recycling is done by lead acid batteries, and this recovered material is reused locally by the same industry.

Beryllium (Be)

Beryllium (Be) with atomic number 4 is a steel-grey, hard and light metal. It is lighter and almost six times stronger than the steel. In addition to the properties of steel and aluminium, Beryllium is non-magnetic and has excellent thermal conductivity with very high melting point. Its exceptional ability to forms alloys with many important materials has increased its importance in the strategic equipment development and production industry. It has been declared as a critical and strategic mineral by many countries including the US, EU and China.

Uses

Because of its unique properties and exceptional qualities, beryllium has wide applications, some which is as listed in Table 2.3. In addition, Figure 2 shows typical beryllium usage across industries in the world.

Table 2.3: Applications of Beryllium

Areas	Uses	Technical Attributes
Electronics & Communications	• In flawless functioning of fibre optic cables • In mobiles and telephone equipment • In battery contacts and electronic connectors • For repeated and constant usage and fatigue-free electrical connections	• Beryllium-copper often referred as 'super-bronze' is an exceptional copper-based alloy in terms of strength, hardness, durability, thermal conductivity and corrosion resistance, and has wide electronic applications. • It resists highly corrosive sea water and extreme pressures • It has low electrical resistance and high thermal conductivity. • It supports denser layers on high-frequency circuits
Transport system	• To improve vehicle fuel efficiency • For traction controls • In transmissions system • In electric motors • In anti-lock braking and fuel injection systems • In aircraft to reduce exhaust emissions	• It has compressive and wear forces. • Nickel-beryllium alloy are used in making tools and forming permanent moulds for casting.

Areas	Uses	Technical Attributes
	• In navigation technology such as Global Positioning System (GPS) for air-traffic control and air route surveillance • In air bag sensors • In engine control electronic systems	
Defence & Aerospace	• In nuclear weaponry • As lightweight alloys in fighter jets, helicopters and satellites • In missile gyroscopes and gimbals • As sensors in satellites and optical systems • As mirrors in infra-red and surveillance equipment • As skin panels for rocket boosters (e.g., Agena) • For inner stage joining of elements in missile systems (e.g., Minuteman) • In rocket nozzles • In explosive ordnance disposal equipment • In Real-time imagery and targeting on surveillance • In heavily loaded brushing in steel mill equipment and housing of submarine cables	• It is stiff. • It is lightweight. • It is six times lighter and stronger than steel reducing weight which is critical to speed and manoeuvrability. • It has the ability to maintain its strength at high temperatures.
Medical	• In pacemakers • In CAT scanners • In Magnetic Resonance Imagery (MRI) machines • In laser scalpels • In springs and membranes for surgical instruments • In medical lasers	• It provides thermal conductivity, strength and dielectric properties.
Nuclear	• To make efficient nuclear fuel • In nuclear industry for moderating and reflecting neutrons • In X rays and radiation-measuring equipment	• High scattering cross section, making it an ideal neutron moderator. It is also an excellent reflector, it reflected back the neutrons from the fission reaction, thereby preventing leakage • It scatters leaked neutrons back into the core hence an excellent component for making blast shields

Source: Compiled using Beryllium Science & Technology Association, Hard assets and other blogs Industrial, Transportation and commercial Aeropspace

Figure 2.2: Typical Beryllium Usage Across the World in Different Industries

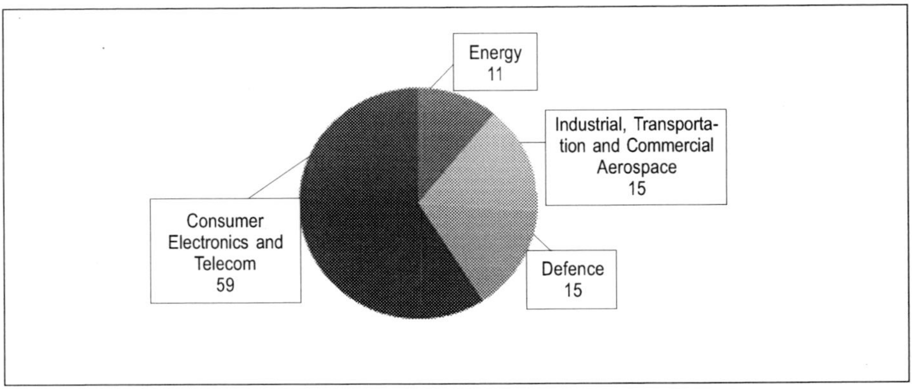

Source: U.S. Geological Survey, Mineral Commodity Summaries, January 2012.

World Production and Reserve

The world production of beryllium is dominated by US producing 90 per cent of world production followed by China (see Table 2.4). Due to escalated demand internationally, in recent times, the US has been developing private partnerships with the industry for creation of more facilities to increase the production.

Table 2.4: Beryllium World Production, Reserves, and Reserve Base (all data is in metric tons)

Countries	Production	Reserve
US	200,000	15,200
China	25,000	-
Other countries	3000	-
World total (rounded)	**230,000**	-

Source: US Geological Survey, Mineral Commodity Summaries, 2013.

Processing[14]

Two typical ores of Beryllium are beryl ($Be_3Al_2(SiO_3)_6$) and bertrandite ($Be_4Si_2O_7(OH)_2$). It can also be extracted by-products of molybdenum or lithium.

The process for 'treating' both the ores is almost similar. Due to extra hardness beryl ore is melted in electric arc, and the slag is converted into power called 'frits', while bertandite is crushed to form frits. On treating with sulphuric acid, frits are converted to form water soluble sulphate. Diluted with water, the solution is transferred to a tank containing hydrophobic organic chemical to retain the iron and aluminium impurities. Process is repeated until the desired beryllium content is obtained.

For highly enriched Beryllium, the hydroxide form is dissolved in ammonium bifluoride and heated to above 1652°F (900°C) to obtain its fluorides. The concentrate is further mixed with molten magnesium in crucibles and heated. The separated beryllium contains 97 per cent of pure beryllium.

Substitution

Due to the high cost, beryllium is used in areas where the special properties of beryllium are crucial for production. For some applications, certain metal matrix or organic composites, high-strength grades of aluminum, pyrolytic graphite, silicon carbide, steel, or titanium may be substituted for beryllium metal or beryllium composites. In some cases, copper alloys containing nickel and silicon, tin, titanium, or other alloying elements or phosphor-bronze alloys (copper-tin-phosphorus) could be used as substitutes.[15] It has been observed that the substitution many a time reduces the effective usage resulting in substantial reduction in performance.

Bismuth (Bi)

Bismuth (Bi) is a hard, brittle, lustrous, and coarsely crystalline material and has atomic number 83. In ancient times, the metal was often confused with lead and tin, which share some of its physical properties. It has the lowest thermal conductivity among all metals, and it is the most diamagnetic of all metals. It is also the useful element type-metal alloy and also used of for castings purposes due to its unique property to expand after solidification.

Uses

Uses of bismuth are as follows (also see Figure 2.3):[16]

- Bismuth is mostly used as an ingredient in pharmaceutical products.
- It is used in solders and fire detection due to low melting point.
- A specific isotope of bismuth is used for treating patients with leukaemia.
- It is used as a carrier for two uranium isotopes in nuclear reactors.
- Bismuth telluride is used in mobile refrigerators and for cooling computer processors.
- Bismuth-tellurium oxide alloy is used in making semiconductor devices.

World Production and Reserve

China with more than 80 per cent of world production holds the monopoly in production of bismuth followed by Mexico (Table 2.5).

Figure 2.3: Typical Bismuth Usage Across Different Industries in the World

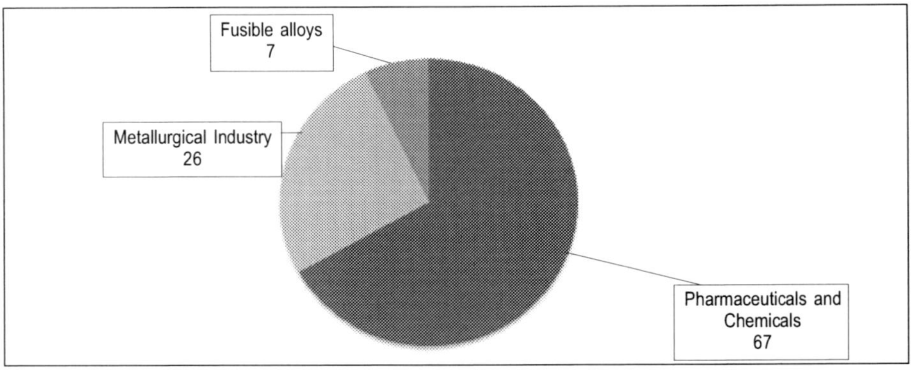

Source: U.S. Geological Survey, Mineral Commodity Summaries, January 2012.

Table 2.5: Bismuth World Production, Reserves, and Reserve Base (all data is in metric tons)

Countries	Production	Reserve
China	6000	240,000
Mexico	1000	10,000
Canada	100	5,000
Bolivia	100	10,000
Other countries	200	50,000
World total (rounded)	7,400	320

Source: US Geological Survey, Mineral Commodity Summaries, 2013.

Processing[17]

Extraction of bismuth from its ores is hardly done as it is rarely economical. Only 0.5 per cent of bismuth is extracted from its original ore; most of it is a by-product of the smelting process of metals such tungsten, zinc, tin, copper, antimony and lead.

The processing and extraction is done mainly by one of two processes: the Betterton-Kroll Process and the Betts Process.

In the Betterton-Kroll process, the bismuth is separated from the molten solution of lead and bismuth; the solution is heated by adding calcium or magnesium into it. Due to its light weight, molten lead rises to the surface as dross (solid impurities). It is then treated with chlorine at temperatures of around 572-932°F (380-500°C) which removes the magnesium and calcium leaving behind bismuth.

The Betts Process involves electrolytic refining of lead bullion. Pure lead deposits on the anode, while impurities in the form of bismuth settle at bottom of the vessel. Additional pure bismuth can be extracted by melting the slag left behind under the presence of carbon.

Substitutes

Bismuth can be replaced in pharmaceutical applications by alumina, antibiotics and magnesia. Titanium dioxide-coated mica flakes and fish scale extracts are substitutes in pigment uses. Indium can replace bismuth in low temperature solders. Free-machining alloys can contain lead, selenium or tellurium as a replacement for bismuth.

Boron (B)

Boron is the Group III A (13) element in the periodic table, occurs as borates and borosilicates in the earth crust. These borates are generally defined as compound containing boric acid (B_2O_3). China was known to have used these compounds in 300 BC to make ceramics, and it has been found that during 8th century they were used primarily as a flux for assaying and refining gold and silver.[18]

Uses

Boron is the second hardest element after diamond and is widely used in industries. The amorphous boron is used as additives in pyrotechnic mixtures, solid rocket propellant fuels and explosives. High-purity boron (>99.99 per cent) is used in electronics.[19] Following are some of the primary uses of boron:[20]

- Glass and porcelain industries are the major consumers of borax and boric acid.
- Borax is used in medicine (boric powder).
- It is used in adhesive and leather processing.
- It is also used in corrosion inhibition.
- It is used in ferrous wire manufacture, flame-proofing and timber preservation.
- Borax used as a flux in the manufacture of artificial gems. Cubic boron nitride (commercially called 'Borazon'), equals diamond in hardness, and boron carbide, titanium boride and tungsten boride are next to diamond in hardness.
- As a fluxing agent, it is used in brazing, welding and soldering.

Other than industries, Boron and its compounds have wide defence and space applications. In the Vietnam War, it was used as light hard bulletproof armour for helicopters and tanks. In space application, diborane (gas), pentaborane (liquid) and decaborane (solid) are used in rocket propellant fuels and also in the processing of shield of space shuttle. In aircraft, oxgano-sodium borate (liquibor) is used in hydraulic brake fluids.[21] Figure 2.4 shows typical Boron usage across industries.

Boron is also a vital element for nuclear application due to its neutron absorbing properties. Boron has two principal isotopes, "10B and 11B and the effectiveness of boron as neutron absorber is due to the high absorption cross sections". "The former Metallurgy Division and the present Materials Processing Division have developed processes for the production of boron, its compounds and components for application as control/shutoff rods in nuclear reactors, sensors for neutron counting, shapes for neutron shielding etc."[22]

Figure 2.4: Typical Boron Usage in Different Industries of the World

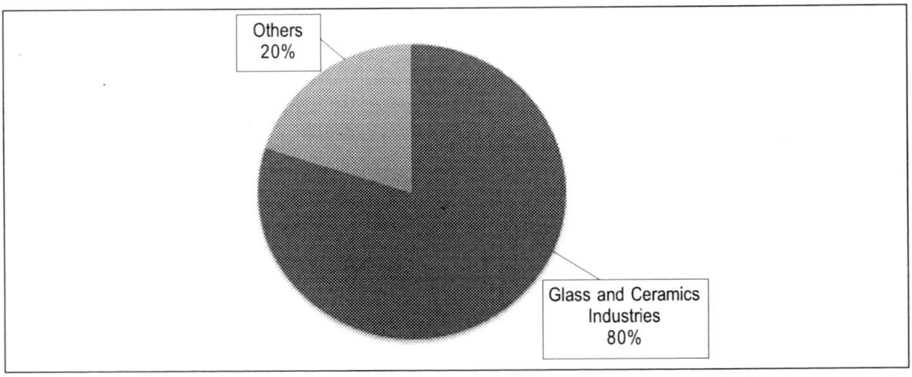

Source: U.S. Geological Survey, Mineral Commodity Summaries, January 2012

World Production and Reserve

The estimated world reserves of Boron are about 210 million tonnes in terms of boric oxide. In terms of world production, Turkey is the leading producer followed by the US; however, the US processed products have less impurities. Table 2.6 shows the production and reserves of Boron.

Table 2.6: Boron World Production, Reserves and Reserve Base (data in thousand metric tons of boric oxide (B_2O_3))

Countries	Production	Reserve
Turkey	2,500	60,000
United States	1230	40,000
Chile	500	35,000
Argentina	600	2,000
Russia	400	40,000
China	100	32,000
Bolivia	140	NA
Kazakhstan	30	NA
Peru	300	4,000
Iran	1	1000
World Total	4,600	210,000

Source: U.S. Geological Survey, Mineral Commodity Summaries 2013.

Processing[23]

Processing technique differs depending on the ore type, but the end product is generally boric acid. Borax-kernite ores (Boron, Kirka, Tincalayu) are crushed to 2.5 cm and then dissolved in hot water/recycled borate liquor. Resultant product is thicker which is fed to vacuum crystallisers, centrifuged and then dried. The final product is refined borax decahydrate or pentahydrate, dehydrated or fused anhydrous borax, which can later be used as feed for boric acid production.

Air dried ulexite combined with local sulphuric acid produces low-grade boric acid. Colemanite concentrates can be used directly, while magnesium borates are generally concentrated, which is then dissolved in acid to remove the magnesium, and then converted to boric acid or sodium borates, which later converted into boric acid. The brine, which is generally produced in China, is recovered by evaporation or carbonisation. The brine is usually bubbled by carbon dioxide and fed to a vacuum crystalliser leading to crystals. In the "evaporation" process, a rapid, controlled cooling selectively crystallises the various salts. These crystals are dehydrated which can be treated to form boric acid.

Substitutes

Substitutions for boron minerals in several applications except glass products are in vogue. Some enamel can use other glass-producing substances, such as phosphates.

Chromium (Cr)

Chromium (Cr) is a steely-grey, lustrous, hard and brittle metal with atomic number 24. Its ability to impart special properties to steel makes it a vital element for making super alloys. Chromium metal has proven of high value because of its high corrosion resistance and hardness.

Uses[24]

Majorly, chromium is used in making steel. It is also used for making special steel alloys, chrome metal super alloys, chrome chemicals and chrome-based refractory products. Figure 2.5 shows chromium usage across different industries. Some of its uses are as follows:

- Making stainless corrosion resistant steel.
- Making carbon steels, full alloy steels, bearing and high speed steels, high-strength low-alloy steels and tool steels, and in some cast irons, superalloys and welding materials.

- Making superalloys used in nuclear reactors.
- Reused in speciality steel for making tools, injection moulds, camshafts, dies, bearings, etc.
- Resistance to wear and tear and high temperature make it a vital component for defence and aerospace industries.
- Used in refractories and foundries such as iron and steel, cement, glass, ceramics, machinery, etc.
- Used in metallurgical industries such as stainless steel, alloyed steel, non-ferrous alloys, etc.

Figure 2.5: Typical Chrome Usage in Various Industries

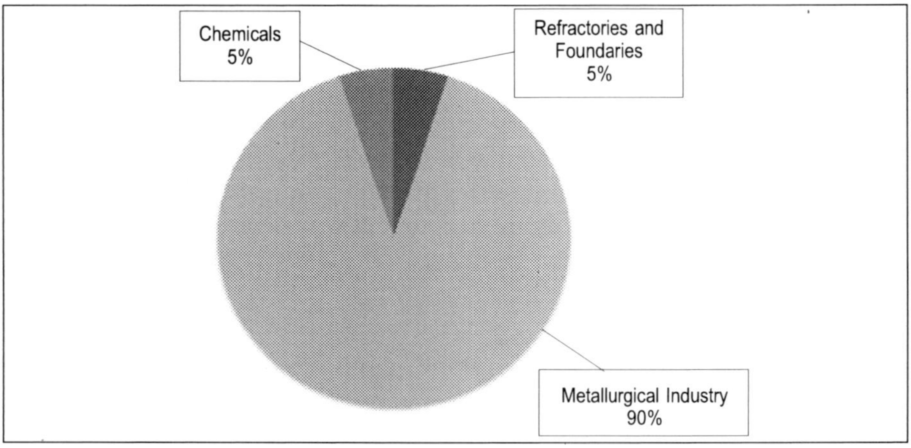

Sources: U.S. Geological Survey, January 2012 and the International Chromium Development Association (ICDA)

World Production and Reserve

According to a survey, world resources have greater than 12 billion tons of shipping-grade chromite, which is sufficient to meet the current demands of the world. South Africa is the highest producer of chromite followed by India and Kazakhstan (also see Table 2.7).

Table 2.7: Chromium World Production, Reserves, and Reserve Base (data in thousand metric tons)

Countries	Production	Reserve
India	3,800	54,000
Kazakhstan	3,800	210,000
South Africa	11,000	200,000
Other countries	5,300	NA
World total (rounded)	24,000	>460,000

Source: U.S. Geological Survey, Mineral Commodity Summaries 2013.

Processing[25]

Chromite ore ($FeCr_2O_4$) is the basic ore from which primary chromium is extracted. Ferrochrome is most widely used component of chromium in the metallurgical industry. The chromite ore is heated in the electric furnace at about 2800°C and is reduced in the presence of coke and coal through carbothermic reaction. After smelting, the molten metal is drained out and solidified in large castings before being crushed.

The pure chromium metal is produced by Aluminothermic production, which accounts for more than 95 per cent of pure chromium metal. In this process, sodium chromate containing calcine is obtained by roasting chromite ore in the presence of soda and lime at 1000°C (2000°F). The waste material is separated by leaching, and the remaining material is further reduced to precipitate chromic oxide (Cr_2O_3). This oxide is mixed with aluminium and Barium peroxide and magnesium powder, and spread on to the mixture. The mixture is ignited; the oxygen present in the chromic oxide reacts with aluminium to form aluminium oxide liberating molten chromium metal that is 97-99 per cent pure.

Substitutes

Because of its vital properties, chromium has no substitutes instainless steel production, the leading end use, or in superalloys, the major strategic end use.

Cobalt (Co)

Cobalt (Co) with atomic number 27 in the periodic table is a brittle, hard, silver-grey transition metal found in association with copper, nickel and arsenic ores.[26] Its alloys possess useful properties such as high temperature melting point (1493°C), ferromagnetic, multivalent, etc. It has the ability to retain its strength and properties even at high temperatures. Cobalt is a vital and strategic alloying material because of its irreplaceable properties and utility in a wide range of industries. Superalloys made of cobalt have improved strength and wear and corrosion-resistance characteristics at elevated temperatures.

Uses

Cobalt is a strategic and critical metal used in diverse industrial and military applications (Figure 6). Some of the critical uses are listed as follows:[27]

- In renewable energy and reusable energy storage systems
- Cobalt-based super alloys are used in turbines and compressors of jet engine
- In precision guided munitions, such as 'smart bombs'[28]
- In Radar systems

- For stealth technology
- In magnets
- In binder material
- In thermal spray coatings
- In orthopaedics
- In rechargeable batteries
- Catalyst in desulphurising crude oil and as a catalyst in hydrogenation, oxidation, reduction and synthesis of hydrocarbons
- In Gas to Liquid Technology (GLT)
- Other uses—as a drying agent in paints, de-colorisers, dyes, pigments and oxidisers, and for promoting adherence of enamel to steel, and steel to rubber in steel belted radial tires

Other than in industries and aerospace technologies, cobalt is also an essential material for nuclear industries. Elemental Cobalt-60 (radioactive isotope, a production of atomic pile) is used in industrial radiography and therapeutics.[29]

Figure 2.6 gives a glimpse of the typical consumption of Cobalt in different industries.

Figure 2.6: Typical Cobalt Usage in Different Industries of the US

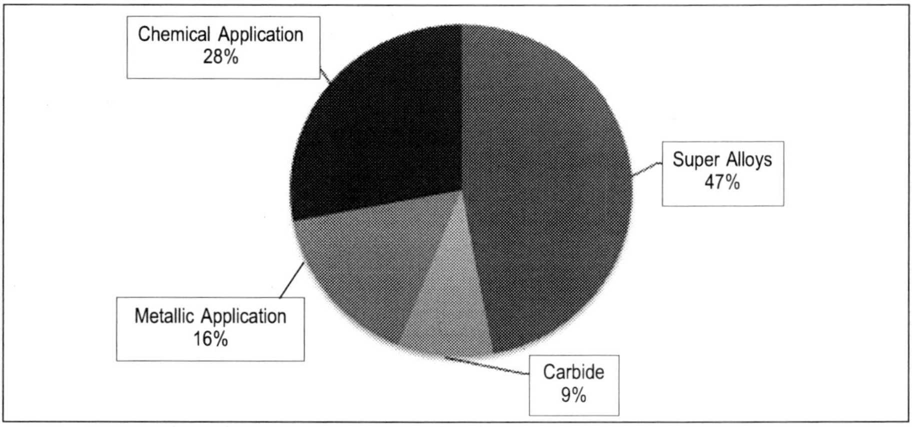

Source: U.S. Geological Survey, Mineral Commodity Summaries, January 2012.

World Production and Reserve

Table 2.8 shows that Congo has the largest production and reserve, but China is the world leading producer of refined cobalt. Most of its cobalt rich ore and partially refined cobalt is imported from Congo.

Table 2.8: Cobalt World Production, Reserves and Reserve Base (all data in metric tons)

Countries	Production	Reserve
Congo (Kinshasa)	60,000	3,400,000
Australia	4,500	1,200,000
Canada	6,700	140,000
Zambia	3,000	270,000
Russia	6,300	250,000
Brazil	1,700	87,000
China	7,000	80,000
Cuba	3,700	500,000
Morocco	1,800	20,000
Other countries	9,000	1,100,000
World Total (rounded)	110,000	7,500,000

Source: U.S. Geological Survey, Mineral Commodity Summaries, 2013.

Processing[30]

Cobalt is always found as a co-product of mining, mainly nickel and copper; hence, its processing depends on the extraction of the primary material.

From Nickel and Copper

During the final conversion of blister copper, cobalt is smelted with the copper concentrate and oxidised along with iron. Cobalt is recovered by reduction with carbon to a copper-iron-cobalt alloy, and treated in an electric funnel. In the case of nickel concentrate, cobalt is recovered in the form of cobalt-hydroxide during the electrolytic refining of nickel smelting. But, cobalt get oxidised before nickel, and can be converted from the final slag. Cobalt can also be recovered from electrowinning after some purification of the concentration formed by the leaching of nickel matte with chloride.

From Ore[31]

In a copper cobalt ore, cobalt sulphide is treated and heated with sulphide concentrate in a controlled condition so as to convert it into soluble sulphate, while minimising the copper and iron into water soluble states. The product is leached, and the resulting solution is treated in order to remove copper and iron, and the cobalt is finally recovered by electrolysis.

Cobalt concentrate from arsenide ore could be obtained by removing arsenic trioxide by the roasting method, as described above for removing the sulphide.

Substitutions

Cobalt is used in specialised applications and cannot be substituted easily. Potential substitutes include barium or strontium ferrites, neodymium-iron-boron or nickel-iron alloys in magnets; nickel, cermets or ceramics in cutting and wear-resistant materials; nickel-based alloys or ceramics in jet engines; nickel in petroleum catalysts and rhodium in hydroformylation catalysts.

Gallium (Ga)[32]

Gallium is a soft, silvery metallic element with atomic number of 31 and the chemical symbol Ga. Gallium was first used in high-temperature thermometers and in designing metals that melt easily because of its unique temperature properties. Ga melts at a low temperature (29.75°C) just about 3°C above the room temperature and has an unusually high boiling point (~2,204°C). Presently, Gallium has wide applications from manufacturing of semiconductors, data-centric networks, to smartphones.

Uses

Figure 2.7 illustrates gallium usage across industries. The following are some uses of gallium:

- The backbone of the electronic industry
- Used in optoelectronic devices such as Light Emitting Diodes (LEDs), laser-diodes, photo-detectors, etc.
- Used in energy sector for making solar cells
- In Gallium Nitride (GaN) transistors, for the ability to operate at much higher temperatures
- Make ideal power amplifiers at microwave frequencies
- In Active Electronically Scanned Array (AESA) and Passive Electronically Scanned Array (PESA) radar applications
- In satellite applications as solar panels
- Use of triple junction gallium arsenide on germanium cells in Mars Exploration Rovers and several satellites
- Used as radiopharmaceutical agents: radioactive isotope ^{67}Ga

World Production and Reserve

Though there is no explicit data available, but, according to the US geological survey, the production was estimated to be 106 metric tons. China, Germany, Kazakhstan, and Ukraine were the leading producers. Since the demand for Gallium Arsenide (GaAs) to make integrated circuits in defence application and in telecommunications is rising; therefore, recycled GaAs is high on demand, and new sources are yet to be explored.

Figure 2.7: Typical Gallium Usage in Industries

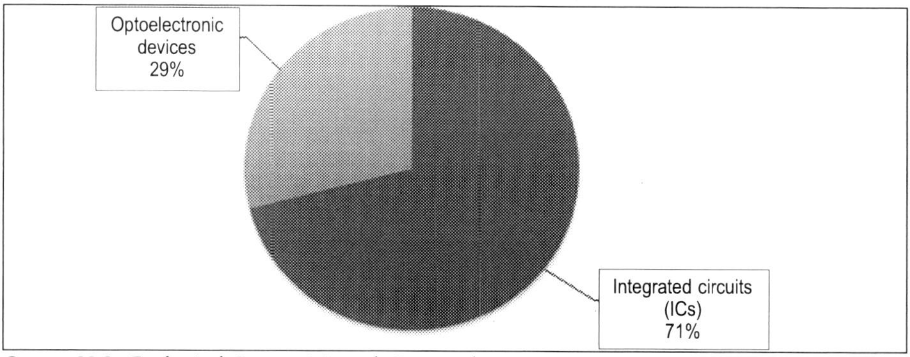

Source: U.S. Geological Survey, Mineral Commodity Summaries, January 2012.

Substitutes[33]

Organic compounds are used in visual displays as substitutes for LEDs. GaAs-based infrared laser diodes can be substituted by Indium phosphide components. Because of gallium's unique properties, GaAs-based Integrated Circuits (IC) used in many defence and energy related applications do not have effective substitutes.

Germanium (Ge)

Germanium (Ge) is a lustrous, hard, greyish-white metalloid with atomic number 32. Germanium is unaffected by acids and alkalis except nitric acid. The properties of germanium is most closely associated with silicon. It easily form compounds with elements like arsenic, gallium or other metals.

Uses[34]

The unique property of germanium as used in semiconductors made it an indispensable metal in the electronic industry. It is widely used in semiconductors, mainly transistors and integrated circuits. Some of the other uses are as follows (also see Figure 2.8):

- Semiconductor industry
- Create alloys and as a phosphor in fluorescent lamps
- Ability of Germanium to filter infrared radiation made it vital element in infrared optical instruments and infrared detectors[35]
- Widely used in sophisticated military electronics systems in IR, thermal imaging and wide angle lenses for night visions etc.
- Energy sectors as a compound Copper-Indium-Gallium-Diselenide (CIGS) to make efficient solar cells. It also used in photovoltaic cells.
- Polyethylene Terephthalate (PET) plastic used in food, beverage and liquid containers.

Figure 2.8: Typical Germanium Usage

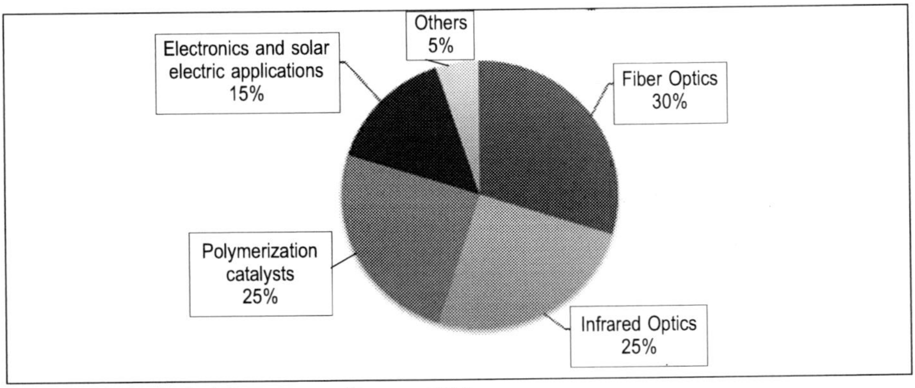

Source: US Geological Department Report, 2012.

World Refinery Production and Reserves

There has been an increasing trend in the demand of germanium due to its specific applications. There has been 46 per cent rise in germanium oxides demand and production since 2011. Countries are relying on recycling to meet the demand and price rise pressure. China produce approximately 70 per cent of world refined germanium followed by Russia and US. World consume 30 per cent of germanium from recycling while 60 per cent of the germanium metal used is routinely recycled as new scrap. Some of the refined oxide producing countries are listed in Table 2.9:

Table 2.9: Germanium World Production, Reserves and Reserve Base (data in kilograms of germanium content)

Countries	Production	Reserve
China	90,000	-
Russia	5,000	-
Other countries	30,000	-
World total (rounded)	128,000	NA

Source: U.S. Geological Survey, Mineral Commodity Summaries, 2012.

Processing[36]

Production of germanium from its ore is highly unlikely due to economic non-feasibility, and therefore produced as a by-product of base metal refining. It is produced from copper ores, but most commonly used from sphalerite zinc ores. The ore is chlorinated and distillate to produce germanium tetrachloride ($GeCl_4$), which is further hydrolysed and dried, producing germanium dioxide (GeO_2). It is heated at 938.25°C to form bars. The impurities are removed by melting and cooling known as zero-refining. It can be crystallised, and can be used in semiconductors and optical lenses.

Substitutions

Silicon can substitute germanium in the electronic industry due to its less expensive advantage. Zinc selenide can be used in infrared applications, but are often very expensive.

Indium (In)

Indium (In) is a rare, soft, malleable and easily fusible heavy metal with atomic number 49. It remain soft at low temperatures and is most suitable for solders.

Uses[37]

Indium has very specific usage, but the most important current use of Indium is in flat panel displays, Plasma Display Panels (PDPs), Liquid Crystal Displays (LCDs), and Organic Light Emitting Diode (OLED) screens, which account for upwards of 80 per cent of all demand. Some others uses are listed as follows:

- Because of its high sensitivity to temperature, Indium is used in nuclear industry to make control rods for batteries in atomic reactors.
- Indium coating solders are used in specific electronics circuits and cryogenics.
- It is used as lubricants on bearings.
- It is used as a glass coating for aircraft windshields.
- It is used in the semiconductor industry for making germanium transistors, thermistors, rectifiers and photocells.
- It is used as a cryogenic seal.

World Production and Reserve

China is the leading Indium producing country in the world. According to the US geological survey 2012 (see Table 2.10), China produced 53 per cent of indium followed by Canada (16 per cent) and Japan (11 per cent).

Table 2.10: Indium World Production, Reserves, and Reserve Base (data in metric tons)

Countries	Production	Reserve
US	30	-
China	380	
Canada	75	-
Japan	70	
Korea	70	
Other countries	35	-
World total (rounded)	670	-

Source: U.S. Geological Survey, Mineral Commodity Summaries, 2013.

Processing

Indium is primarily obtained mainly as a by-product of lead and zinc smelting. It is also found in the residue of copper, lead and tin. It is obtained from zinc waste by leaching with sulphuric and hydrochloric acid, which removes zinc and lead leaving behind Indium concentrate.

Molybdenum (Mo)

Molybdenum (Mo) is an element of the second transition series and has atomic number 42. It has very high melting point of around 2623°C with a higher density than iron. It's one of the important elements that enhances the properties of steel. Its coefficient of thermal expansion is lowest in all industrial materials, and hence, when fused with certain materials, it will enhance their properties.

Uses

Molybdenum's most vital usage is in steel industries to enhance strength, toughness, weldability, hardenability, elevated temperature strength and corrosion resistance. Some of the other uses are as follows:

- In nickel-based alloys, it improves resistance to both corrosion and high-temperature creep deformation.
- It's a versatile alloying agent for alloy steel, cast iron, nickel, cobalt and titanium alloys.
- It is used for imparting desired properties, such as increased strength, hardness and resistance to corrosion, temperature and chipping.
- It also finds application in permanent magnet alloys.
- It is used as a lubricant.
- It is used to enhance super alloys.
- It is used in manufacturing armour and aircraft parts.[38]
- It is used in solid rocket motors, and molybdenum-based products are used to guide propulsion though vanes and nozzles.[39]
- Molybdenum is used in alloys in the piping and tubing of nuclear plants.[40]

The typical industry-wise usage of Mo is shown in Figure 2.9.

World Production and Reserves

World estimated reserve is about 11 million tonnes, while China, the US and Chile together accounted for about 77 per cent of world production.[41] China (43 per cent), the US (27 per cent), Chile (12 per cent) and Peru (5 per cent) have high reserves of Molybdenum in the world as shown in Table 2.11.

Figure 2.9: Molybdenum Usage

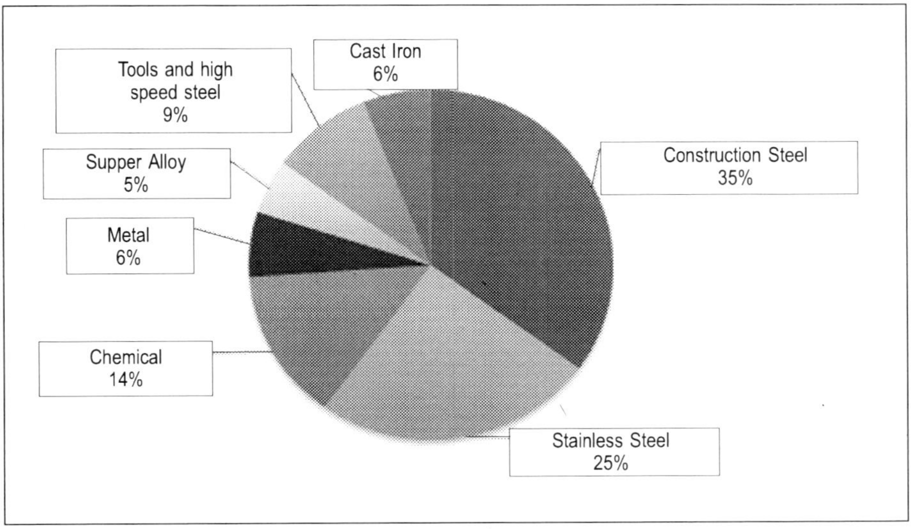

Source: Pidgeon Molybdenum Deposit Project Mph Venture Crop.

Table 2.11: Molybdenum World Production, Reserves and Reserve Base (data in metric tons)

Countries	Production	Reserve (thousand metric tons)
China	105,000	4,300
United States	57,000	2,700
Chile	35,300	2,300
Mexico	10,900	130
Mongolia	1,950	160
Peru	19,500	450
Russia	3,900	250
Iran	4,000	50
Canada	9,400	220
World total (Est.)	250,000	11,000

Source: U.S. Geological Survey, Mineral Commodity Summaries, 2013.

Processing[42]

The primary and commercially viable ore concentration for Mo is bisulfide (MoS_2), but it has to be separated from mined gravels.[43] The final product from the given ore can be obtained from various conventional processes. The processing of ores can be seen in flow chart below:

Figure 2.10: Typical Flow Diagram of Molybdenum Processing

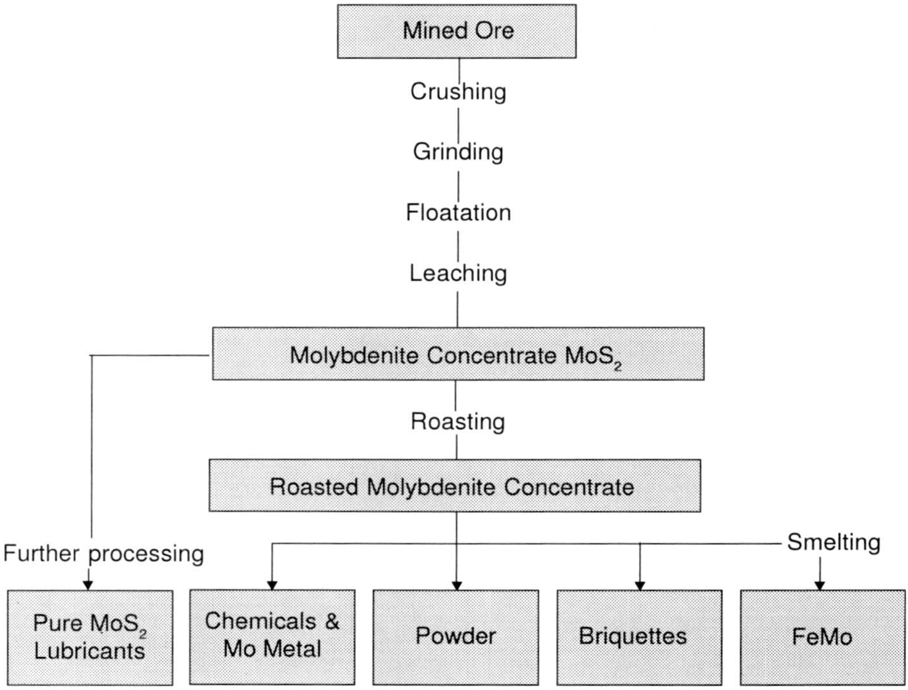

Source: The International Molybdenum Association (IMOA).

Basically, for the final production, the ore after mining is crushed and grounded in fine particles that are only microns (10^{-3} mm) in diameter, releasing molybdenite from the gangue (worthless rock). Subsequently, the following processes are carried out:

Floating

After crushing and grinding, the ore is then processed by floating. In this process, the ground ore is mixed with a liquid and aerated. The gauge sinks and settles at the bottom while the less dense ore floats. The concentrate obtained contains between 85 per cent and 92 per cent MoS_2. Further treatment by acid leaching can be used to dissolve impurities like copper and lead if necessary.

Roasting

Roasting is done at about 500-600°C, which converts MoS_2 into molybdenite (MoO_3) concentrate. In multi-level hearth furnaces, the concentrate, which moves from top to bottom is heated by air and gases blown from the bottom.

Lime scrubber removes sulphur dioxide resulting 57 per cent molybdenum, and less than 0.1 per cent sulphur.

Smelting
About 25 per cent of the resulting molybdenite concentrate is processed to form different chemical products. Smelting is processed into ferromolybdenum (FeMo). Mixed with iron, the concentrate is reduced by aluminium in a thermite reaction. Resultant product contains between 60 and 75 per cent molybdenum, balance is essentially iron.

Substitutions[44]
Because of the versatile properties of Mo, the scope for substitution in cast iron and steel industry is minimal. Potential substitutes for "molybdenum include chromium, vanadium, niobium (columbium), and boron in alloy steels; tungsten in tool steels; graphite, tungsten, and tantalum".[45]

Nickel (Ni)[46]

Nickel with chemical symbol Ni and atomic number 28 is a lustrous, silvery-white metallic element. It is hard, ductile and malleable and can take a high polish. It has very high melting and boiling points. It has fairly low thermal and electrical conductivity and can be easily magnetised.

Uses[47]
Nickel and nickel-based material plays a crucial role from everyday material usage to high-end critical materials. Nickel acts as a critical material for the production of stainless steel and corrosion-resistant alloys. Some of the other important uses of nickel are as follows:

- Nickel alloys have critical usage in defence-related technology, such as in the production of turbine blades, helicopter rotors, and fuselage sections of aircrafts.
- It is used in applications as rolled steel strips and extrusion dies.
- Nickel combined with cadmium, as Nickel-Cadmium batteries, is used in Space Vehicles.
- It is used for Nickel Plated Invar.[48]
- It is used in the heat transfer and cooling systems as well as in the reactor vessel internals.
- Copper-nickel alloys are used for coinage and marine engineering.
- It is used as a material for stealth technology in modern fighters.
- Its commercial uses are in ceramics, special chemical vessels. etc.
- It is used in rechargeable nickel-cadmium storage batteries.
- It is used in electronic circuits in computer hard discs.

Typical usage of nickel worldwide is shown in Figure 2.11.[49]

Figure 2.11: Typical Worldwide Usage of Nickel

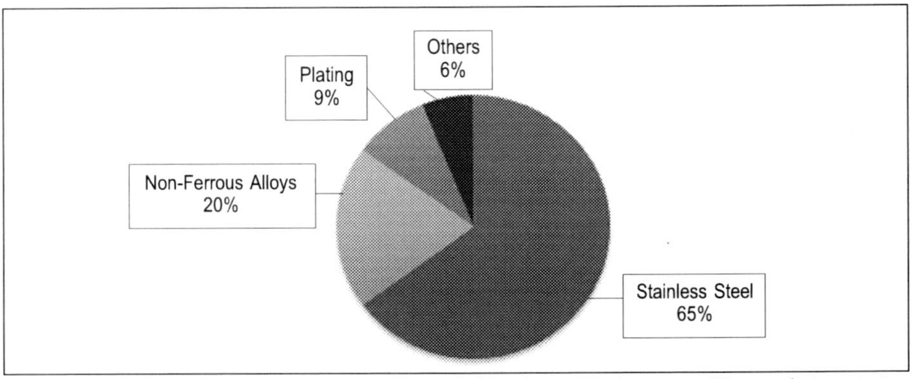

Source: Nickel Development Institute under Nickel Producers Environmental Research Association (NiPERA).

World Production and Reserve

About 70 per cent of nickel reserves are in form of laterites and 30 per cent in sulphide deposits. World's highest reserve for nickel was estimated in Australia (37 per cent) followed by New Caledonia (10 per cent), together contributing for almost half the world reserves and production. Table 2.12 shows the world reserve and producing countries.

Table 2.12: Nickel World Production, Reserves and Reserve Base (data in thousand metric tons)

Countries	Production	Reserve
Australia	230	20,000
New Caledonia	140	12,000
Indonesia	320	3,900
Brazil	140	7,500
Canada	220	3,300
China	91	3,000
Colombia	80	1,100
Cuba	72	5,500
Russia	270	6,100
South Africa	42	3,700
Other countries	1,200	4,600
World total (rounded)	2,100	75,000

Source: U.S. Geological Survey, Mineral Commodity Summaries, 2013.

Processing

Primary nickel is produced from two very different ores, lateritic and sulphidic. Lateritic ore are found in tropical regions, while sulphidic ores are found in conjunction with copper-bearing ores.

Lateritic Ore[50]

A reduction furnace is used to reduce nickel oxide and to remove moisture from the ore. In order to impart fuel value, ore is heated in an electric furnace to accommodate the high magnesia content of the ore. Sometimes sulphur is added to the lateritic ore to form matte, which can be processed further. Hydro metallurgical processes based on ammonia or sulphuric acid leach are also used.

Sulphide Ore Processing[51]

Flash smelting (modern technology) or electric smelting (conventional technology) is used in this process. In order to reduce the sulphur content and volatile matter, electric smelting is used. In flash smelting, dry sulfide ore containing less than 1 per cent moisture is fed to the furnace along with pre heated air, oxygen-enriched air (30–40 per cent oxygen), or pure oxygen. This process results in oxidising iron and sulphur while forming a liquid matte (up to 45 per cent nickel) and a fluid slag. Slags are processed in an electric furnace, before discarding, to recover nickel.

Refining Matte[52]

There are number of methods to refine nickel matte. Matte refining begins with crushing, leaching and separation of matte. Roasting and chlorine-hydrogen reduction produce high-grade nickel oxides (more than 95 per cent nickel). Use of inert cathode technology with electric cell in a solution of sulphuric acid or chloride electrolytes is the most common technology used in this process.

Substitutes[53]

Direct substitution of nickel in the production of stainless steel is less likely because of its unique properties. Nickel metal hydride in batteries can however be replaced by lithium-ion. Speciality steel can be used in power generation and petrochemical industries to replace nickel-based alloys. Corrosion-resistance alloys can be replaced by titanium-based alloys in some applications.

Niobium (Nb)

Niobium (Nb), previously called Columbium (Cb), is a soft, rare, transition metal with atomic number 41. It is a very good alloying agent, which when added to another material especially steel creates a material with substantial benefits. With the increasing utility of high-grade steel and superalloys, there has been arise in demand for niobium in international market.

Uses

Niobium is mainly used in the production of steel and superalloys. It was reported that 54 per cent of the world's consumption of Niobium is for making steel. Some of the uses are listed in Table 2.13 and Figure 2.12.

Table 2.13: Typical Niobium Usage

Niobium Products	Applications	Technical Attributes/Benefits
SLA Ferro-niobium (~60 per cent Nb)	Niobium additive to: - High strength low alloy. - Steel and stainless steel for oil and gas pipelines, car and truck bodies, architectural requirements, tool steels, ships - Hulls, railroad tracks.	Imparts a doubling of strength and toughness due to grain refining. Weight reduction.
Niobium oxide	- Manufacture lithium niobate for surface acoustic wave filters. - Camera lenses. - Coating on glass for computer screens. - Ceramic capacitors.	- High index of refraction. - High dielectric constant. - Increase light transmittance.
Niobium carbide	Cutting tool compositions.	High temperature deformation, controls grain growth.
Niobium powder	Niobium capacitors for electronic circuits.	High dielectric constant, stability of oxide dielectric.
Niobium metal plates, sheets, wire, rod, tubing	- Sputtering targets. - Cathode protection systems for large steel structures. - Chemical processing equipment.	Corrosion resistance, formation of oxide and nitride films. Increase in high temperature resistance and corrosion resistance, oxidation resistance, improved creep resistance, reduced erosion at high temperatures.
Niobium-titanium alloy Niobium-tin alloy	Superconducting magnetic coils in MRI, magnetoencephalography, magnetic levitation transport systems, particle physics experiments.	Electrical resistance of alloy wire drops to virtually zero at or below temperature of liquid helium (-268.8°C).
Niobium-1 per centzirconium alloy	- Sodium vapour lamps - Chemical processing equipment	Corrosion resistance, fixation of oxygen, resistance to embrittlement.
Vacuum-grade ferro-niobium and nickel-niobium	Superalloy additions for turbine blade applications in jet engines and land-based turbines. Inconel family of alloys, superalloys.	Increase in high temperature resistance and corrosion resistance, oxidation resistance, improved creep resistance, reduced erosion at high temperatures.

Source: Tantalum-Niobium International Study Centre, 2012.[54]

Figure 2.12: Typical Worldwide Usage of Niobium

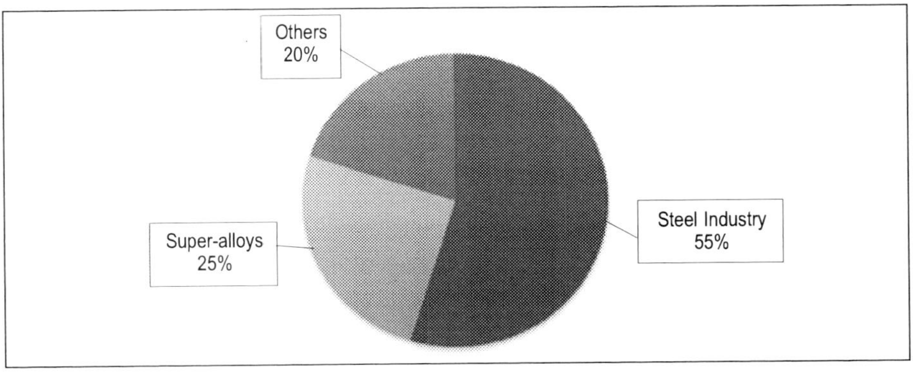

Source: US Geological Department Report, 2012.

World Production and Reserve[55]

Brazil is the highest producer of Niobium in the world followed by the Canada (see Table 2.14). The leading suppliers of niobium in ore and concentrate were Australia (54 per cent), Mozambique (13 per cent), and Canada and Brazil.

Table 2.14: Niobium World Production, Reserves and Reserve Base (data in metric tons of niobium content)

Countries	Production	Reserve
Brazil	63,000	4,100,000
Canada	140,000	200,000
Other countries	700	NA
World total (rounded)	69,000	>4,000,000

Source: U.S. Geological Survey, Mineral Commodity Summaries, 2013.

Processing[56]

The primary ore for niobium is known as pyrochlore, which has strong geochemical coherence with tantalum. Pyrochlore concentrates are reduced to ferroniobium through an aluminothermic process. In this process, the concentrate is mixed with hematite (an iron ore), aluminum powder and small quantities of fluorspar and lime fluxes. The resulting pyrochlore concentrate has 55-60 per cent Nb_2O_5.

Substitutes

Some materials can be substituted for niobium, but it may include a performance or cost penalty. The possible substitutes are molybdenum and vanadium, as alloying elements in high-strength low-alloy steels; tantalum and titanium, as alloying elements in stainless and high-strength steels and ceramics, molybdenum, tantalum, and tungsten in high temperature applications.

Silver (Ag)

Silver with chemical symbol Ag and atomic number 47 is a soft, white, lustrous transition metal with the highest electrical and thermal conductivity. It has high malleability and is resistant to atmospheric oxidation.[57] Silver is second to gold in terms of high-value ornaments, jewelleries, currency coins and bullions.

Uses[58]

Some of the unique properties of silver and its utility and capability have made it one of the strategic and vital material of modern era. It has wide usage from industrial and medical sectors to energy sector and space. Some of the vital uses of silver are as follows:

- Because of its high electrical conductivity, it has found wide applications, viz., in printed electric circuits and coating for electronic equipment.
- It is used in conductors and in alloys of gold and copper for electrical contacts.
- When exposed to light, the silver-halide crystals change to record a latent image; accuracy of this process makes it useful for non-digital consumer photography, film and X-rays.
- Silver plating is used in aluminium waveguide and communication systems.
- Silver-plated waveguides are used in communication payloads of satellites.
- Silver plating on aluminium is required to obtain good Radio Frequency (RF) performance.
- Silver provides the best known electrical conductivity and is solder able.
- It's antimicrobial, non-toxic qualities make it useful in medicine and consumer products.
- It is widely used in mirrors and silverwares.
- It is used in photovoltaic cells to enhance the efficiency of solar cells solar panels. It is used in rid lines that draw electrical current from the semiconducting surface of a photovoltaic cell.
- Silver-coated ball bearings reduce friction in engines.
- Modern skyscrapers have window glass that is coated with silver to reflect sunlight in order to enhance the air-conditioning efficiency hence reducing cost.
- Silver-based ionic liquids can be used to clean up petroleum waste products.[59]

Other than industrial usage, silver is highly used in photography, as when silver is exposed to light, the silver-halide crystals change to record a latent image that can be developed into a photograph. Thus, it is useful for non-digital consumer photography, film and X-rays. Jewellery and silverware is the second most important sector in the worldwide usage of silver. Figure 2.13 gives a breakdown of silver usage worldwide.

Figure 2.13: Breakdown of Silver Usage

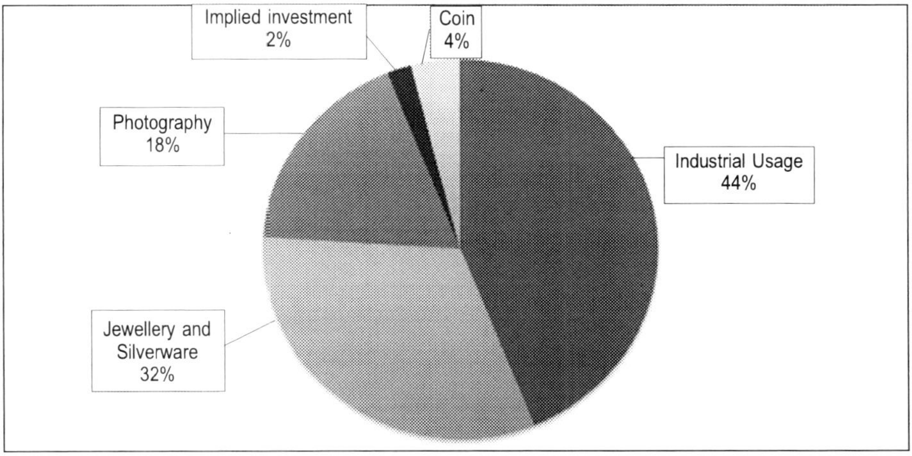

Source: Wealth wire special report.[60]

World Production and Reserves

The total reserves of silver are estimated at 540,000 metric tonnes. Chile, Peru, Poland, Mexico, China and Australia are the main countries having silver reserves as shown in Table 2.15.

Table 2.15: Silver World Production, Reserves and Reserve Base (data in metric tons of silver content: 1 metric ton = 1,000 kilograms = 32,150.7 troy ounces)

Countries	Production	Reserve
Mexico	4,250	37,000
China	3,800	43,000
Peru	3,450	120,000
Australia	1,900	69,000
Russia	1,500	NA
United States	1,050	25,000
Bolivia	300	22,000
Poland	1,170	85,000
Chile	1,130	77,000
Canada	530	7,000
Other countries	3,900	50,000
World total (rounded)	24,000	540,000

Source: U.S. Geological Survey, Mineral Commodity Summaries, 2013.

Processing

Silver ore generally exists in association with major metals such as copper, lead or zinc. It is found in sulphide, zinc and copper forms as galena (PbS), sphalerite (ZnS) and chalcopyrite (CuFeS2), respectively. To remove sulphide, the floating process is carried out, and the mineral is extracted.

From Copper

By smelting the copper sulphide concentrate, 'blister' copper is obtained, which has maximum silver present in concentrate form. Insoluble impurities called 'slimes' are accumulated at the bottom after electrolytic refining, which contain a high concentration of silver originally present in the ore.

From Lead

A lead bullion is formed by roasting and smelting the lead concentrate, which still contains impurities such as antimony, arsenic and sliver. To remove silver, zinc is added to lead bullion; the process is called the Parkes process. After reacting with silver, zinc produces an insoluble compound that can be removed by vacuum process. Remaining concentrate is removed by cupellation process in which concentrate is heated at a very high temperature (800°C) under oxidising condition. The lead oxidises, while the silver alloy thus produced is refined by the Moebius or Thum Balbach process.

From Zinc

Zinc concentrates are roasted and then leached with sulphuric acid to dissolve their zinc content, leaving a residue that contains lead, silver and gold. Zinc is further reduced and vaporised from the slag by a process called slag fuming (in which powdered coal or coke is blown along with air). Lead is converted into metallic form containing silver, which is processed by the above method Parkes process.

Substitutions[61]

Tantalum and titanium can be used in place of silver for surgical pins and plate. Aluminium and rhodium can replace silver in mirrors. Xerography can be used for black-and-white as well as colour printing applications.

Tantalum (Ta)

Tantalum (Ta) with atomic number 73 is a hard, blue-gray, lustrous transition metal. It is highly corrosion resistant and is closely related to niobium in terms of physical and chemical properties, often even considered identical.

Uses

Table 2.16 gives the applications and attributes of various tantalum products.

Table 2.16: Typical Tantalum Usage

Tantalum Products	Applications	Technical Attributes/Benefits
Tantalum carbide	Cutting tools	Increased high temperature deformation, control of grain growth
Lithium tantalate	Surface Acoustic Wave (SAW) filters in mobile phones, hi-fi stereos and televisions.	Electronic signal wave dampening provides for clearer and crisper audio and video output.
Tantalum oxide	- Lenses for spectacles, digital cameras and mobile phones - X-ray film - Ink jet printers	- Ta_2O_5 provides a high index of refraction so lenses for a given focal strength can be thinner and smaller - Yttrium tantalate phosphor reduces X-ray exposure and enhances image quality - Wear resistance characteristics. Integrated capacitors in ICs
Tantalum powder	Tantalum capacitors for electronic circuits in: - medical appliances such as hearing aids and pacemakers; - automotive components such as ABS, airbag activation, engine management modules, GPS; - portable electronics (e.g., laptop computers, cellular/mobile phones, video cameras, digital still cameras); - other equipment such as DVD players, flat screen TVs, games consoles, battery chargers, power rectifiers, cellular/mobile phone signal masts, oil well probes	High reliability characteristics and low failure rates, operation over a wide temperature range from -55 to +200°C, can withstand severe vibrational forces, small size per microfarad rating/electrical storage capability
Tantalum fabricated sheets and plates	- Chemical process equipment including lining, cladding, tanks, valves, heat exchangers - Cathodic protection systems for steel structures such as bridges, water tanks - Corrosion resistant fasteners, screws, nuts, bolts - Spinnerettes in synthetic textile manufacture	Superior corrosion resistance - equivalent in performance to glass

Tantalum Products	Applications	Technical Attributes/Benefits
Tantalum fabricated sheets, plates, rods, wires	- Prosthetic devices for humans - hip joints, skull plates, mesh to repair bone removed after damage by cancer, suture clips, stents for blood vessels	Attack by body fluids is non-existent; highly bio-compatible
Tantalum fabricated sheets, plates, rods, wires	- High temperature furnace parts	Melting point is 2996°C although protective atmosphere or high vacuum required
Tantalum ingot	- Sputtering targets	Applications of thin coatings of tantalum, tantalum oxide or nitride coatings to semi-conductors to prevent copper migration
Tantalum ingot	- High temperature alloys for: - air and land based turbines (e.g., jet engine discs, blades and vanes) - rocket nozzles	Alloy compositions containing 3-11 per cent tantalum offer resistance to corrosion by hot gases, allow higher operating temperatures and thus efficiency and fuel economy
Tantalum ingot	- Computer hard drive discs	An alloy containing 6 per cent tantalum has shape memory properties
Tantalum ingot	- Explosively Formed Projectile for TOW-2 missile	Balance of density and formability allow for a lighter and more efficient system

Source: Tantalum-Niobium International Study Centre, 2012.

World Production and Reserve

Mozambique remains the highest producer of tantalum followed by the Brazil (see Table 2.17).

Table 2.17: Tantalum World Production, Reserves, and Reserve Base (data in metric tons of tantalum content)

Countries	Production	Reserve
Brazil	180	88000
Mozambique	260	200,000
Congo	46	4000
Other countries	280	NA
World total (rounded)	765	>150,000

Source: U.S. Geological Survey, Mineral Commodity Summaries 2013.

Processing[62]

The tantalum ore is processed by heating the mixture with sulphuric acid and hydrofluoric acid at elevated temperatures. Using Methyl Isobutyl Ketone (MIBK), or liquid ion exchange, using an amine extractant in keroses, the slurry is further processed to produce highly purified solutions of tantalum. This process also separates impurities and niobium from the process, and refined tantalum is recovered.

Substitutes

Some substitutes are available; however, generally, they are found less effective. Substitutes available are niobium in carbides; aluminium and ceramics in electronic capacitors; glass, niobium, platinum, titanium, and zirconium in corrosion-resistant equipment and hafnium, iridium, molybdenum for high temperature applications.

Tin (Sn)

Tin with the chemical symbol as Sn is the main metal in group 14 of the periodic table and has the atomic number 50. Easy to recycle, tin has a low melting point, is malleable, is resistant to corrosion and fatigue and has the ability to alloy with other metals. Tin is one of the oldest metals known to mankind and is used in combination with copper to make bronze.

Uses

Tin can be used in both in industry and also in the form of chemical compounds. Some of the uses of tin are as follows (see Figure 2.14):[63]

- Electroplating is an important application of tin.
- Its usage lies in electrical components such as in capacitors electrodes, fuse-wires and major usage in soldering wires make it a vital mineral in the electronic industry.

Figure 2.14: Typical Tin Usage in Different Industries

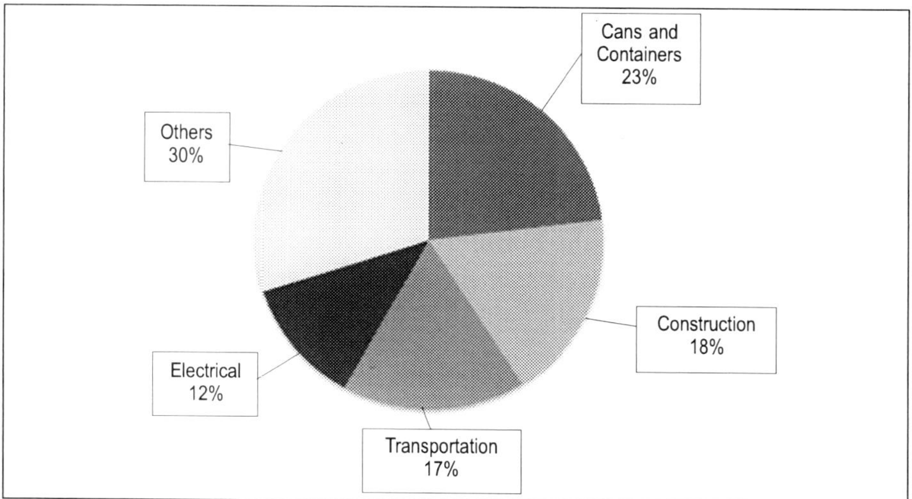

Source: U.S. Geological Survey, Mineral Commodity Summaries, January 2012.

- It's a non-toxic compound; hence, it is used in various food packaging industries such as tin cans and foils.
- It is used in organic compounds and has several applications as fungicides and insecticides for the agriculture industry.

World Production and Reserve

China is the world's largest producer of tin. Its production in recent years have declined due to drought conditions and pollution control measures adopted by local administrations in China. Nevertheless, China continues to remain the highest producer in the world followed by Indonesia and Peru (Table 2.18).

Table 2.18: Tin World Production, Reserves, and Reserve Base (data in metric tons of tin content)

Countries	Production	Reserve
China	100,000	1,500,000
Indonesia	41,000	800,000
Peru	29,000	310,000
Malaysia	29,000	310,000
Bolivia	20,000	400,000
Brazil	11,500	710,000
Other countries	2,000	180,000
World total (rounded)	230,000	4,900,000

Source: U.S. Geological Survey, Mineral Commodity Summaries 2013.

Processing[64]

Cassiterite (SnO_2) is the primary and most important ore for tin. Cassiterite concentrates is separated with the help of magnetic or electrostatic separation. Smelting further processes the ore.

Smelting[65]

Cassiterite is reduced to tin by heating the ore with carbon at about 1200-1300°C. Smelting is done in a Reverberatory furnace under the presence of carbon-reducing agent, limestone and silica fluxes for around 10-12 hours. The refined tin is left at the bottom, which is separated by forming slab while cooled slag is reheated and re-smelted to extract 10-20 per cent tin present in the slag.

Refining

Tin recovered from slag has metallic impurities which are removed by refining. Refining is generally done by heat treatment or electrolytic processes. In heat treatment, tin is heated just above its melting point and collected while leaving behind residue. Electrolytic refining is done only for specialised purpose high purity tin as the method is not cost effective.

Substitutes

Aluminium, glass, paper, plastic or tin-free steel substitute for tin cans and containers. Other materials that substitute for tin are epoxy resins for solder; aluminium alloys, copper-base alloys, and plastics for bronze; plastics for bearing metals that contain tin and compounds of lead and sodium for some tin chemicals.

Tungsten (W)[66]

Tungsten, also called "wolfram", has chemical formula W and atomic number 74. Tungsten has the highest melting point (3,422±15°C) and boiling point (5,700°C) of all metals. The coefficient of thermal expansion of tungsten is lowest in all metals; hence, it is widely used in the filament of bulb and high-speed cutting tools with carbide. Presence of carbon and oxygen gives tungsten considerable hardness and brittleness.

Uses

Tungsten's unique properties and wide application make it a vital component of wide industrial applications. Following are some of its vital uses in different industries:[67]

- Tungsten is used in making special and alloy steels.[68]
- It is widely used in cutting and wear-resistant materials.
- Tungsten wires form the filament in incandescent light bulbs and cathodes for electronic tubes.
- It is used in armour plate and armour-piercing ordnance.
- It is an important element to make Super Alloy which is further used in aircraft engines, rocket nozzle, marine vehicles, turbine blades vanes, exhaust gas assemblies and burner liners.
- Tungsten alloy used in balancing components, henceforth reducing vibrations.[69]
- Tungsten alloys balance weights for missile bodies and sensor arrays.[70]
- Tungsten Heavy alloys counterweights are incorporated into the pitch control system of many propeller designs as a fail-safe device to ensure that over speeding is prevented.[71]
- Tungsten and tungsten alloys are presently considered as main candidate materials for helium cooled divert or designs for the next nuclear fusion reactor generation (DEMO).[72]
- Crystal tungstates are used as scintillation detectors in nuclear physics and nuclear medicine.[73]

Figure 2.15 gives a broader breakdown of tungsten usage in different industries of the major tungsten consuming countries.

Figure 2.15: Breakdown of Tungsten Usage in Different Industries

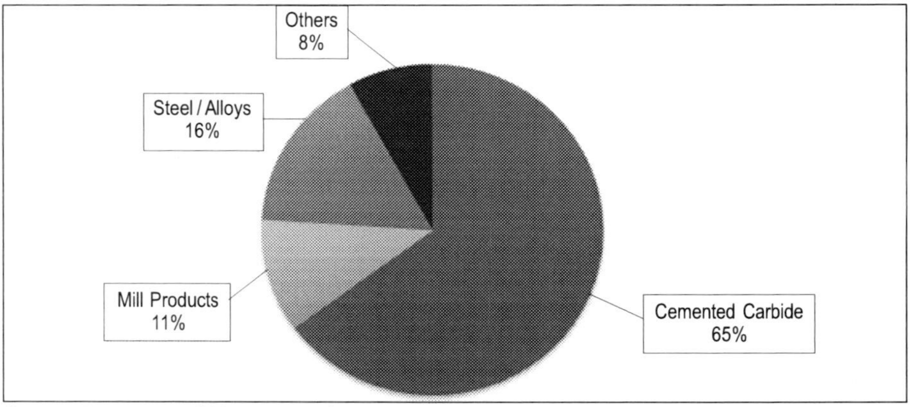

Source: International Tungsten Industry Association.

World Production and Reserve

The world reserves of tungsten in terms of metal content are 3.2 million tonnes, distributed broadly amongst China (64 per cent), Russia (9 per cent), Canada (4 per cent) and the US (5 per cent). China was the leading producer (80 per cent), followed by Canada (4 per cent) and Russia (4 per cent) in 2012, as shown in Table 2.19.

Table 2.19: Tungsten World Production, Reserves, and Reserve Base (data in metric tons of tungsten content)

Countries	Production	Reserve
China	62,000	1,900,000
Russia	3,500	250,000
United States	NA	140,000
Austria	1,100	10,000
Canada	2,000	120,000
Bolivia	1,100	53,000
Other countries	3,000	760,000
World total (rounded)	73,000	3,200,000

Source: U.S. Geological Survey, Mineral Commodity Summaries, 2013.

Processing

There are two major ores of tungsten: wolframite [(Fe, Mn)WO_4], which contains iron and manganese tungstates, and scheelite ($CaWO_4$).During processing, the ore is dissolved in alkaline pressure digestion, using either soda or concentrated NaOH solution. This process produces sodium tungstate solution, later converted to ammonium tungstate solution by solvent extraction or ion exchange resins. Before converting into ammonium tungstate into sodium tungstate, the solution is precipitated, purified and filtered. Finally, high purity Ammonium-Paratungstate (APT) is obtained by crystallisation, with the formula $(NH_4)10(H_2W_{12}O_{42}) \cdot 4H_2O$ which can be filtered to get tungsten.

Substitutes[74]

Molybdenum tool steels and tungsten tool steels are interchangeable. Moreover, in future the development of a new metal shaping methods, such as laser is possible. Tungsten remains essentially non-substitutable for filaments, electrodes and contacts in lamp and lighting applications. In some applications, substitutions of any other material might result in increased cost or in some cases loss in product performance.

Gas Helium

In this context, mentioning called Gas Helium[75] as a 'material' might seem inessential, because it is not a 'solid' substance extracted from the earth. However, it is important to discuss it since it is one of the world's most critical raw materials. Helium's strategic importance was recognised during the First World War, when it was used as a safer alternative to hydrogen to lift reconnaissance and weather balloons.

Helium is a unique material especially in liquid form. It is commonly used as a coolant in various applications, for example, to run superconducting magnets inter alia in MRI (a safer alternative to x-ray body scanners) applications and computer chip and optical fibre manufacturing. It is also used as a blanket-gas to shield sensitive materials from atmospheric oxygen, and enable certain chemical reactions to be performed, and in specialist welding operations in which the weld is stronger when the metal surface has not been exposed to reactive atmospheric gases. Helium finds further application in gas-cooled nuclear reactors as a heat-transfer agent. It has relevance for the space industry (space rockets) too. For many of these uses, there is no substitute for helium. It is also important to note that helium is a non-renewable natural resource. Industries like the semiconductor manufacturer units could come to a standstill in case of any shortage of helium.

Most of the world's helium is found in the US, and it has the largest stock reserve of gas helium. In recent times, the prices for refined helium sold to end-users have quadrupled from US$ 40 per thousand cubic feet in 2000 to US$ 160 per thousand cubic feet in 2012. It is reasoned that the low prices and the stability of helium market during 1980s has significantly contributed to the rapid growth of MRI as a (medical) diagnostic tool. However, now, understating the importance of helium both for civilian and strategic purposes, the 'politics of helium' is taking shape. The US is taking the issue of helium production and exports very seriously. On October 2, 2013, President Obama signed into law the Helium Stewardship Act of 2013. This act has replaced the Helium Privatization Act of 1996.

NOTES

1. Sergey V. Krivovichev (ed.), *Minerals as Advanced Materials II*, Springer, Berlin Heidelberg, 2012, p. v.
2. Wulf Depmeier, "From Minerals to Materials", in Sergey V. Krivovichev (ed.), *Minerals as Advanced Materials II*, Springer, Berlin Heidelberg, 2012, p. 1.
3. Interestingly, however, many organic processes result in the formation of minerals. For instance, seashells are made of minerals, as are coral reefs and the bones and teeth of animals. An easy rule of thumb is that if a material is associated with the "soft-parts" of a plant or animal it cannot be a mineral, while if that material is part of the skeleton or rigid support structure, then it might be composed of minerals.
4. "Minerals", IPFW Geosciences Department, at http://www.geosci.ipfw.edu/PhysSys/Unit_3/minerals.html (Accessed July 14, 2013).
5. "Minerals, Rocks & Rock Forming Processes", Indiana University, at http://www.indiana.edu/~geol105/1425chap5.htm (Accessed July 14, 2013).
6. The information regarding these materials has been taken from multiple sources. For some of the materials, significant amount of information is available, while in some cases limited information is available. While describing various materials, care has been to taken to follow similar pattern for every mineral as far as possible; however, in some cases, because of the information limitation, it has not been possible to follow the format strictly.
7. Rae Weston, *Strategic Materials: A World Survey*.
8. "Antimony Uses, Production & Prices", Home Tristar http://www.google.co.in/url?sa=t&rct=j&q=&esrc=s&source=web&cd=2&cad=rja&uact=8&ved=0CD4QFjAB&url=http%3A%2F%2Fwww.tri-starresources.com%2FTRISTAR%2520ANTIMONY%2520PRIMER%2520JAN%25202012.pdf &ei=rrpMU7CrMMHWrQfym4H4Dg&usg= AFQjCNGwBFdCEphPC2cG3k2-J-F9Dolosg&sig2=kB-z1USKZSZbpZ9huPo3Nw&bvm=bv.64764171,d.bmk (Accessed July 7, 2013).
9. "Antimony History", Bristol University | School of Chemistry, at http://www.chm.bris.ac.uk/webprojects2004/tabor/uses.html (Accessed July 9, 2013).
10. "Antimony", USGS Mineral Resources Program, at http://minerals.usgs.gov/minerals/pubs/commodity/antimony/mcs-2012-antim.pdf (Accessed July 8, 2013).
11. Ibid.
12. G. Anderson, Corby, "The Metallurgy of Antimony", MIT - Massachusetts Institute of Technology, at http://web.mit.edu/12.000/www/m2016/pdf/antimony.pdf (Accessed July 9, 2013).
13. The pH value is a measure of the acidity or basicity of the solution. The natural pH value is generally 7 and can exceed maximum up to 10; pH below 7 makes the solution acidic while above makes it basic.
14. "Metal Profile: Beryllium", at http://metals.about.com/od/properties/a/Metal-Profile-Beryllium.htm (Accessed July 14, 2013).
15. "Beryllium", USGS Mineral Resources Program, at http://minerals.usgs.gov/minerals/pubs/commodity/beryllium/mcs-2013-beryl.pdf (Accessed July 16, 2013).

16. "Want to Know it? Answers to Life's Questions: Uses of Bismuth", at http://wanttoknowit.com/uses-of-bismuth/ (Accessed July 16, 2013).
17. "Bismuth Metal", at http://www.slideshare.net/angelica_terrado/bismuth-metal# (Accessed July 16, 2013).
18. G. Önal and F. Burat, "Boron Mining and Processing in Turkey", Instytut Gospodarki Surowcami Mineralnymi i Energi[1] Polskiej Akademii Nauk, at http://www.min-pan.krakow.pl/Wydawnictwa/GSM2443/onal-burat.pdf (Accessed July 18, 2013).
19. "Boron: Physical and Chemical Properties", at http://www.springerreference.com/docs/html/chapterdbid/332754.html (Accessed July 18, 2013).
20. "Boron Minerals", Indian Bureau of Mines, at http://ibm.nic.in/IMYB%202011_Boron%20Minerals.pdf (Accessed July 18, 2013).
21. "Boron in Materials Technology", at http://biotsavart.tripod.com/bmt.htm (Accessed July 19, 2013).
22. C. Subramanian, A.K. Suri and T.S.R. Ch. Murthy, "Development of Boron-based Materials for Nuclear Applications", Bhabha Atomic Research Centre (BARC), at http://www.barc.gov.in/publications/nl/2010/2010030403.pdf (Accessed July 19, 2013).
23. Robert B. Kistler and Cahlt Helvaci, "Boron and Borates", at http://kisi.deu.edu.tr/cahit.helvaci/Boron.pdf (Accessed July 19, 2013).
24. "Uses of Chromium", at http://www.icdacr.com/index.php?option=com_content&view=article&id=104&Itemid=167&lang=en (Accessed July 19, 2013).
25. "Metal Profile: Chromium", at http://metals.about.com/od/properties/a/Metal-Profile-Chromium.htm (Accessed July 20, 2013).
26. "Cobalt | Physical Properties", at http://www.webelements.com/cobalt/physics.html (Accessed July 19, 2013).
27. "Cobalt & Other Critical Raw Materials", at http://www.resourceinvestor.com/2011/06/23/cobalt-other-critical-raw-materials (Accessed July 20, 2013).
28. "Cobalt", Indian Bureau of Mines, at http://ibm.gov.in/IMYB%202011_Cobalt.pdf (Accessed July 21, 2013).
29. "Cobalt | Radiation Protection", US Environmental Protection Agency, at http://www.epa.gov/rpdweb00/radionuclides/cobalt.html (Accessed July 21, 2013).
30. Cobalt Commodity Profile, British Geological Survey Profile, 2011.
31. "Cobalt Processing", *Encyclopaedia Britannica*, at http://www.britannica.com/EBchecked/topic/123274/cobalt-processing (Accessed July 22, 2013).
32. "Gallium: A Smart Metal", USGS Publications, at http://pubs.usgs.gov/fs/2013/3006/pdf/fs2013-3006.pdf (Accessed July 22, 2013).
33. "Gallium", USGS Mineral Resources Program, at http://minerals.usgs.gov/minerals/pubs/commodity/gallium/mcs-2013-galli.pdf (Accessed July 22, 2013).
34. "Germanium (Ge) - Chemical properties and Environmental effects", Lenntech, at http://www.lenntech.com/periodic/elements/ge.htm#ixzz2mfe9FUm8 (Accessed July 24, 2013).
35. Ibid.
36. "Metal Profile: Germanium", at http://metals.about.com/od/properties/a/Metal-Profile-Germanium.htm (Accessed July 24, 2013).
37. "Indium Uses", at http://www.chemicool.com/elements/indium.html (Accessed December 30, 2013).
38. "The Uses of Molybdenum", at http://www.useofmolybdenum.net/ (Accessed July 25, 2013).
39. "Defense and Aerospace Applications of Molybdenum, Tungsten and Tantalum Products", *AZo Journal of Materials Online*, at http://www.azom.com/article.aspx?ArticleID=9073 (Accessed July 25, 2013).
40. "Critical and Strategic Minerals. Can Colorado Play a Role?", White Paper, AIPG - American Institute of Professional Geologists, at http://www.aipg.org/education/pdf/white%20paper%20Critical%20and%20Strategic%20Minerals.pdf (Accessed July 25, 2013).

41. "Molybdenum", Indian Bureau of Mines, 2011.
42. "Molybdenum Processing", IMOA: International Molybdenum Association, at http://www.imoa.info/molybdenum/molybdenum_processing.php (Accessed July 26, 2013).
43. "Molybdenum processing", *Encyclopaedia Britannica*, at http://www.britannica.com/EBchecked/topic/388593/molybdenum-processing#toc82042 (Accessed July 26, 2013).
44. "Molybdenum", US Geological Survey, 2013.
45. Ibid.
46. "Nickel Metal", Nickel Institute, at http://www.nickelinstitute.org/NickelUseInSociety/AboutNickel/NickelMetaltheFacts.aspx (Accessed July 29, 2013).
47. "Where & Why Nickel is Used", Nickel Institute, at http://www.nickelinstitute.org/en/NickelUseInSociety/AboutNickel/WhereWhyNickelIsUsed.aspx (Accessed December 30, 2013).
48. "Advanced Technologies", Indian Space Research Organisation, at http://www.isro.gov.in/ttg/pdfuploads/TT%20_SAC_%201002ThermalControlCoating.pdf (Accessed July 29, 2013).
49. Ibid.
50. "Nickel Smelting and Refining", World Bank Group, at http://www.ifc.org/wps/wcm/connect/469da18048855b7f891cdb6a6515bb18/nickel_PPAH.pdf?MOD=AJPERES (Accessed July 30, 2013).
51. "Nickel Processing", *Encyclopaedia Britannica*, at http://www.britannica.com/EBchecked/topic/414313/nickel-processing/81474/From-sulfide-ores (Accessed July 30, 2013).
52. "Refining Methods of Nickel", Nickel Institute, at http://www.nickelinstitute.org/~/media/Files/NickelUseInSociety/AboutNickel/Production/Refining.ashx (Accessed July 30, 2013).
53. "Nickel", British Geological Survey, September 2008.
54. "Niobium - Raw Materials and Processing", Tantalum-Niobium International Study Center, at http://tanb.org/niobium (Accessed July 30, 2013).
55. "Niobium", USGS Mineral Resources Program, at http://minerals.usgs.gov/minerals/pubs/commodity/antimony/mcs-2012-antim.pdf (Accessed July 30, 2013).
56. "Niobium 101", at http://www.iamgold.com/files/pdf/Niobium%20101%20Final%20March%202012.pdf (Accessed July 30, 2013).
57. "Silver Mineral | Uses and Properties", at http://geology.com/minerals/silver.shtml (Accessed July 30, 2013).
58. Uses of Silver in Electronics", at http://geology.com/articles/uses-of-silver/ (Accessed July 30, 2013).
59. "World Silver Survey 2013 A Summary", Thomson Reuters GFMS and the Silver Institute, at https://www.silverinstitute.org/site/wp-content/uploads/2013/06/WSS2013Summary.pdf (Accessed August 1, 2013).
60. www.silverwire.com (Accessed August 1, 2013).
61. Ibid.
62. "How Tantalum Is Mined", at http://www.ehow.com/about_6136148_tantalum-mined.html#ixzz2lpzE7RwD (Accessed August 1, 2013).
63. "Tin", at http://www.carondelet.pvt.k12.ca.us/Family/Science/GroupIVA/tin.htm (Accessed August 2, 2013).
64. "Tin - Mineral Fact Sheets", Australian Mines Atlas, at http://www.australianminesatlas.gov.au/education/fact_sheets/tin.html (Accessed August 3, 2013).
65. "Tin processing", *Encyclopaedia Britannica*, at http://www.britannica.com/EBchecked/topic/596496/tin-processing/82122/Refining (Accessed August 3, 2013).
66. "Tungsten Processing", International Tungsten Industry Association (ITIA), at http://www.itia.info/tungsten-processing.html (Accessed August 3, 2013).
67. "Tungsten Uses", International Tungsten Industry Association (ITIA), at http://www.itia.info/tungsten-properties.html (Accessed August 3, 2013).
68. "Primary Uses of Tungsten", International Tungsten Industry Association (ITIA), at http://

www.itia.info/tungsten-primary-uses.html(Accessed August 3, 2013).

69. "Tungsten", at http://www.wolfmet.com/applications/aerospace (Accessed August 4, 2013).
70. "Defence and Aerospace Applications of Molybdenum, Tungsten and Tantalum Products", No. 39.
71. "Tungsten." www.tungstenchina.com/product/Tungsten-Alloy-713.html (Accessed August 5, 2013).
72. "Tungsten Industry", International Tungsten Industry Association (ITIA), at http:// www.itia.info/thermonuclear-energy.html (Accessed August 5, 2013).
73. "Tungsten", at http://en.wikipedia.org/wiki/Tungsten#Alloys, (Accessed August 5, 2013).
74. "Tungsten Material", Indian Bureau of Mines and US geological survey 2013.
75. John Kemp, "U.S. Strategic Helium Reserve Dwindles, Prompting Supply Concerns and Legislative Action", at http://www.huffingtonpost.com/2013/03/27/us-strategic-helium-reserve_n_2961771.html (Accessed March 18, 2014).

    Chris Rhodes, "Peak Minerals: Shortage of Rare Earth Metals Threatens Renewable Energy", July 30, 2012, at http://oilprice.com/Alternative-Energy/Renewable-Energy/Peak-Minerals-Shortage-of-Rare-Earth-Metals-Threatens-Renewable-Energy.html (Accessed on March 20, 2014).

    "Helium", at http://www.blm.gov/nm/st/en/prog/energy/helium.html (Accessed on March 27, 2014).

    "Selling the Nation's Helium Reserve", a report by the Committee on Understanding the Impact of Selling the Helium Reserve, The National Academies Press, Washington D.C., 2010.

REFERENCES

"Mineral Deposit", *Encyclopaedia Britannica, Rocks and Minerals*, at http://www.britannica.com/ EBchecked/topic/383726/mineral-deposit (Last Accessed March 2014).

"Metal Profiles", at http://metals.about.com/od/properties/a/Metal-Profiles.htm (Last Accessed March 2014).

Mineral Year Book, US Geological Survey, at http://minerals.usgs.gov/minerals/pubs/commodity/ myb (Last Accessed March 2014).

Indian Minerals Year Book 2012, Indian Bureau of Mines, at http://ibm.nic.in/imyb2012.htm (Last Accessed March 2014).

World Mineral Statistics, British Geological Survey, at http://www.bgs.ac.uk/mineralsuk/statistics/ worldStatistics.html.(Last Accessed March 2014).

3

Global Distribution of Strategic Mineral Resources

This chapter provides the contours of investments made by a few important states in strategic minerals/materials. However, the information available (in open source) about the wealth of mineral assets and activities undertaken by them varies in content from state to state. In this chapter, an attempt has been made to project this information and coherently as possible (depending on the nature of information available). Also, for the purposes of trade figures and other important statistics, 2012 has been taken as a cut-off year; however, at places it has not been possible to retain it due to the non-availability of information.

The following sections provide profiles of various important countries/ regions.

Africa

The second largest continent in the world encompassing 56 independent nations and adjacent islands, Africa has the largest mineral industry in the world. The mineral reserves in this region are found in large quantities; moreover, it has the highest mineral reserves of some strategic minerals such as manganese, chromium, cobalt, lead, vanadium and titanium (an important light metal for aerospace and defence industries); precious metals like gold, diamond and platinum and a whole range of other non-fuel minerals. The quality of the minerals available is also very significant. For last few decades, various western and Asian countries have been dependent on Africa for the supply of minerals. Today, various states in the world are freshly formalising their Africa policy because of the capacity of this region to supply strategic minerals. There is a rising scramble over these resources from Africa partly because of the presence of emerging economies like China, India, and Brazil. Also, western countries are feeling the heat of the competition for the resources, particularly, of strategic mineral supplies owning to the increasing demand from additional states.

Mineral Industry in Africa

The share of world production from Africa for various minerals is as follows: bauxite 9 per cent; aluminium 5 per cent; chromite 44 per cent; cobalt 57 per cent; copper 5 per cent; gold 21 per cent; iron ore 4 per cent; steel 2 per cent; lead 3 per cent; manganese 39 per cent; zinc 2 per cent; cement 4 per cent; natural diamond 46 per cent; graphite 2 per cent; phosphate rock 31 per cent; coal 5 per cent; mineral fuels (including coal) and petroleum 13 per cent; uranium 16 per cent.[1] The mineral industry in recent times has emerged as an important source of export earnings for many African nations. According to an estimate, Gross Domestic Product (GDP) of sub-Saharan Africa has increased from 2.5 per cent in 2009 to 5.4 per cent in 2011 and estimated to reach 5.8 per cent[2] by the end of 2013. This significant growth has had an evident effect partly because of growing requirement of emerging economy on increasing demand for strategic minerals from Africa. It may be noted that it is difficult to provide precise information about exports from Africa because various states in this region have their individual business strategies and interests. Also, owning to complex security situation in various states, the authenticity of the data made available at times remains questionable. Figure 3.1 shows the physical locations of the minerals in the African continent.

Commodity Review

Aluminium, Bauxite and Alumina

Accounting the 8 per cent of world's total bauxite production, African bauxite production has increased by nearly 13 per cent in 2010. Nation of Guinea by producing 17,593,100 metric tons in 2011 accounted for about 90 per cent of African bauxite production followed by Sierra Leone and Ghana with 6 per cent and 3 per cent, respectively.

African production of refined aluminium is significant. South Africa with the production of around 810000 metric tons in 2011 accounted for 44 per

Figure 3.1: Map of African Minerals[3]

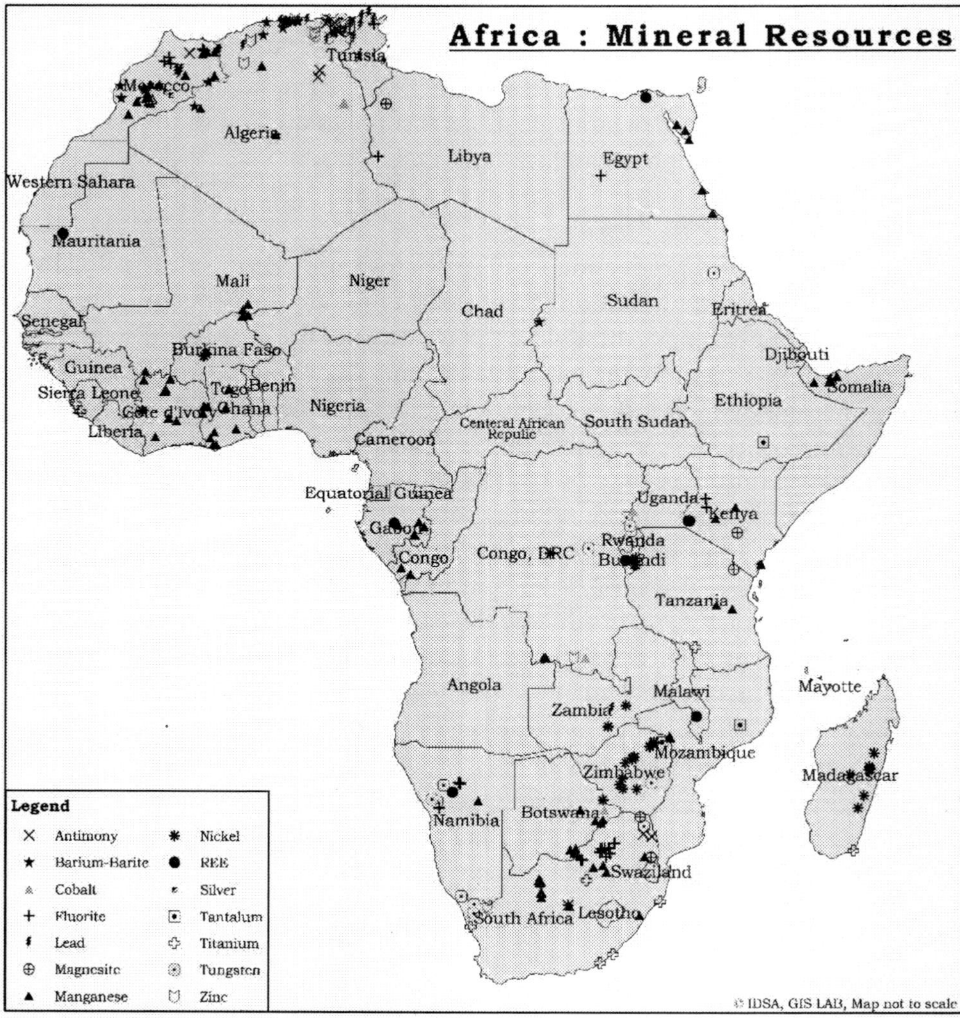

cent of African aluminium output, followed by Mozambique and Egypt with 30 per cent (5,62,000 tons) 22 per cent (3,53,904 tons), respectively.

Cobalt (Co)

Africa's share of world cobalt production is estimated to be about 70 per cent. Congo (Kinshasa) accounts for approximately 86 per cent of African cobalt mine production with 108,888 metric tons followed by Zambia and Morocco with 8 per cent and 4 per cent, respectively.

Chromium (Cr)

Africa has a share of approximately about 40 per cent of world's total chromium production. South Africa alone shared almost 54 per cent of world total chromium production in 2012. South Africa also shares about 95 per cent of Africa's total chromium production, while additional ores get mined in Madagascar, Sudan and Zimbabwe (see Figure 3.2).

Figure 3.2: Chromium Production

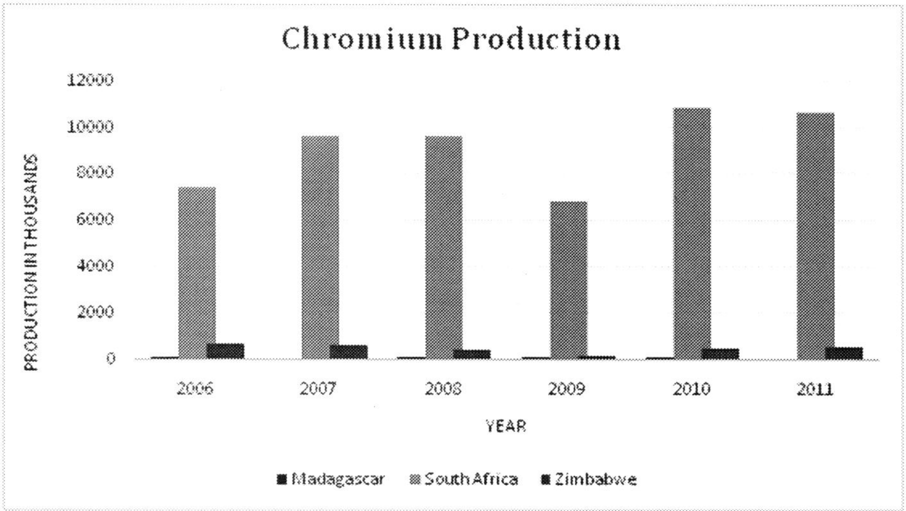

Source: Mineral Commodity British Geological Survey.

Copper (Co)

Africa's world share of total copper production is around 7 per cent. Some increase in Africa's copper mine production has been witnessed post 2010. In 2010, Zambia with 7, 39,759 metric tons accounted for 56 per cent of the African copper mine production followed by Congo (Kinshasa) 30 per cent (4, 80,000 metric tons) and South Africa, 7 per cent (96,500 metric tons). Africa's copper production is expected to increase by 7 percent in coming year with substantial investment by China in Zambia and Congo.

Lithium (Li)

Probably, Zimbabwe is the only country to produce lithium in Africa. Africa's lithium production was 700 metric tons (t) in 2011, which is expected to reach 900-1000 metric tons (t) by 2014.

Manganese (Mg)[4]

According to 2010 report of the US Geological Survey (USGS), Africa shared about 29 per cent of world manganese ore output. South Africa shared about 24 per cent of world total manganese production in 2012. South Africa shared about 55 per cent of total African output in 2010 followed by Gabon (25 per cent), and Ghana (about 13 per cent).

Nickel (Ni)

Africa has significant amount of nickel production with South Africa and Madagascar as the major players. During the last few years, certain country specific fluctuations are being witnessed in respect of production of nickel. While the output of South Africa has increased marginally by 8 per cent, there has been significant increase in Madagascar output, which was reported to be 40 per cent increase from 15,000 in 2010 to 25,000 in 2011. There has been slight decrease in the outputs of Zimbabwe and Zambia. Zambia which has joined nickel production in recent period contributed around 2,869 tons of nickel in 2011. South Africa contributed 45 per cent of the total nickel output of Africa followed by Madagascar 26 per cent and Botswana 16 per cent. The output of Zimbabwe is expected to decrease due to closure of one of its major nickel mines, the Shangani Mine. The African nickel output is expected to increase significantly due to development activities in various countries which might strive for mineral production in the coming decade.

Tin (Sn)

African mining for tin production has shown some decline in recent past. Cassiterite in Congo (Kinshasa) of is one of the major producers of tin in Africa contributing 53 per cent of total production followed by Rwanda, which accounts for around 40 per cent output, and Nigeria, which accounts for about 7 per cent. With the announcement of Abu Dabbab alluvial tin project and tantalum mine, both in Egypt, in 2013. The continent is expected to increase its total production by 30 per cent by 2014.

Zinc (Zn)

Africa's mine production of zinc has decreased since 2008. According to USGS 2009, Morocco accounted for 53 per cent of the total African zinc mine production followed by Namibia, 21 per cent; South Africa, 16 per cent and Congo (Kinshasa), 10 per cent. While Africa's zinc production has reduced to about 7 per cent since 2009, its overall world share is about 2 per cent, which as per a mineral rich continent like Africa is comparatively less.

According to International Lead and Zinc Study Group (ILZSG) Lead and Zinc Statistics' Bulletin,[5] Africa's consumption till 2010 was 2 per cent of total world consumption. African zinc mine production is expected to increase by about 8 per cent by 2015 as the long-halted Algeria zinc production has started.

Australia

Australia is one of the sixth largest countries in the world in respect of geographical area and is the world's third largest ocean territory. It is also the only nation continent with a population of only 23 million, which is relatively small compared to its total land area. Australia is one of the richest countries in the world with 12th largest economy and fifth highest per capita income. Mining is one of the strongest pillars in Australian economy, and it contributed US$ 100 billion in 2011, which is about 10 per cent of its total GDP; mining-related component comprises 9 per cent making the total contribution to about 19 per cent.[6] It is also one of the leading mineral producing countries in the world, ranking within the top 10 countries in the production of minerals like bauxite, coal, cobalt, copper, gem and near-gem diamond, gold, iron ore, lithium, manganese ore, tantalum and uranium (see Figure 3.3).[7]

Mineral Trade

With a total trade of US$ 637.7 billion in 2011, of which exports constitute about US$ 329.0 billion and imports constitute about US$ 308.7 billion.[8] Minerals contributed 58 per cent of the total exports generating high revenue for the country. Australia's investment in the mineral industry is significant. It spent approximately US$ 3.1 billion in the fiscal year 2011, of which 65 per cent was spent on known deposits while 35 per cent was spent on new exploration projects. Table 3.1 shows the major Australian mineral exports.

Commodity Review

Antimony (Sb)[10]

Antimony production is not very significant. It was around 1800 tons in 2012 while import was around 769 tons. The major producer of this ore is Mandalay Resources Ltd.'s Costerfield Mine in Victoria.

Figure 3.3: Australian Mineral Map

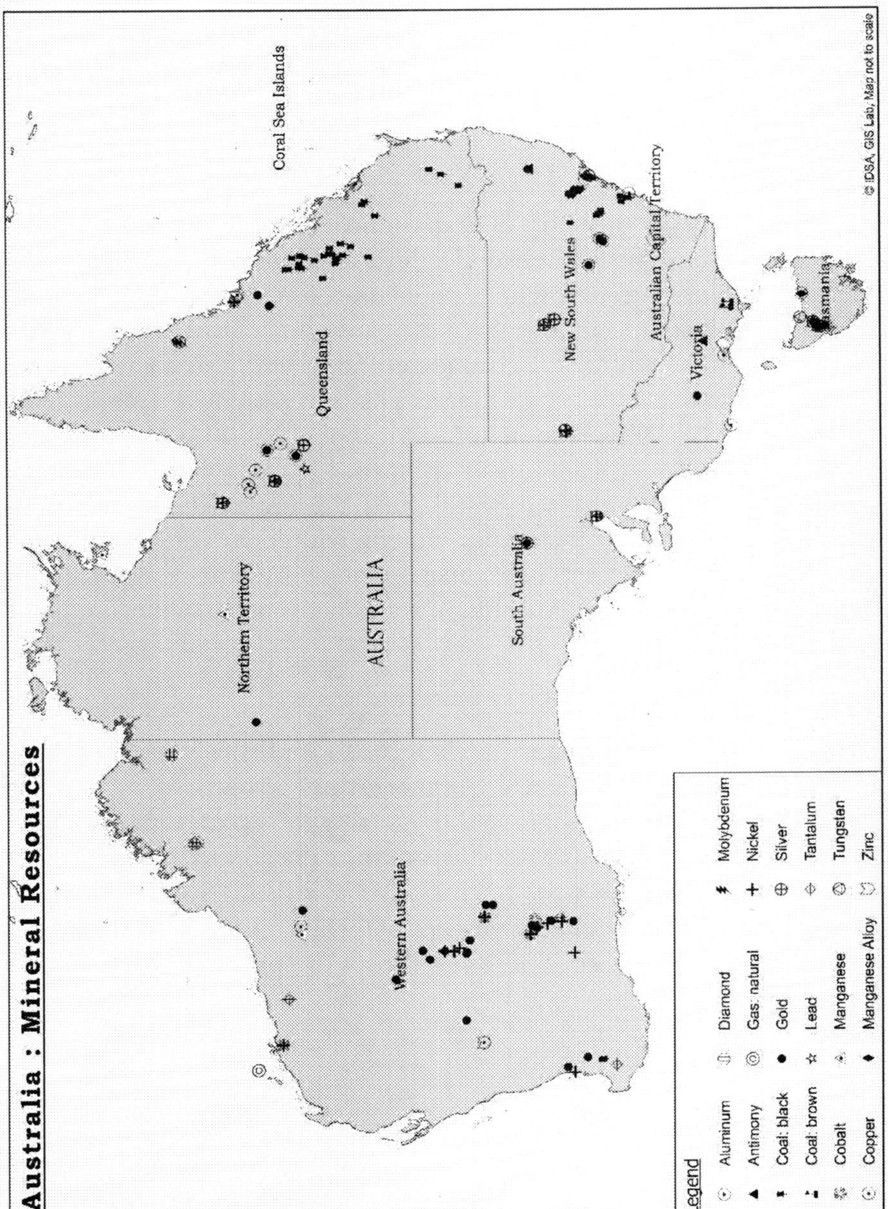

Table 3.1: **Major Mineral Exports of Australia**

Australia Major Mineral Exports[9]

Commodity	Units	Quantity	Value (thousands US$)
Alumina	kt	16,653	4,969
Aluminium (ingot metal)	kt	1624	3,838
Coal, black			
Metallurgical	Metric tons	24 526	
Thermal	Metric tons	11 886	
Copper	kt	805	8,506
Diamonds	'000 c	10 355	471
Gold, refined	t	335	12,996
Iron and steel			
Iron ore and pellets	Metric tons	34 515	
Iron and steel	kt	1 120	
Lead	kt	658	1,833
Manganese ore and concentrate	kt	5 648	1 395
Nickel	kt	221	3,875
Oil and gas			
Crude oil and other refinery feedstock	ML	9 534	
LNG	Metric tons	7 789	
LPG	ML	1 105	
Salt kt	11 185	247	
Tin t	6 031	101	
Titanium minerals			
Ilmenite concentrate	kt	197	
Rutile concentrate	kt	382	
Uranium oxide	t	7555	751
Zinc	kt	1482	2 214
Zircon concentrate	kt	748	370

Sources: *Australian Bureau of Statistics*; Australian Bureau of Agricultural and Resource Economics and Sciences (ABARES); Australian Mineral Statistics, March Quarter 2011.

Cobalt (Co) and Nickel (Ni)

Cobalt deposits are found in close association with nickel and copper ores. Cobalt and nickel are vital strategic minerals and have very a high demand in the commodity market. Country holds the highest reserve of cobalt estimating to be about 24 million tons of nickel deposits, which is a share of about 26.8 per cent of world nickel production. According to Australian Bureau of Statistics, the country invested about US$ 262.1 million for nickel-cobalt exploration in 2011.[11] Western Australia has the highest reserve contributing around 90 per cent of the country's output.

Copper (Co)

Australia has vast copper reserves and is ranked as the third largest economic resource (13 per cent) after Chile (28 per cent) and Peru (13 per cent). It is also ranked fifth in the world sharing about 6 per cent of the world copper production. In 2011, the country's total copper production was around 961 kilo-tons. South Australia accounted 33 per cent of total production followed by Queensland 31 per cent. China was the leading destination of the country's exports sharing 35 per cent of the total exports followed by India, 31 per cent; Japan, 21 per cent and the Republic of Korea, 11 per cent.

Lead (Sb), Silver (Ag) and Zinc (Zn)

Usually, Zinc is the major component of the ore, while silver and lead are the by-products. With one of the largest resources of zinc (about 26 per cent), Australia is the second largest producer of zinc ores after China, and the fourth largest producer of silver. Australia has produced 15,000 tons of zinc and 62,000 tons of lead in 2011. China is the leading export destination for zinc, while India is the leading export destination for refined lead. The Economic Demonstrated Resource (EDR)[12] of silver was about 88kT representing 16 per cent of the world economic resource.

Tantalum (Ta)

Estimated production of tantalum is around 790 tons. Australia is also estimated to have the second largest resource of tantalum after Brazil. Green bushes and the Wodgina Mines in Western Australia are supposed to be producing most of the Australian tantalum.

Tin (Sn)

The world production of tin was estimated to be 250kT in 2011, of which Australia produced 5 per cent of the total world production. Australia was estimated to have exported 11,049 tons of tin concentrates and 19 tons of refined tin in 2011. Metal X Ltd. was one of the highest producing company in Tasmania, which has 50 per cent share of Yunnan Tin Group of China. Renison Bell deposit in Western Tas (the West Coast of Tasmania) has the highest reserves of Australia's total tin production. The country was estimated to have produced 5,000 tons of tin in 2011. Australia was ranked seventh in terms of tin production in the world.

Tungsten (W)

Australia produced 72,000 tons of tungsten in 2011, which is about 11.4 per cent of world total production of tungsten. Initial production of wolframite concentrates as the primary ore began at both Wolfram Camp and Mount Carbine in north Queensland in 2012 producing 27 tons of high-grade concentrates.

Brazil[13]

Brazil is the fifth largest country in the world in terms of geographical area as well as population. It is also one of the largest countries in South America and the Latin American region. As a free market economy, and the fastest growing economy, Brazil has the sixth largest economy in the world in terms of nominal GDP. With 8,870 mining companies operating in the country in 2011, it is one of the largest mineral producing countries in the world. Mining industry contributed 4.5 per cent of the GDP in 2011 (Figure 3.4).

Mineral Trade

In 2011, Brazil's exports and imports were around US$ 236 billion and US$ 209 billion, respectively. The mineral trade in the country contributes significantly to the country's trade balance. In 2011, the mineral trade surplus was around US$ 48 billion. The total export and import share of some of the minerals is shown in Figures 3.5 and 3.6.

Commodity Review

Copper (Co)

Brazil's total copper production was 218,670 tons in 2011. Brazil imported 484,800 tons of copper ore mainly from Chile (95 per cent) and Portugal (4 per cent), while 63,100 tons of copper metal in 2011 mainly from Chile (81 per cent) and Peru (18 per cent). Due to high investment in the copper industry, Brazil is expected to increase its domestic production to regulate the trade balance by reducing the imports. Brazil is expected to be self-reliant in copper production shortly.

Manganese (Mg)

Brazil was ranked as the sixth largest producer of manganese in the world. With the production of 3.2 metric tons of manganese in 2011, the country shared 11.6 per cent of world production. Ferroalloys industry was the major

Figure 3.4: Brazil's Mineral Map

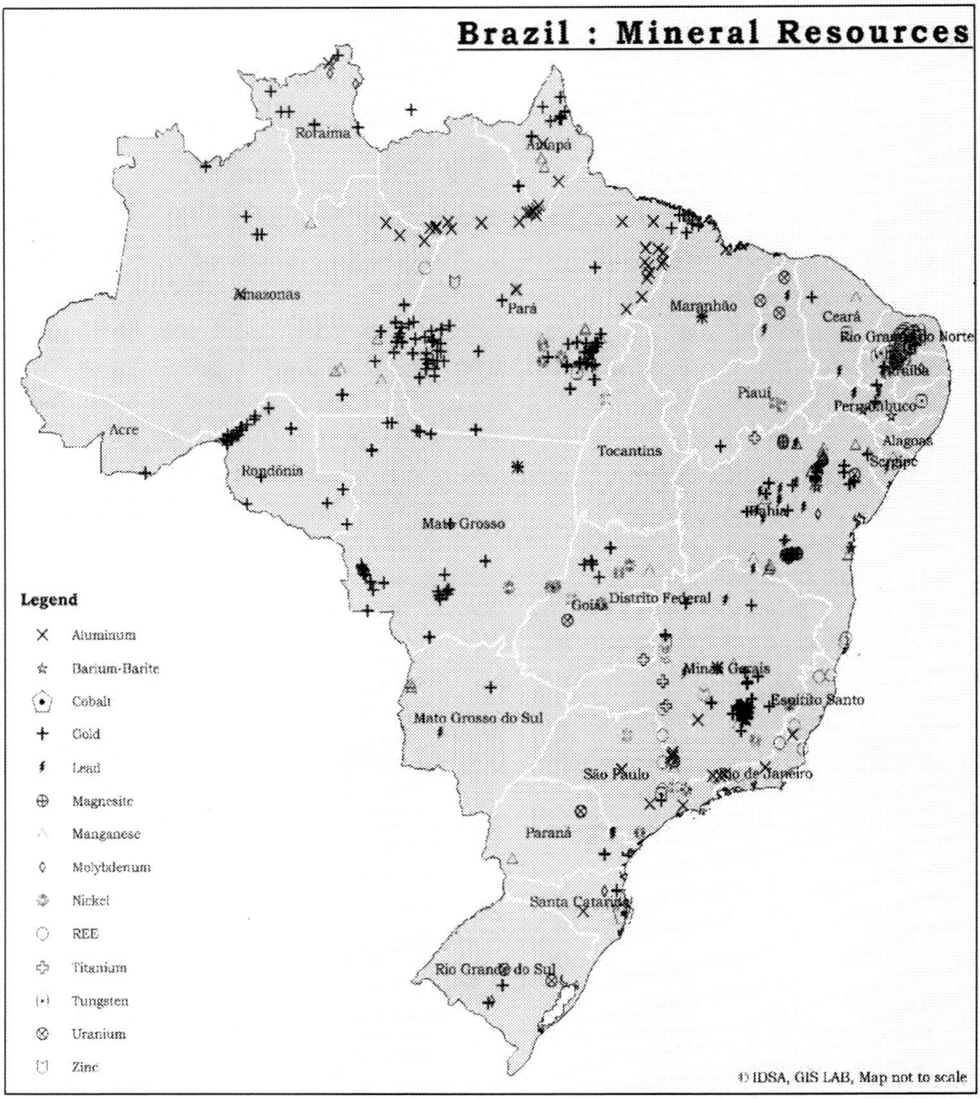

consumer of manganese consuming 85 per cent of total consumption in Brazil followed by the electrical batteries (15 per cent) industry. There was a slight increase in the production of manganese in 2011 from 2010. The trend of production is as shown in Figure 3.7.

Figure 3.5: Brazil's Mining Trade Balance – Exports (per cent of amount in US$)

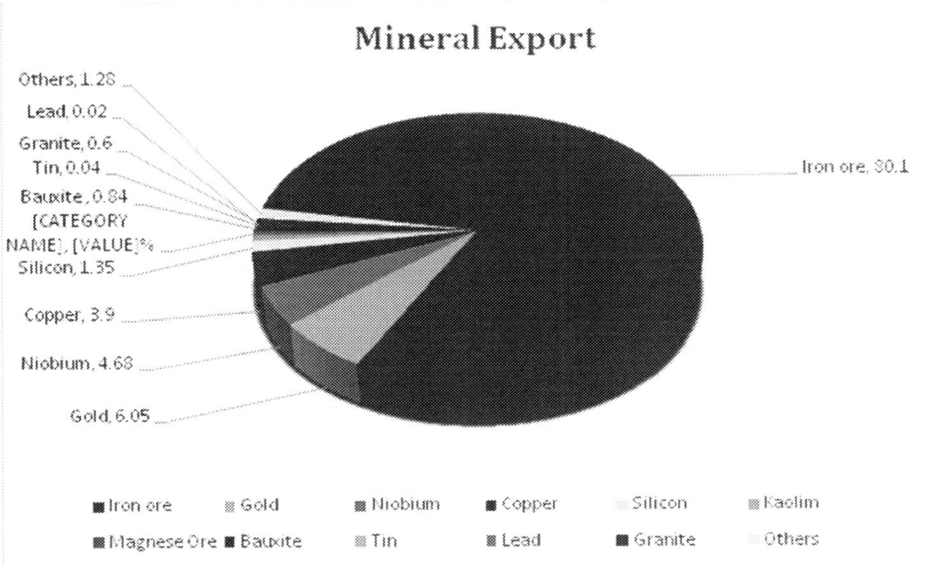

Source: Information and Analyses on the Brazilian Mineral, 2012.

Figure 3.6: Brazil's Mining Trade Balance – Imports (per cent of amount in US$)

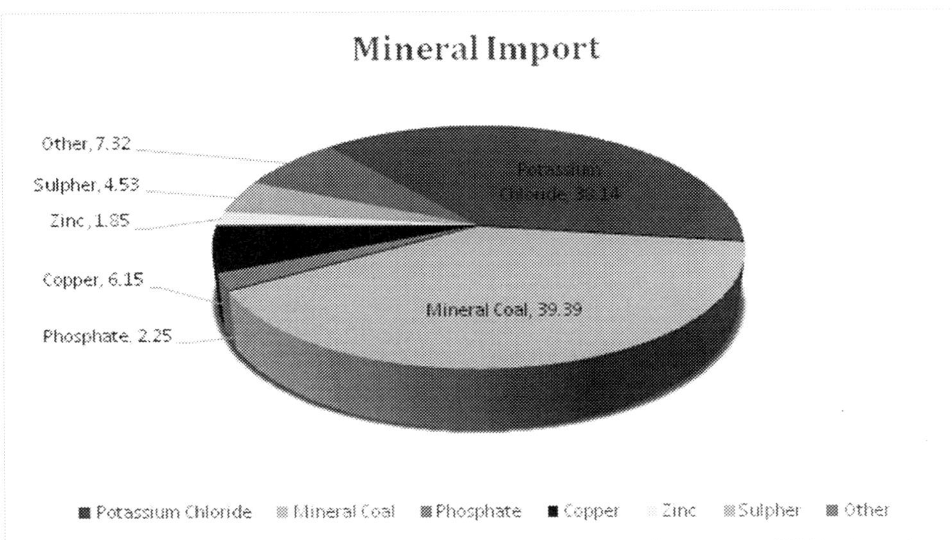

Source: Information and Analyses on the Brazilian Mineral, 2012.

Figure 3.7: Production of Manganese in Brazil

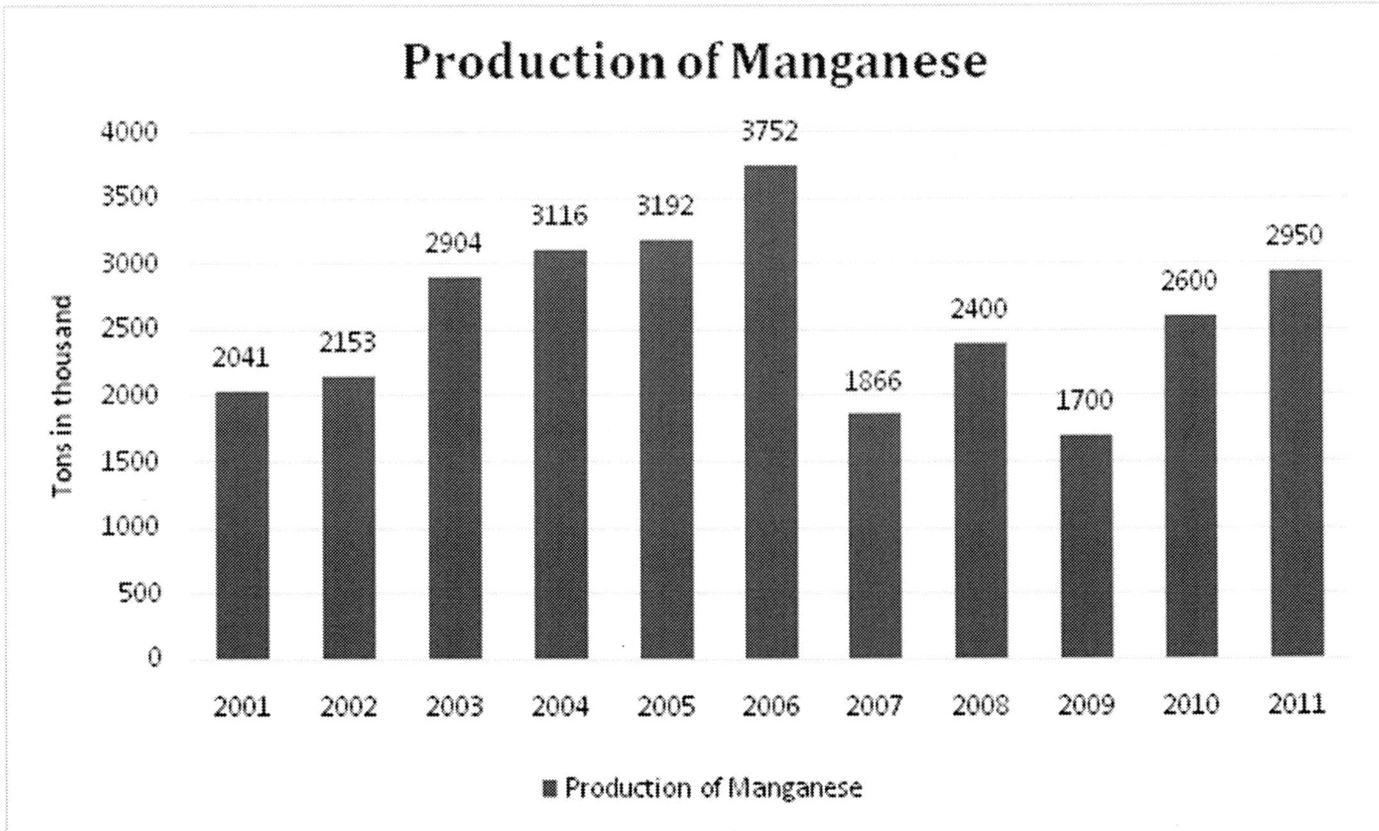

Source: Information and Analyses on the Brazilian Mineral, 2012; LME, 2012.

Nickel (Ni)

Brazil is the seventh largest producer of nickel in the world, and produced 110,960 tons of nickel ore in 2011. The production of the most widely used form of nickel, ferronickel alloys, was around 8,600 tons. Vale, one of the biggest multinational mining corporations in Brazil produced 1.5 metric tons of nickel.

Tin (Sn)

With 12,000 tons of production in 2011, the country was ranked the fifth largest producer of Zinc ore in the world. The main producers in the country were Mineração Taboca (66 per cent), Coopersanta (20 per cent) and others (14 per cent). Brazil has the third largest reserve of tin in the world share, that is, 12.5 per cent of the total reserve following China 31.25 per cent and Indonesia 16.66 per cent.

Zinc (Zn)

Brazil is the 12th largest producer of Zinc in the world with an output of around 206,130 tons in 2011. It also shared 2.5 per cent of the total world production of zinc in 2011. The zinc ore reserves accounted for 6.5 million tons. There were two main metallurgy operations (Juiz de Fora and Tres Marias) located in Minas Gerais State which produced 211,800 tons of zinc metal.

China

In geographical terms, the People's Republic of China (PRC) is the fourth largest country in the world after Russia, Canada and the US with land area of 9.6 million square kilometres. With population of about 1,359 million, it's the world's most populous nation contributing about 20 per cent of world population. It's also the second largest economy in the world after the US with an unprecedented economic growth of approximately 8 per cent per year which was higher than the expected growth of 7 per cent in its 12th five-year plan.[14] To sustain the massive economic growth, its demand for energy, minerals, and metals have grown substantially making the country the leading mineral producing and consuming country in the world.

China has some of the world's richest strategic mineral reserves; it was the leading producer of aluminium, antimony, barite, bismuth, cement, coal, fluorspar, gold, graphite, iron and steel, lead, magnesium, mercury, molybdenum, phosphate rock, rare earths, salt, talc, tin, tungsten and zinc in 2011.[15] China has also come up as the world producer of 37 minerals and metals and produces more than 50 per cent of the world's total output of 12

Figure 3.8: Major Mines and Important Deposits in China

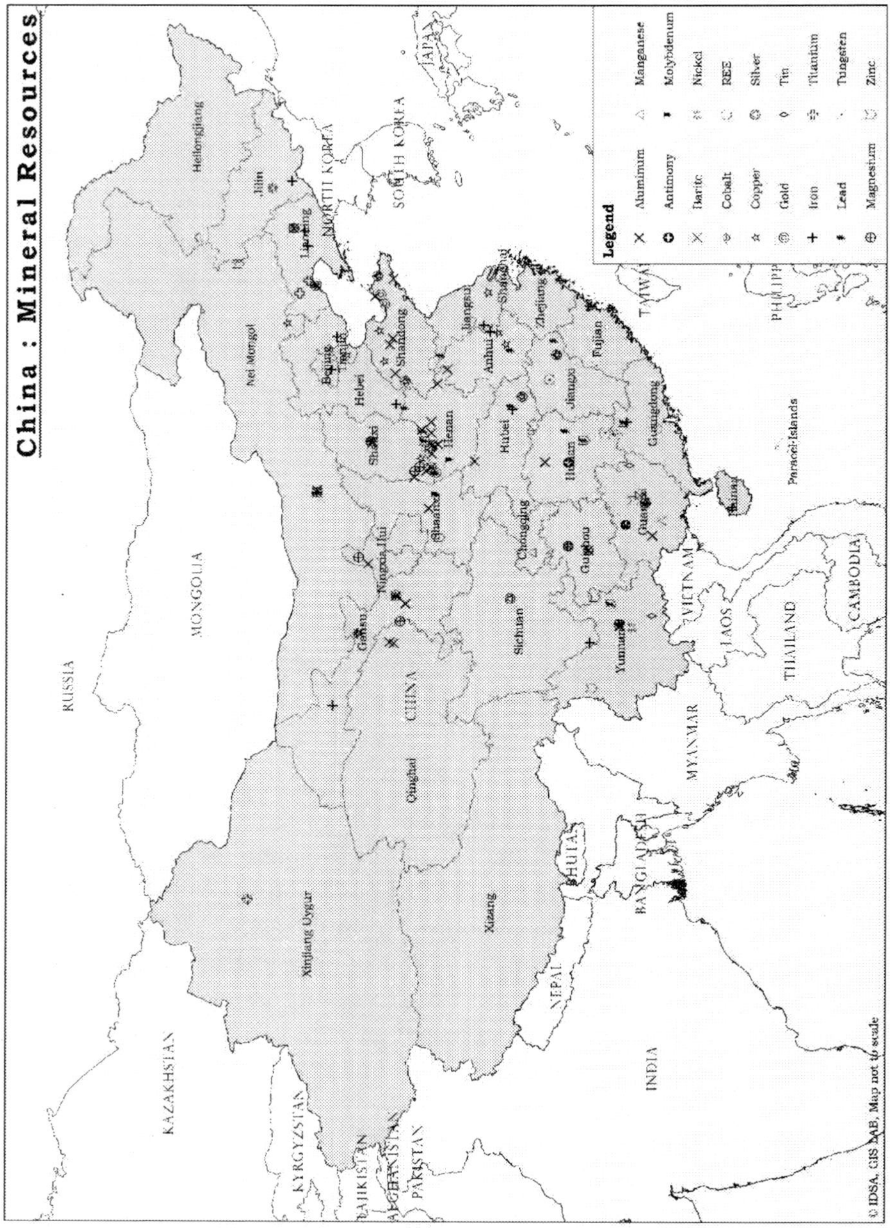

of these.[16] China's share of world production is 85 per cent of rare earths (this value shows variations for source to source, and at places it has also been put to around 95 per cent), 32 per cent of tin and 83 per cent of tungsten. With such deposits in hand, China is in a position to control the price of minerals at the global level. Figure 8 shows the major metallic mineral resources in China.

Overall, the mining sector is a vital sector to shape Chinese economy. China has made significant amount of investments into this sector both domestically and globally. According to the USGS 2010 report, "China's fixed-asset investment increased by 24.5 per cent to US$ 3.7 trillion, of which the mining sector (including coal) received US$ 148.5 billion and the natural gas and oil sector received US$ 44.5 billion".[17] The labour force in the mining sector was 5.62 million, or 4.3 per cent of the country's total workforce in 2010.[18]

Mineral Trade[19]

China is one of the top three mineral and metal product trade dominating country in the world. In 2010, its total trade was US$ 712.5 billion, which accounted for 24.0 per cent of the country's total trade. There was an increase of 34.7 per cent in trade in 2011, as compared to 2009 accounting for US$ 2.97 trillion. The major destination for Chinese trade is mainly the US, as it imports 80 per cent of strategic minerals from China, followed by the European Union (EU), Hong Kong and Japan. Table 3.2 lists China's mineral exports in 2011.

Table 3.2: China's Export Minerals in 2011

Commodity	Quantity (metric tons)	Value (thousands US$)
METALS		
Aluminium:		
Alumina	76,280	53,506
Metal and alloys:		
Unwrought	7,66,122	17,89,057
Semi manufactures	30,00,000	1,03,61,684
Antimony:		
Metal, unwrought	5,062	66,317
Oxide	41,995	5,12,728
Barium sulphate	28,90,000	2,41,911
Copper, metal and alloys:		
Unwrought	1,56,516	14,90,847
Semi-manufactures	5,00,347	45,25,882
Indium, unwrought, including powder	105	69,025

Commodity	Quantity (metric tons)	Value (thousands US$)
Iron and steel:		
Pig iron and cast iron	8,70,000	4,40,978
Steel:		
Bars and rods	66,90,000	59,87,326
Shapes and sections	27,00,000	20,94,512
Sheets and plates	2,65,80,000	2,55,62,875
Tube and pipe	14,40,000	37,52,393
Wire of steel or iron	17,00,000	21,49,800
Ferroalloys	9,30,000	36,11,795
Scrap	25,095	12,813
Magnesium, metal and alloy:		
Unwrought, Mg not less than 99.8 per cent	1,85,879	5,55,104
Other unwrought	99,362	3,28,377
Manganese, unwrought	56,386	2,01,768
Molybdenum, ores and concentrates	18,732	3,74,994
Silver, unwrought	1,178	13,03,603
Tin, metal and alloys, unwrought	1,227	38,222
Tungsten, tungstates	5,136	1,82,165
Zinc:		
Metal and alloys, unwrought	48,369	1,15,648
Oxide and peroxide	17,608	32,979
INDUSTRIAL MINERALS		
Cement	1,06,10,000	6,20,353
Fluorspar	7,20,000	1,33,809
Granite	80,40,000	2,56,840
Graphite, natural	4,40,000	3,65,181
Magnesia, fused	20,70,000	6,62,229
Rare-earth products	16,900	26,67,140

Source: US and British Geological Survey, 2012.

China's expanding economy and rising per capita income has certainly raised the imbalance between supply and demand for some of the resources due to rising domestic demand for minerals: from metallic and non-metallic minerals to energy minerals. According to World Watch Institute report, in 2005 alone China consumed 26 per cent of world steel and 47 per cent of cement. China is the world's largest producer and consumer of coal contributing 3.5 billion metric tons of coal in 2011, and also the world's largest consumer of refined lead. There has been acute shortage of certain important strategic minerals such as chromium, cobalt, copper, iron ore, manganese, nickel, petroleum, platinum-group metals and potash; hence, exceeding "domestic supply, and imports which were estimated to account for more than 40 per cent of domestic consumption".[20] Table 3.3 lists China's mineral imports in 2011.

Table 3.3: China's Import of Selected Minerals in 2011
(Metric tons unless otherwise specified)

Commodity	Quantity	Value (thousands US$)
METALS		
Aluminium:		
Bauxite	4,48,44,914	20,57,746
Alumina	18,80,000	7,77,809
Metal and alloys, unwrought	3,33,123	8,27,960
Semi manufactures	5,77,364	35,92,775
Scrap	26,90,000	46,25,509
Chromium, chromite	94,40,000	26,63,791
Cobalt:		
Ore and concentrates	3,48,191	8,50,937
Unwrought and powder	11,057	1,75,504
Copper:		
Ore and concentrates	63,80,000	1,55,18,135
Anode	4,16,332	37,80,616
Metal and alloys, unwrought	32,91,469	2,89,76,396
Semi manufactures	7,81,623	78,28,354
Scrap	46,90,000	1,63,51,959
Iron and steel:		
Iron ore	68,60,80,000	11,24,06,539
Steel:		
Bars and rods	11,50,000	19,26,600
Seamless pipe	5,20,000	19,79,468
Shapes and sections	3,90,000	4,16,672
Sheets and plates	1,32,00,000	1,56,94,346
Scrap	67,70,000	41,36,390
Manganese ore	1,29,70,000	26,74,563
Nickel:		
Ore and concentrates	4,80,55,678	49,04,203
Metal, refined greater than 99.95 per cent Ni	11,169	2,69,007
Metal, other refined	2,01,310	46,45,652
Titanium dioxide	2,28,528	7,03,812
INDUSTRIAL MINERALS		
Diamond (kilograms)	3,342	61,47,250

Commodity	Quantity	Value (thousands US$)
Nitrogen, phosphorus, and potassium fertilizers:		
Compound fertilizers	10,20,000	5,31,911
Di-ammonium phosphate	90,000	58,573
Potassium chloride	64,00,000	26,91,321
Potassium sulphate	1,50,000	75,505

Source: US and British Geological Survey 2012.

Aluminium (Al)

Aluminium is obtained from its most common ores, that is, bauxite, alumina and aluminium. In 2008, China replaced Brazil to be the second largest aluminium producer in the world after Australia by increasing the production by 37 per cent in five years and 19 per cent in 2009 compared to 2008. In 2009, it accounted for around 15 per cent of the total world output and shared 37 per cent of total world aluminium production. However, China remains world's leading aluminium importer due to its insufficiency to meet the domestic demand. Chinese production in 2011 was nearly 89.23 million tons and imports was 34.87 million tons.[21] China's unwrought aluminium imports came mainly from Russia, Oman, Australia, South Africa, India and North Korea. Figure 9 shows the aluminium imports of China.

Figure 3.9: Aluminium Imports of China 2011

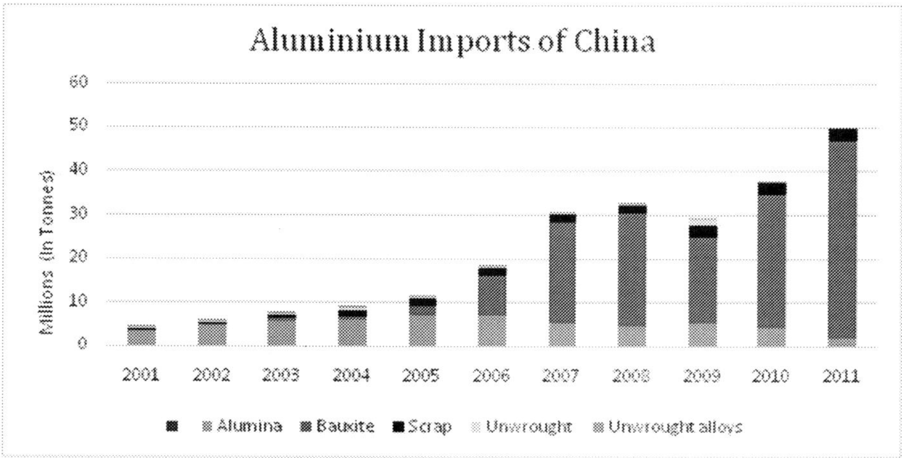

Source: Centre for Sustainable Mineral Development (BGS); US Geological Survey and *World Mineral Year book 2011.*

Figure 3.10 shows sector-wise consumption of aluminium in China.

Figure 3.10: Consumption of Aluminium in China

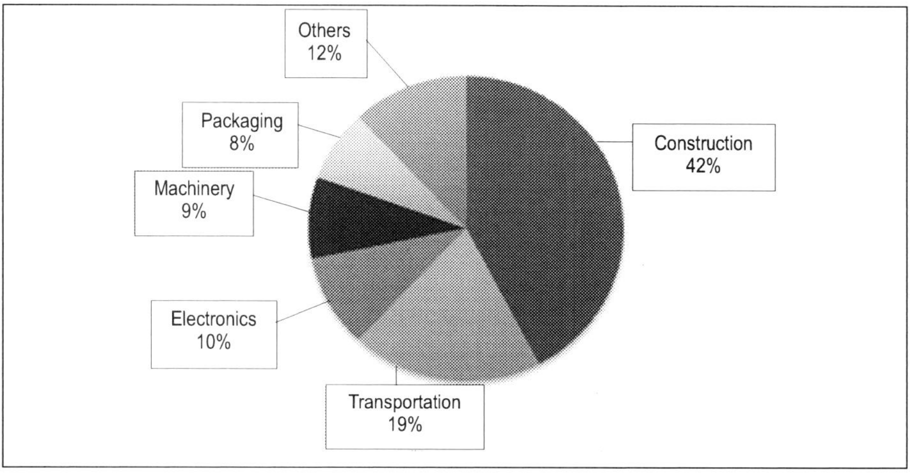

Source: US Geological Survey; Alumina and Aluminium Monthly, 2012a; China Metals, 2012.

Commodity Review

Antimony (Sb)

China has been one of the leading producers of cobalt in the world. In 2011, China produced 128,017 tonnes of antimony. Even though the Chinese Government came down heavily on illegal mining in the provinces of Guangxi, Hunan and Yunnan, the country was still insufficient to meet the domestic demand of antimony concentrates. Therefore, China imported 60,151 tons of ores and concentrates, 491tons of metal and 3,215 tons of oxides in 2011. But, subsequently the government has strictly restricted further exploitation of antimony and has taken over complete control as it is a strategic mineral.

Cobalt (Co)

China's cobalt resource is limited; hence, its maximum demand is met by imports. In 2011, the country's production was 128,017 tons while the net import of China was around 417,615 tons, comprising 348,191 tons of ore and concentrates and 11,057 tons of unwrought and powder. The Democratic Republic of the Congo and South Africa accounted for 93 per cent of the total imports.[22] The consumption of cobalt is dominated by battery industries followed by cement carbide and magnets (see Figure 3.11).

Figure 3.11: Cobalt Consumption in China

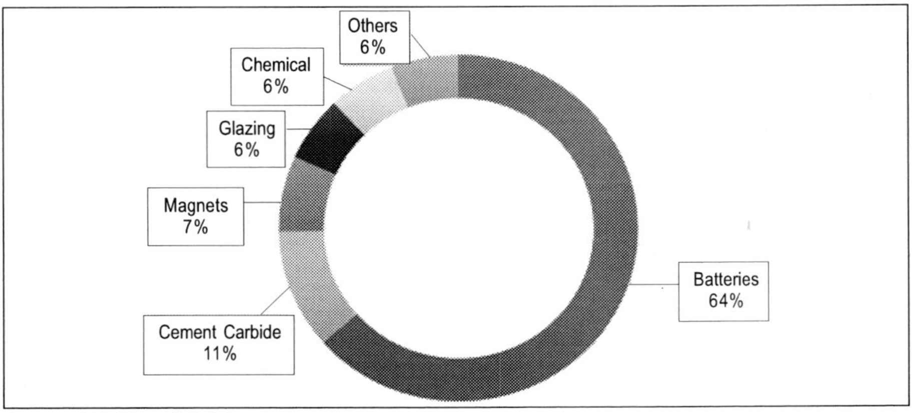

Source: USGS and BGS.

Nickel (Ni)

90 per cent of China's nickel resource is in the form of copper-nickel sulphide as there is no primary source of nickel in the country. China consumes three times the average production of mined nickel; therefore, the gap is filled mostly by imports. The most vital use of nickel is in the stainless steel industry, which creates a greater demand and high price of refined nickel in the international market. Therefore, China imports 90 per cent of laterite form of ore which contains 2 per cent nickel content from Indonesia and the Philippines. China is probably one of the fastest growing markets for stainless steel in the world. Its production was 89,800 tons in 2011. About 70 per cent of nickel was consumed by the stainless steel sector in China in 2011. China is also using nickel pig iron to replace pure nickel content in stainless steel production. Chinese investment in other part of the world is also rising as the Indonesian Government has been planning to ban the export of laterite ore containing 6 per cent of nickel content.[23]

Copper (Cu)

Copper is a critical and strategic material for China. China's refined and mined copper production in 2011 was estimated to be 5.1 million tons and 1.2 million tons, respectively, which is 30 per cent of the total demand of copper in the country. Hence, China imports considerable amount of copper concentrates, scrap anode and refined metal from foreign markets. The main imports of copper concentrates are from Chile (22.2 per cent), copper scrap from the US (13.8 per cent) and refined copper from Chile (45.0 per cent).[24] According to China Nonferrous Metals Industry Association, the "country's average ore grade was 0.77 per cent copper. Owing to lower ore grade and

Figure 3.12: Copper Imports of China

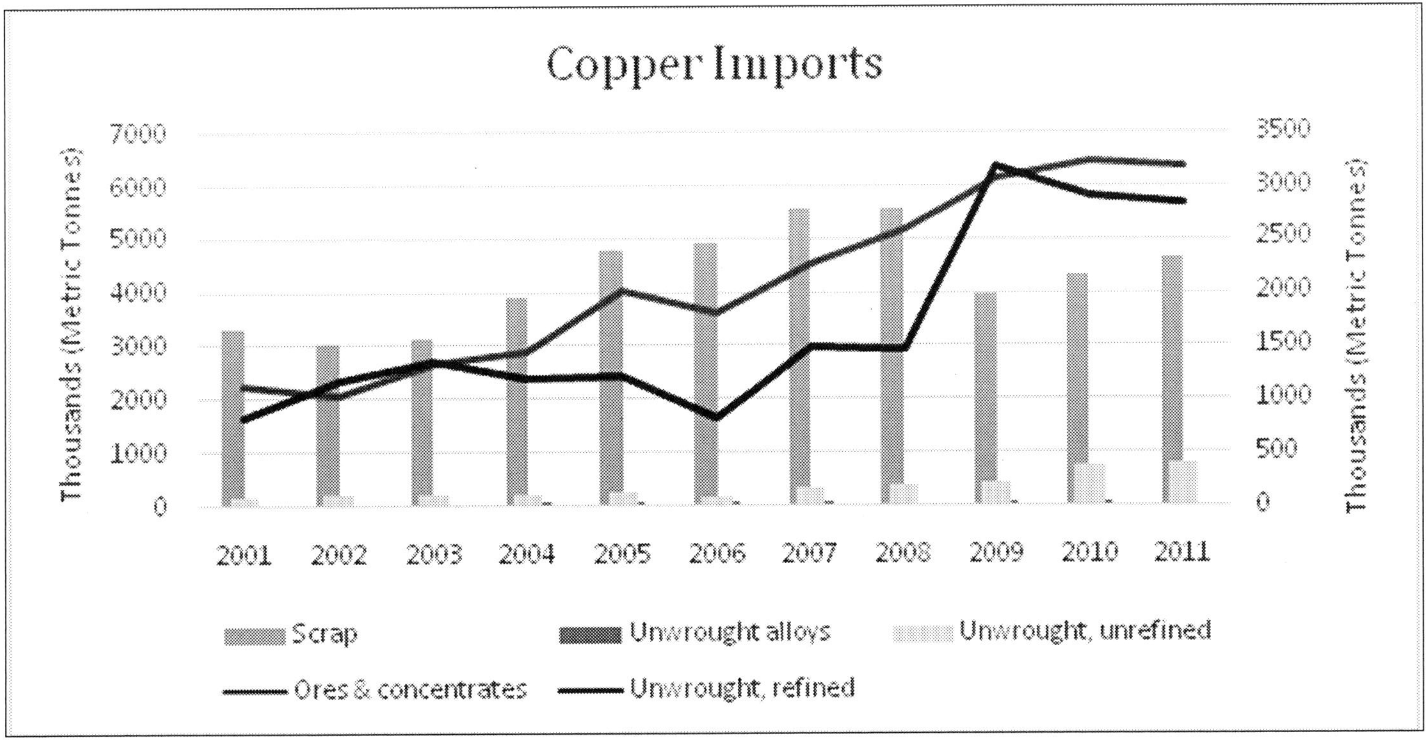

Sources: Centre for Sustainable Mineral Development (BGS), US Geological Survey and *World Mineral Year book 2011*.

more complicated elemental composition in the ore, the processing recovery rate decreased to 86.58 per cent."[25]

The consumption of copper in china is mainly dominated by the power sector contributing 46 per cent, followed by home goods and appliances as 11 per cent and electronics as 9 per cent.

Iron and Steel

Accounting for about 57 per cent of the world's pig iron production and 45 per cent[26] of the world's crude steel production in 2011, China remains the world's leading iron and steel producer. While the private sector accounts 80 per cent of the investment, iron and steel making output capacity has increased to 700 metric tons and 850 metric tons, respectively, in 2011. China is also the net steel product exporter accounting 33.2 metric tons of exports of which 55 per cent alone was exported within Asia. Due to low iron content and high impurities of domestic ores, industries import pig iron ore from other parts of the world too. While estimated "50 per cent of seaborne ore in the world was destined for China",[27] Australia, Brazil, India, South Africa and Canada remain the net exporters of iron ore to China accounting for the rise in imports to 686 million tons in 2011 from 618 million tons in 2010. Due to this massive import figures, the international pricing is highly driven by China as the demand is driven by Chinese imports.[28] Figure 3.13 shows how steel and iron production is met by iron imports.

Figure 3.13: Iron Imports and Steel and Iron Production in China

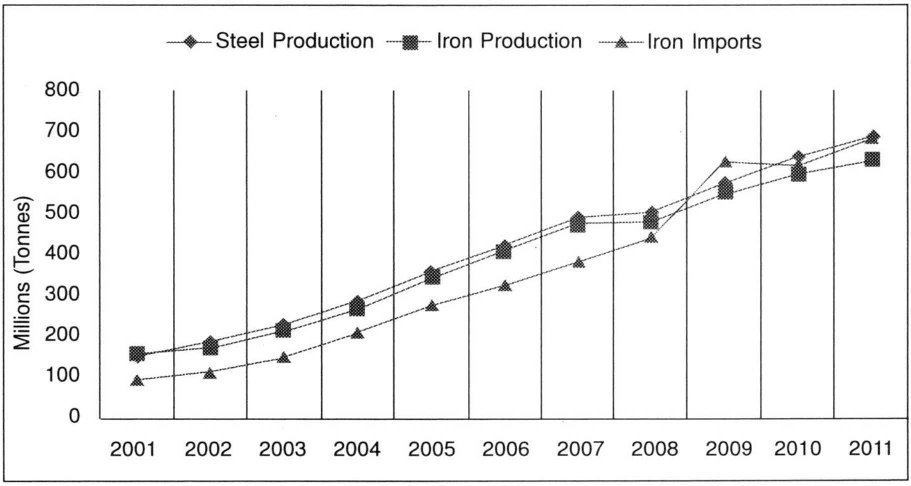

Source: Centre for Sustainable mineral development (BGS), US Geological survey and World Mineral Year book 2011.

China imported about 70 per cent of high-value-added steel products from overseas in 2011. The major consumption of iron and steel in China is by the construction industry, which accounted for as much as "54.4 per cent of the total iron and steel consumption in China in the year 2011".[29]

Titanium (Ti)

China is one of the largest titanium producing countries in the world. The major producing grade in China is sponge titanium and small volume of soft sponge (MHT–95 grade). China had more than 20 titanium sponge plants, and the total output production was estimated to be more than 130,000 t/yr till 2011. The high quality rutile ore is limited in the country, and most of it is in the form of iron and vanadium. It has also been estimated that Chinese ores have low quality; hence only "70 per cent of titanium producers could produce MHT–100 grade titanium sponge (Brinell hardness[30] of less than 100, or mild sponge), which contains between 99.5 per cent and 99.6 per cent titanium. China produced a small volume of soft sponge (MHT–95 grade), which contains 99.7 per cent titanium". Chinese imported 2.3 million tons of titanium ore and concentrates in 2011, mainly from Australia, India and Vietnam.

Tungsten (Sn)

China is estimated to have 1.8 million tons of tungsten reserves, which is approximately 64 per cent of the world's mineable reserves, and it provides the tungsten supply of "about 85 per cent for the global use every year". It is also the world largest tungsten producing country, and at the same time, the largest importer of tungsten ores and concentrates in world accounting 9,905 tons. However, it also remains one of the leading tungsten exporters accounting 27,524 tons (tungsten content) of tungsten products mainly to the EU, Japan, the Republic of Korea, and the US. It consumed about 37,000 tons of tungsten, while mining and processing capacity reached 2, 20, 00,000 and 4,00,00,000 metric tons, respectively.[31]

India

With a population of about 1.2 billion, India is the second largest populous country in the world after China. It also the seventh largest country in terms of area and has some of the most diverse geography in the world. With the 10th largest economy in the world in terms of nominal GDP and third largest in terms of Purchasing Power Parity (PPP), it is one of the fastest emerging economies in the world.[32] To sustain such an economy, the industrial and manufacturing industry plays an indispensable role; moreover, minerals play a vital role in sustaining this strategic industry. With its diverse geographical attributes, the country is endowed with significant mineral resources. Mining sector is an important segment of the Indian economy. Mining contributed about US$ 45 billion which was 2.63 per cent of the country's GDP in 2011. India produces as many as 87 minerals, which include 4 fuel, 10 metallic,

Figure 3.14: India's Mineral Map

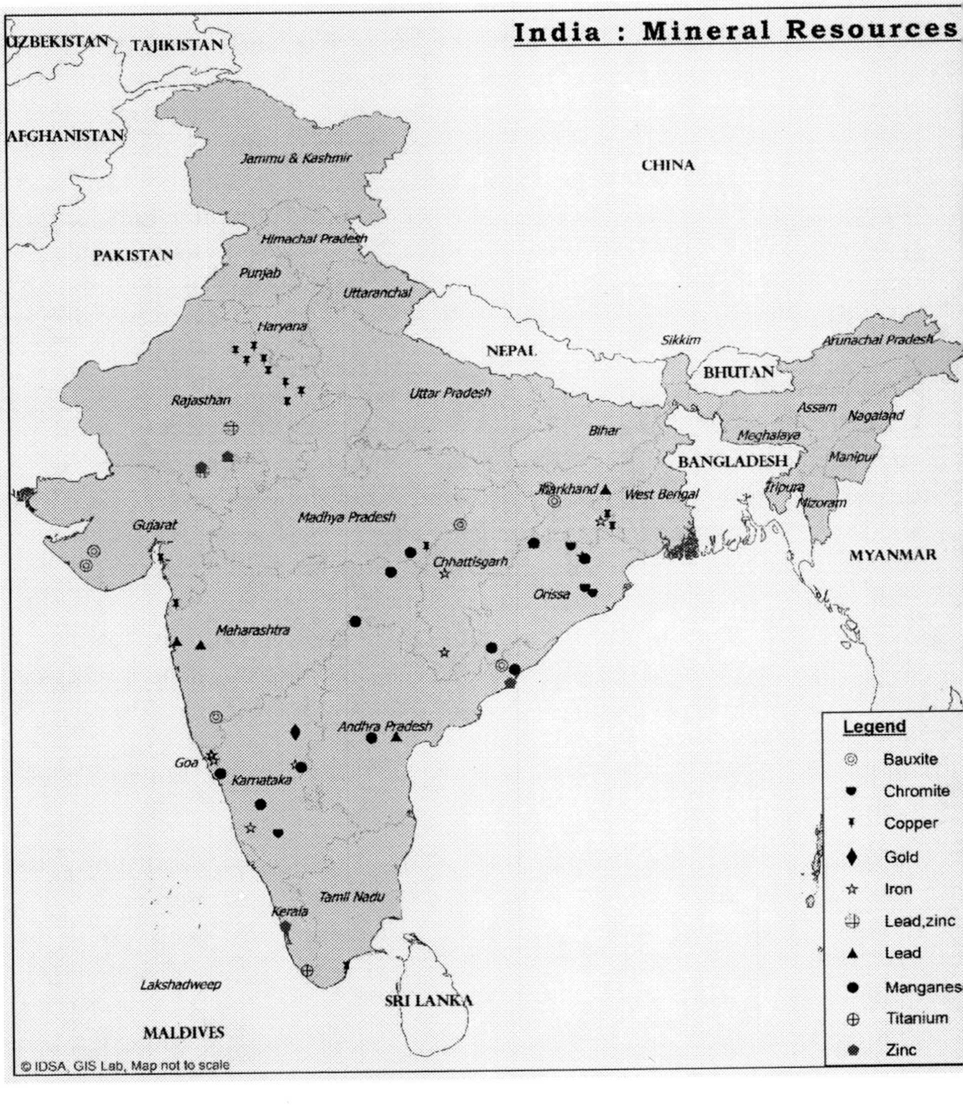

47 non-metallic, 3 atomic and 23 minor minerals (including building and other materials).[33] India also contributes significantly towards minerals such as barite, bauxite, chromium, coal, iron ore, limestone and manganese ore in terms of output, which was among the 10th largest in the world.[34] Figure 3.14 shows minerals found across India.

Mineral Industry in India

In 2011, the Indian mining industry contributed about 2.63 per cent to the GDP which is one of the lowest vis-à-vis some of the larger emerging economies such as China (20 per cent), Australia (8 per cent) and Russia (14.7 per cent).[35] However, this percentage is expected to increase between 7 per cent and 8 per cent in the near future due to increasing demand. The total number of mines in 2011-12 was estimated to be around 3,236 mainly dominated by larger number of small operational mines. The public sector companies account for 66.5 per cent of the total value of mineral production. The open cast mining[36] is the main practice for mining in India accounting 80 per cent of the total mining. During 2011-12, estimated value for fuel minerals accounted for US$ 28.69 billion or 68.22 per cent; metallic minerals, US$ 8.39 billion or 19.94 per cent of the total value and non-metallic minerals including minor minerals US$ 4.97 billion or 11.83 per cent of the total value.[37] Some of the major minerals imported by India are listed in Table 3.4. Please read this table along the Mineral Trade discussed on next page.

Table 3.4: India Imports of Selected Ores and Concentrates in 2012

Commodity	Quantity (metric tons)	Value (thousands US$)
Manganese ores and concentrates etc.	2,822,131	486,730
Copper ores and concentrates	2,387,465	4,884,537
Chromium ores and concentrates	1,922,919	50,266
Borates	112,225	
Zinc ores and concentrates	212,185	89,534
Titanium ores and concentrates	112,834	49,968
Aluminium ores and concentrates	76,707	31,425
Lead ores and concentrates	75,978	149,725
Ash residues containing metals of metallic compounds	59,186	48,703
Niobium, tantalum, vanadium or zirconium ores and concentrates	45,285	71,237
Granulated slag from the manufacture of iron or steel	28,580	999
Slag & ash nes, including sea wood ash (kelp)	9,422	1,995
Slag, dross other than granulated slag	9,141	827
Molybdenum ores and concentrates	7,735	138,559
Ores and concentrates, nes	6,683	25,730

Commodity	Quantity (metric tons)	Value (thousands US$)
Nickel ores and concentrates	5,123	13,849
Cobalt ores and concentrates	5,041	12,895
Tungsten ores and concentrates	327	534
Tin ores and concentrates	369	264
Precious metal ores and concentrates	21	-
Antimony	3,712	-

Source: Mineral Trade (trademap.org)[38]

Overall, India's mining industry constitutes a large number of small operational mines. The number of mines which reported mineral production [excluding minor minerals, petroleum (crude), natural gas and atomic minerals] in India was 2,076 in 2011-12 as against 2,355 in the previous year. Table 3.5 provides information on the state-wise distribution of the number of mines and their contribution towards mineral production. This table provides information on 11states which together account for 93.64 per cent of the total number of mines. In respect of the total value of mineral production apart from the regions mentioned, the rest of the country's contribution is less than 9 per cent (2011-12).

Table 3.5: Number of Mines and Shared Percentage Value Distribution (State-wise)

Name of the State	No. of mines	Shared Value of mineral production (per cent)
Andhra Pradesh	354	6.99
Gujarat	308	6.83
Rajasthan	241	9.01
Madhya Pradesh	225	4.69
Karnataka	180	3.13
Tamil Nadu	156	-
Odisha	119	12.02
Jharkhand	106	5.86
Chhattisgarh	99	9.15
Maharashtra	86	-
Goa	70	3.30
Offshore areas, Assam	-	25.79, 4.63

Source: Mining industry in India, 2013.[39]

Mineral Trade

In 2010, the total export of ores and minerals was estimated to be around US$ 27.6 billion. "Diamond (mostly cut and polished) was the principal item of export, accounting for 71.3 per cent of all mineral and ore exports; iron ore, 13.0 per cent; alumina, 5.6 per cent; and granite, 3.3 per cent".[40] In terms of metals and alloys, Iron and Steel export remained the highest sharing about 46.6 per cent of the total export followed by copper and alloys (including brass and bronze) which accounted for 28.5 per cent.[41] The total value of imports of ores, minerals and fuels was about US$113 billion.

India is heading to become one of the largest economies in the world; however, the per capita consumption of most of the metals remains the lowest in the world, which is likely to increase exponentially in next few decades. While India remains self-sufficient with regard to most of the minerals, there are a few minerals whose resources are limited and may not be sufficient to meet the domestic demand in the future. These minerals are the backbone of strategic industries like defence, space, nuclear, energy, etc. Hence, the availability of these minerals in the future to meet the domestic demand of strategic industries is crucial.

Commodity Review

Antimony (Sb)

As per the United Nations Framework Classification (UNFC) system, as on April 1, 2010, total resources are estimated at 10,588 tons ore with metal content of around 174 tons. The antimony resources in India are reported to be inferior in quality. The occurrence of antimony is reported to be in Andhra Pradesh, Bihar, Jammu & Kashmir, Karnataka and Uttar Pradesh. Presently, India does not produce antimony and the entire demand is met through imports. India imported 3,712 tons of antimony in 2011-12, 83 per cent of which was imported from South Africa alone followed by China (3 per cent). Import of alloys and scrap was mainly from China (90 per cent). Figure 3.15 shows the antimony imports of India over the last few years.

Borates[42]

As per the UNFC system,[43] total resources of borax as on April 2010, were estimated at 74,204 tons in Jammu & Kashmir; however, they are still under survey. Borax is not produced in India presently as economically workable deposits could not be established so far. All the domestic need is solely met through imports of raw borax. The total borax imports were around 112,225 tons in 2011 mainly imported from Turkey (43 per cent), the US (25 per cent), Bolivia (15 per cent) and Argentina (8 per cent). The future demand might increase because of a probable shift to fibre glass reinforcement by industries to enhance efficiency by reducing weight.

Figure 3.15: Antimony Imports of India

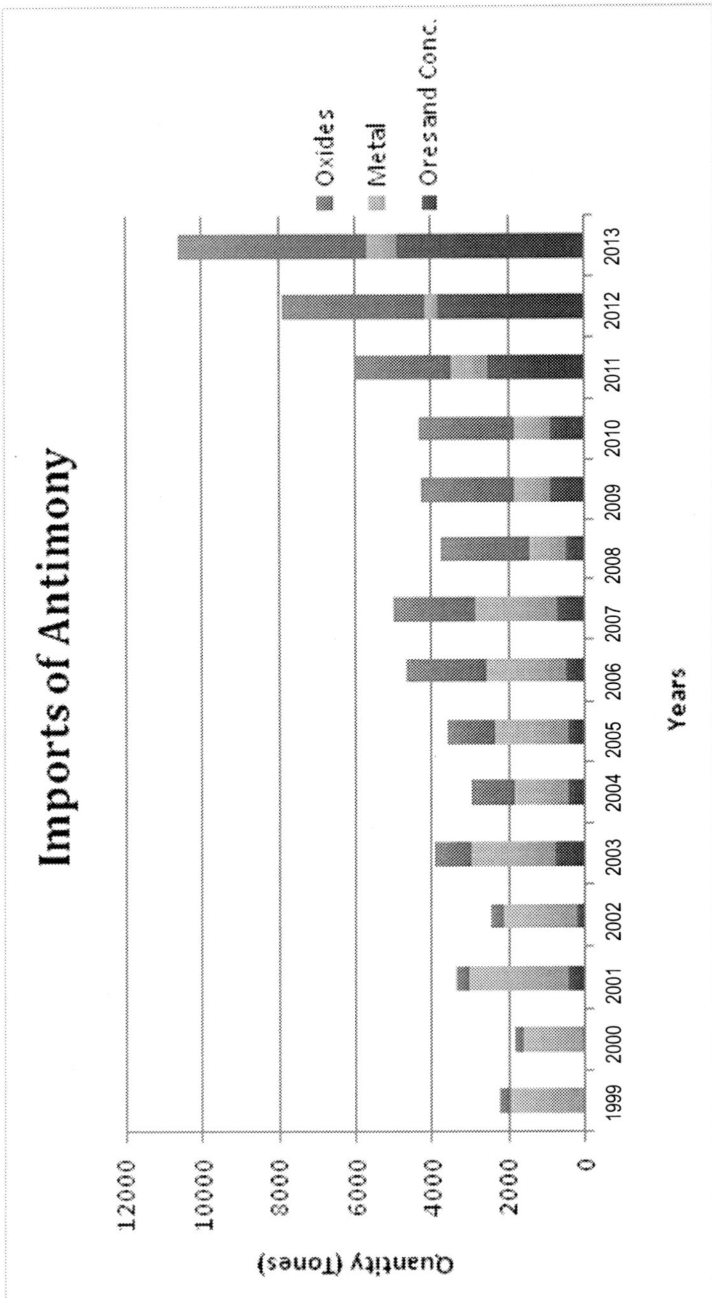

Source: Indian Bureau of Mines and Export-Import data bank.

Cobalt (Co)

Associated mainly with copper, nickel and arsenic oxide, cobalt is an important strategic mineral with wide usage and unique properties. Most of the cobalt in India is recovered during copper and nickel processing as there is no production of cobalt from indigenous ores. The remaining demand for refined cobalt is met through imports. India's cobalt ores and concentrates were estimated to be around 5,041 tons, while alloys were around 748 tons in 2011. Imports were mainly from Zaire/Democratic Rep. of Congo (74 per cent) and People's Rep. of Congo (22 per cent) (see Table 3.6).

Table 3.6: India's Cobalt Imports in 2011

Countries	Quantity
Zaire Rep./Congo, Dem. Rep. of	1,059,679
People Republic of Congo	370,673
USA	27,283
Uganda	13,639
UK	3,097
Unspecified	41,033
All Countries	1,515,404

Source: *Indian Bureau of Mines Year Book 2011.*

Cobalt's unique properties make it an indispensable mineral in many strategic industries. Owing to its usage in a number of industries, the future domestic and global demand is likely to have an exponential increasing trend. The demand of cobalt is likely to go up with use of "super-alloys in civil aviation, catalysts for gas-to-liquid production of synthetic liquid fuels, rechargeable batteries for hybrid electric vehicles, cellular telephones, aerospace and energy generation industries which use cobalt-bearing super alloy gas turbine engine parts".[44] India does not have any primary cobalt production facility. The secondary production comes from nickel-bearing laterite deposits in Odisha (state on the east coast of India) and declining copper slag produced by Hindustan Copper Limited (HCL), but its commercial viable usage is still under Research and Development (R&D). Though the recycling of cobalt is used to meet the domestic demand; however, the future demand is expected to increase. It's therefore vital to clearly identify the future demand and diversify import risk from particular countries.

Fluorite (CaF_2)[45]

As per the UNFC system, the total resources of fluorite in the country, as on April 2005, were estimated at 20.17 million tons. By regions, Gujarat

Figure 3.16: Fluorite Usage

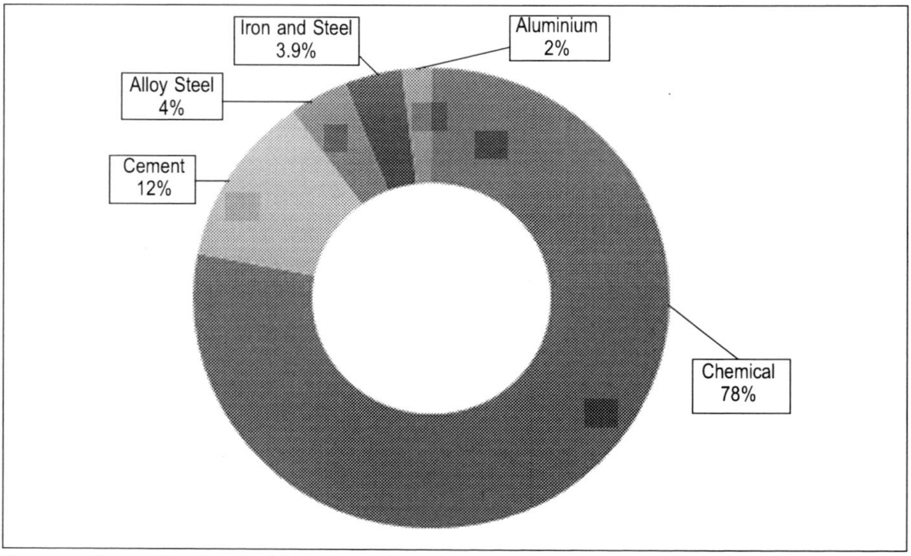

Sources: Centre for Sustainable Mineral Development (BGS), US Geological Survey and *World Mineral Yearbook 2011.*

accounted for 69 per cent of the total resources having 13.93 million tons, followed by Rajasthan with 5.24 million tons (26 per cent). Fluorite plays a vital role in the manufacture of aluminium, gasoline, insulating foams, refrigerants, steel, chemical and uranium fuel. The production of fluorite is scarce in the country and mainly fulfilled as a by-product in phosphoric acid production during the processing of phosphate rock. However, the chemical and aluminium industry requires a more refined and purified form; hence, the demand is solely met by imports. The sector-wise usage of fluorite is shown in Figure 3.16.

India imported 147138 tons of fluorite in 2011 mainly from China (54 per cent) and Kenya (31 per cent). The production of fluorite is limited in India, and as discussed earlier, grades of fluorite produced do not meet the specifications of the chemical industry, which is the biggest user of fluorite; hence, India will remain dependent on imports owing to both quality and quantity issues.

Molybdenum (Mo)[46]

As per the UNFC System, the provisional resources of molybdenum ore in the country as on April 1, 2010 are estimated at about 19.29 million tons containing about 12,640 tons Molybdenite (MoS_2). The above resources are located in Tamil Nadu (9.97 million tons), Madhya Pradesh (8 million tons) and Karnataka (1.32 million tons). Molybdenite (MoS_2) is the principle ore of molybdenum and usually extracted as a by-product of copper mining. The domestic demand is high; therefore, molybdenum demand in India is mostly met by imports. India's ores and concentrates imports were around 7,735 tons, while alloys and scrap was 297 tons in 2012. Imports were mainly from Chile (33 per cent), the US (18 per cent), Netherlands (15 per cent) and Canada (8 per cent). The principle use of molybdenum is in stainless steel and in chemicals/catalysts. The global and domestic demand is expected to go high as considerable growth in super alloys and stainless steel sector is expected in the near future. India is expected to depend more on imports to meet the increasing domestic demand.

Nickel (Ni)

Nickel is one of the most important elements that enhances the properties of iron manifold and makes products hard; it is used in stainless steel production too. As per UNFC, as on April 4, 2010, the total provisional resources of nickel ore have been estimated at 189 million tons. The 66 per cent of world nickel production is used in the stainless steel industry. In 2011-12, domestic consumption of nickel in India was estimated to be 2,235 tons mostly consumed in alloy-steel industry. There is no primary source of nickel production in India; however, nickel is recovered as nickel sulphate crystals, a by-product obtained during copper production. Most of the domestic demand is met by processing alloys and scraps, while the remaining by imports. India's nickel import in 2011-12 was round 41,729 tons of which, nickel alloys were 33,658 tons, while nickel waste & scrap was 1,129 tons. Imports in 2011-12 were mainly from Russia contributing 34 per cent of the total imports followed by Australia (12 per cent), Norway (11 per cent) and the UK (6 per cent). The estimated demand of the country is expected to increase exponentially. According to the 12th year plan, the estimated steel production is expected to reach 5 million tons; hence, with the development of strategic industry in India, the demand is expected to rise further. Therefore, India would have no choice but to be depend on imports to meet the domestic demand.

Selenium (Se)

Selenium gets recovered as a by-product during copper, lead-zinc, gold and platinum ore processing, and does not have any primary source available for extraction. Selenium is expected to be recovered from Copper Smelter of HCL in Jharkhand; however, HCL has not confirmed further production of selenium 2006-07 (further data is not available). Imports of selenium decreased to 194 tons in 2011-12, as compared to 209 tons in the previous year. Imports were mainly from Japan, Belgium and the Republic of Korea in 2011-12.

Tungsten (W)

Tungsten is an important strategic mineral in India owing to its usage in high-end technology industries. The total resources of tungsten ore in India, as per UNFC system, as on April 1, 2010, have been estimated at 87.4 million tons; however, all these resources are placed under 'remaining resources' category due to probable technological constraint to extraction. The entire demand is mainly met by imports and recycling of alloys and scrap. Imports of tungsten ores and concentrates have seen a drastic increased to 327 tons in 2011-12 from 27 tons in the previous year. Imports were mainly from China (34 per cent), the US (15 per cent), Korea (11 per cent) and Japan (8 per cent). Owing to lack of primary source, there is no indigenous production of tungsten concentrates; hence, India will continue to meet its entire demand only through imports.

United States

The third largest country in the world in terms of geographical area and highest economy in the world in terms of purchasing power parity, the US is one of the most developed countries in the world. Being a superpower which has been involved in various conflicts since the World War II era till the present, the US dependence on minerals has been significant. Its various industries, especially the defence industry, are crucially dependent on strategic minerals. In recent times, as many emerging economies are becoming both significant producers and consumers of various raw mineral products, the US is keen to ensure that its supply chain of strategic materials does not get affected. The US was the first country to realise the vitality of materials to sustain economic growth. It was the only country to come up with National Strategic Material Act, 1939 followed by Critical Material Stockpiling Act, 1945.[47] During the period "1900-1929 the United States produced nearly 90 per cent of all the minerals it consumed. Since about World War II, however, the mineral position of the United States has deteriorated".[48] Presently, the US imports dependency has increased significantly, for instance, "one-half of U.S. apparent consumption of the 41 mineral commodities shown in the figure below came from imports, and the United States was 100 percent import reliant for 18 of those". However, it has reduced its

Figure 3.17: 2012 US Net Import Reliance

Commodity	Percent	Major Import Sources (2008–11)[2]
ARSENIC (trioxide)	100	Morocco, China, Belgium
ASBESTOS	100	Canada, Zimbabwe
BAUXITE and ALUMINA	100	Jamaica, Brazil, Guinea, Australia
CESIUM	100	Canada
FLUORSPAR	100	Mexico, China, South Africa
GRAPHITE (natural)	100	China, Mexico, Canada, Brazil
INDIUM	100	China, Canada, Japan, Belgium
MANGANESE	100	South Africa, Gabon, Australia, China
MICA, sheet (natural)	100	China, Brazil, Belgium, India
NIOBIUM (columbium)	100	Brazil, Canada, Germany
QUARTZ CRYSTAL (industrial)	100	China, Japan, Russia
RUBIDIUM	100	Canada
SCANDIUM	100	China
STRONTIUM	100	Mexico, Germany, China
TANTALUM	100	China, Estonia, Germany, Kazakhstan
THALLIUM	100	Germany, Russia
THORIUM	100	India, France
GALLIUM	99	Germany, United Kingdom, China, Canada
GEMSTONES	99	Israel, India, Belgium, South Africa
VANADIUM	96	Rep. of Korea, Canada, Austria, Czech Republic
BISMUTH	92	China, Belgium, United Kingdom
PLATINUM	91	Germany, South Africa, United Kingdom, Canada
GERMANIUM	90	China, Belgium, Russia, Germany
IODINE	88	Chile, Japan
ANTIMONY	87	China, Mexico, Belgium, Bolivia
DIAMOND (dust, grit, and powder)	85	China, Ireland, Republic of Korea, Russia
STONE (dimension)	85	China, Brazil, Italy, Turkey
POTASH	81	Canada, Russia
BARITE	80	China, India, Morocco
COBALT	78	China, Norway, Russia, Finland
RHENIUM	78	Chile, Netherlands, Germany
TITANIUM MINERAL CONCENTRATES	77	South Africa, Australia, Canada, Mozambique
TIN	75	Peru, Bolivia, Indonesia, China
SILICON CARBIDE (crude)	73	China, South Africa, Romania, Netherlands
ZINC	72	Canada, Mexico, Peru, Spain
CHROMIUM	70	South Africa, Kazakhstan, Russia, Mexico
GARNET (industrial)	65	India, Australia, China, Canada
TITANIUM (sponge)	64	Japan, Kazakhstan, China, Ukraine,
PEAT	62	Canada
SILVER	57	Mexico, Canada, Peru, Poland
PALLADIUM	54	Russia, South Africa, United Kingdom, Norway
NICKEL	49	Canada, Russia, Australia, Norway
MAGNESIUM COMPOUNDS	46	China, Canada, Brazil, Australia
TUNGSTEN	42	China, Bolivia, Canada, Germany
SILICON	38	Brazil, Russia, China, Canada
COPPER	35	Chile, Canada, Peru, Mexico
NITROGEN (fixed), AMMONIA	35	Trinidad and Tobago, Russia, Canada, Ukraine
MAGNESIUM METAL	31	Israel, Canada, China
MICA, scrap and flake (natural)	31	Canada, China, India, Finland
VERMICULITE	30	South Africa, China, Brazil, Australia
PERLITE	24	Greece
ALUMINUM	20	Canada, Russia, China, Mexico
SALT	19	Canada, Chile, Mexico, The Bahamas
SULFUR	19	Canada, Mexico, Venezuela

Source: US Geological Survey.

Figure 3.18: US Selected Mineral Map

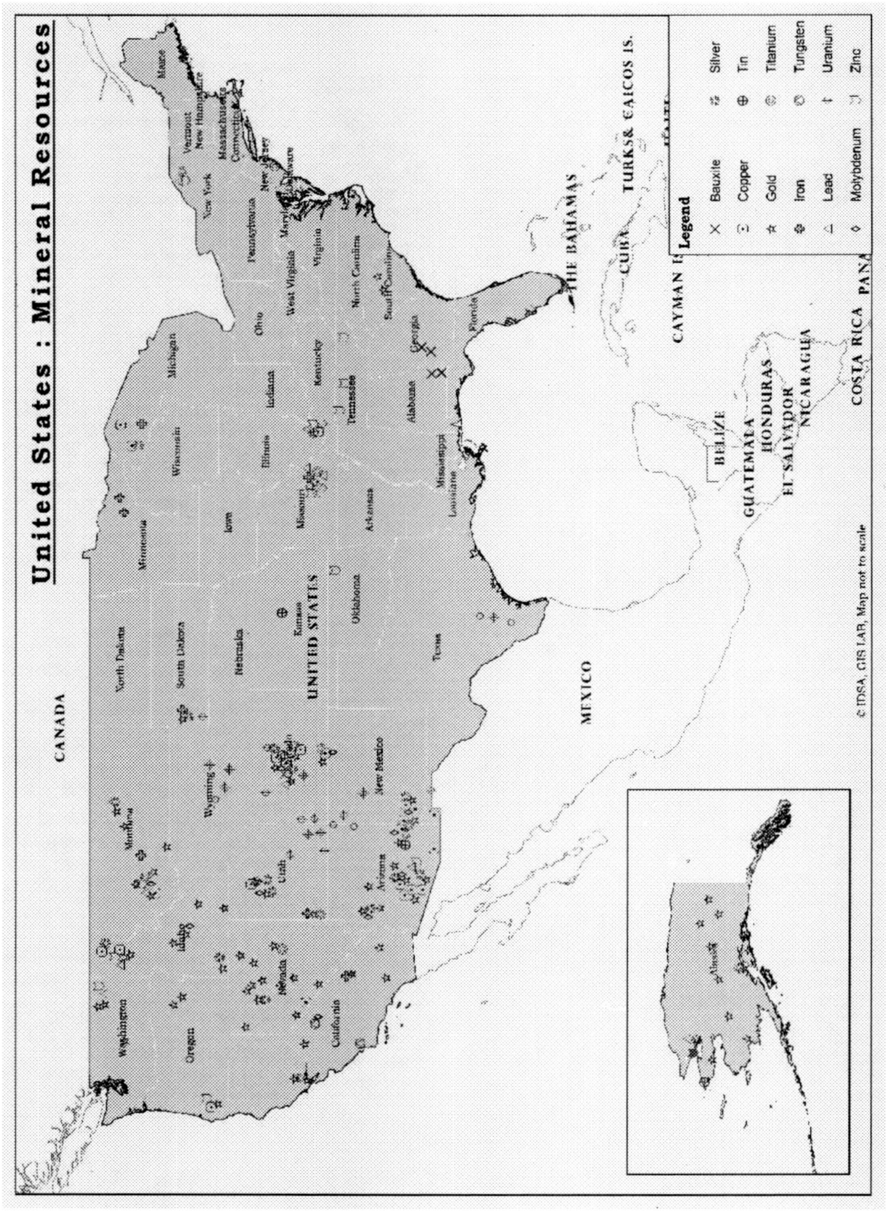

dependency from 100 per cent in 2002 to 85 per cent in 2012-13; the reduction in import dependency predominantly on China is rather significant.

Nevertheless, the US dependency on imports has increased in recent years, often because it is economically advantageous to do so. Some developing countries not only bear the advantage of having rich source of mineral deposits, but also have cheap energy source and cheap labour to economically extract them. Hence, all the minerals imported by the country is not meant to be completely considered under the risk of high import dependence. In recent years, as there is a surge in domestic demand, the employability for greener technology and enhancement of present technology is increasing. Therefore, in many cases, there is a partial or complete insufficiency of these minerals. Currently, the US depends upon overseas suppliers for over 80 percent of its most important strategic minerals of which "47 per cent of the 19 minerals on which the United States is 100 per cent import dependent upon are produced in China".[49]

Depending on the risk factor and high dependency on imports in above figure, the US has defined its strategic material in the risk pyramid shown in Figure 3.18: from very high risk at top to very low risk at the bottom. These also includes rare earth materials.

Figure 3.19: Resources Risk Pyramid for the US

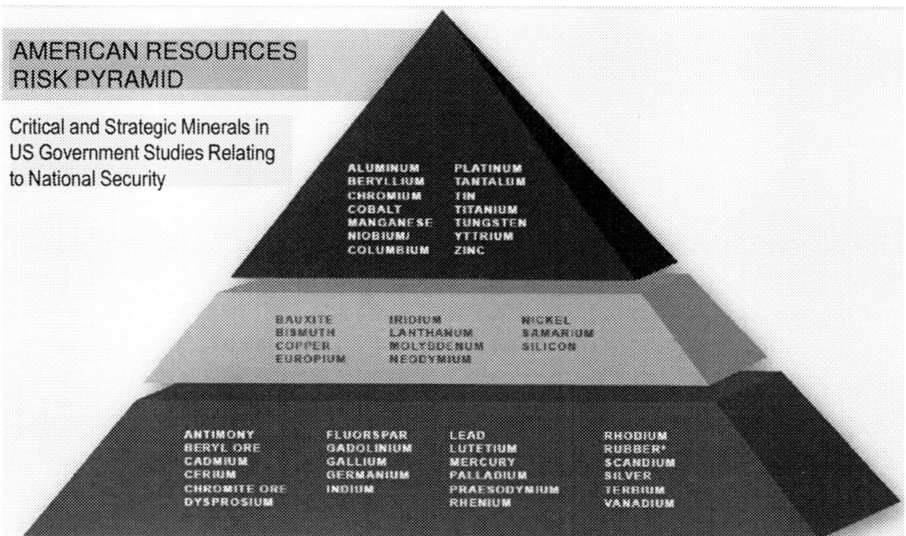

Source: http://americanresources.org/

Commodity Review

Antimony (Sb)

There was no production of antimony reported in 2012, and therefore, the state was 100 per cent dependent on imports: mainly from China, 74 per cent; followed by Mexico, 12 per cent; Peru, 3 per cent and others, 11 per cent. The antimony in the US was mainly used in flame retardants, 35 per cent; transportation as used in batteries, 29 per cent; chemicals, 16 per cent; ceramics and glass, 12 per cent and others, 8 per cent.

Arsenic (As)

There is no primary reserve of arsenic in the US, and limited metal is extracted from Gallium-Arsenide (GaAs) semiconductor scrap. The net imports of arsenic in the US was around 6,900, of which consumption was around 6,680 metric tons; hence, there is a trend of complete imports reliance. Arsenic has wide applications in the US, such as in the enhancement of lead batteries, solar cells for satellites, anti-frictional additives in bearings and telecommunications. It is imported mainly from China, constituting around 86 per cent of the net imports, followed by Japan with 13 per cent.

Bauxite and Alumina

The US production of bauxite is around 5.6 million tons, which is not enough to meet domestic consumption. In case of alumina, the US is almost 100 percent dependent on imports. The alumina imports were around 1,850 metric tons in 2012, 90 per cent of which is consumed in aluminium smelters. Nearly half of US bauxite imports are from Jamaica constituting 43 per cent, while 34 per cent of alumina comes from Australia.

Chromium (Cr)

Since 1948, the US has been a major producer of chromium ore in the world, but in recent times the country relies heavily on imports. In 2012, the US import reliance was 70 per cent with a net import of 139,095 metric tons.[50] It was estimated that the US consumes 6 per cent of the world's total chromium production, mainly in the form of chromite ore, chromium chemicals, chromium ferroalloys, chromium metal and stainless steel. Chromium is mainly imported from South Africa, 34 per cent; Kazakhstan, 17 per cent; Russia, 10 per cent; Mexico, 5 per cent and others, 34 per cent. Since 2010, the US consumption of chromium was distributed as shown in Figure 3.19.[51]

Figure 3.20: Chromium Consuming Sectors

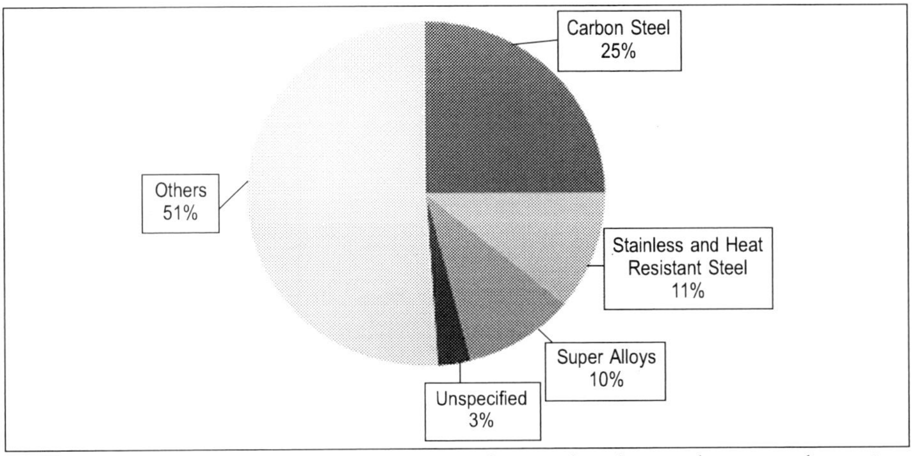

* **'Others'** include cast irons, welding and alloy hard-facing rods and materials, wear- and corrosion-resistant alloys and aluminum.

Sources: US Geological Survey Mineral Plans.

Cobalt (Co)

The US production of cobalt has not seen significant growth in a decade, and country has 78 per cent dependency on imports. The US imports in 2012 were around 12,214 metric tons: mainly from China, 20 per cent; followed by Norway, 14 per cent; Russia, 12 per cent and others, 44 per cent. Cobalt is a vital mineral in for the US defence, space and manufacturing industry. Its utility in making superalloys, mainly required for the manufacturing gas turbine engines, is well-known. Figure 3.20 shows the consumption of cobalt in various vital industries.

Figure 3.21: Cobalt Consumption in Various Vital Sectors

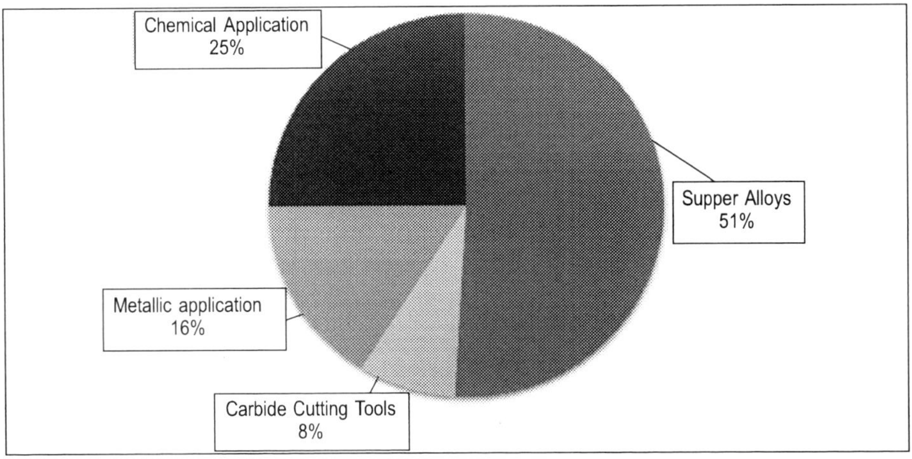

Source: US and UK Geological Survey, 2012.

Gallium (Ga)

There is no primary production of gallium in the US, and so it is completely dependent on imports. Gallium is an essential mineral for the production of GaAs and Gallium Nitride (GaN), constituting 99 per cent in electronic circuits. This mineral is vital for the production of Integrated Circuit (IC) chips used in most of the defence and space applications. In 2012, the US imported 58 tons of pure gallium, mainly from Germany, 32 per cent, followed by the UK, 27 per cent and China, 15 per cent.

Lithium (Li)

Lithium is widely used in rechargeable batteries and lubricants. The US does not have any major lithium production facility and its dependence on imports is more than 70 per cent. Domestic lithium is mainly extracted from scraps and recycled. The US imported 1,070 metric tons of lithium in 2012, more than half of which was imported from Argentina, 52 per cent, followed by Chile, 44 per cent and China, 3 per cent.

Niobium (Nb)

Niobium is a vital strategic material for the US mainly for two reasons: First, there is no domestic production, and the country is 100 per cent dependent on imports. Secondly, the major usage of this mineral is in production of high grade steel constituting about 52 per cent and for supper alloys as 48 per cent to be used in aerospace industries. The state imported 47,000 metric tons of niobium in 2012 and estimated value of niobium consumption was US$ 424 million and was expected to be about US$ 500 million in 2012.[52] Brazil is the highest net exporter of niobium to the country contributing about 82 per cent of net export followed by Canada with 10per cent.

Vanadium (V)

The major usage of vanadium as an alloying agent, in the iron and steel industry, amounts to about 93 per cent of the total vanadium domestic consumption. The US has about 96 per cent of import dependency importing about 8,330 metric tons of mineral in 2011 of which ferrovanadium constituted the highest. Ferrovanadium was imported mainly from Republic of Korea, 43 per cent, and Canada, 33 per cent; Vanadium pentoxide was imported from Russia, 47 per cent, followed by South Africa, 32 per cent and China, 19 per cent.

NOTES

\# Maps of Africa, Australia, Brazil, China, India and US are compiled from US geological (USGS) and British geological (BGS) survey using GIS map data at http://mrdata.usgs.gov/ (Accessed on 20th April 2014)

1. Hanns W. Maull, "South Africa's Minerals: the Achilles Heel of Western Economic Security?" *International Affairs (London),* 62 (4), Chatham House, autumn, 1986, pp. 619-626.
2. "Sub-Saharan African GDP Growth Forecasts", *The Economist*, October 13, 2011, at http://www.economist.com/node/21533441 (Accessed December 22, 2013).
3. "Map of Africa", at http://teacherweb.ftl.pinecrest.edu/snyderd/APHG/projects/MUN-BC/maps/minerals.jpg (Accessed December 24, 2013).
4. "Manganese Production 2012", USGS Mineral Resources Program, at http://minerals.usgs.gov/minerals/pubs/commodity/manganese/mcs-2012-manga.pdf (Accessed December 24, 2013).
5. Publications List, International Study Group of Lead and Zinc, at http://www.ilzsg.org/generic/pages/list.aspx?table=document&ff_aa_docume (Accessed December 24, 2013).
6. "Economic Irrationalism", *The Sydney Morning Herald*, at http://www.smh.com.au/federal-politics/political-opinion/our-economic-irrationalism-20120312-1uwde.html (Accessed December 24, 2013).
7. "Australia's Trade with East Asia, the Americas, and the European Union: 2010", Australian Government Department of Foreign Affairs and Trade, at http://www.dfat.gov.au/media/releases/department/2011/dfat-release-20110817.html (Accessed December 21, 2013).
8. "RBA: Statement on Monetary Policy-November 2013", Reserve Bank of Australia, at http://www.rba.gov.au/publications/smp/2013/nov/html/index.html (Accessed December 22, 2013).
9. "Production and Trade – Minerals, Oil and Gas", Australian Bureau of Statistics, at http://www.abs.gov.au/ausstats/abs@.nsf/Lookup/by%20Subject/1301.0~2012~Main%20Features~Production%20and% 20trade%20%E2%80%93%20minerals,%20oil%20and%20gas~153 (Accessed December 24, 2013).
10. Artemis Resources, at http://www.artemisresources.com.au/IRM/Company/ShowPage.aspx/PDFs/1527-22308941/ShowmetheAntimony (Accessed December 24, 2013).
11. "Nickel", Geoscience Australia, at http://www.ga.gov.au/minerals/mineral-resources/nickel.html (Accessed December 24, 2013).
12. **Economic Demonstrated Resources** are the sum of measured resources and indicated resources. Indicative resource is economic, where there is a reasonable level of confidence, of their contained metal, grade, tonnage, shape, densities, physical characteristics, while measured resources are indicated resources that have undergone enough further sampling and are acceptable estimates.
13. *Information and Analyses on the Brazilian Mineral Economy*, Instituto Brasileiro de Mineração – IBRAM, at http://www.ibram.org.br/sites/1400/1457/00000365.pdf (Accessed December 24, 2013).
14. "China's Twelfth Five Year Plan (2011-2015) - the Full English Version", British Chamber of Commerce in China–Brit Cham, Beijing, at http://www.britishchamber.cn/content/chinas-twelfth-five-year-plan-2011-2015-full-english-version (Accessed December 24, 2013).
15. Report on Chinese Mineral Reserves, 2011, US Geological Survey.
16. David Adams, "China Mines", May 23r, 2006, at http://www.nexis.com (Accessed December 24, 2013).
17. Chinese Mineral Report, USGS Mineral Resources Program, at http://minerals.usgs.gov/minerals/pubs/country/2010/myb3-2010-ch.pdf (Accessed December 24, 2013).
18. Ministry of Land and Resources, report from National Bureau of Statistics China 2011d, p. 3–7. National Bureau of Statistics of China, 2011b, p. 115
19. *Mineral Year Book for China*, USGS Mineral Resources Program.

Jennifer C. Li, "China's Rising Demand for Minerals and Emerging Global Norms and Practices in the Mining Industry", Foundation for Environmental Security & Sustainability, at http://www.fess-global.org/workingpapers/chinas_rising_demand_for_minerals.pdf (Accessed December 24, 2013).http://minerals.usgs.gov/minerals/pubs/country/2010/myb3-2010-ch.pdf (Accessed December 24, 2013).

20. World Bank Report, 2010.
21. World Mineral Production Report, British Geological Survey, 2007-2011.
22. World Mining Reports, United States Geological Survey, British Geological Survey (BGS), 2011.
23. *China Mining and Metals Weekly*, 2011.
24. *Copper and Nickel Monthly*, 2011a.
25. "Copper", Metal Bulletin, at http://www.metalbulletin.com/Base-metals/Copper-all.html?Year=2011 (Accessed March 27, 2014).
26. "Surging Chinese Steel Exports Put Pressure on World Prices", *Wall Street Journal*, May 16, 2013.
27. Zhang Changfu, Secretary General of China Iron and Steel Association, "The Role of the Iron & Steel Industry in China's Future Economic Development", July 19, 2012.
28. Global Iron and Steel Production, at http://www.issb.co.uk/global.html (Accessed December 24, 2013).
29. Ibid.
30. The Brinell hardness test is commonly used to determine the hardness of materials like metals and alloys.
31. "Research on Global and China Tungsten Industry", at www.prnewswire.com/news-releases/research-on-global-and-china-tungsten-industry-2013-2017- 214292931.htmlChrome HTML.2UYD3FAPGFJ5KGVCKF5QFHSG3I/Shell/Open/Command (Accessed December 24, 2013).
32. Report for Selected Countries and Subjects, IMF — International Monetary Fund, at http://www.imf.org/external/pubs/ft/weo/2013/01/weodata/weorept.aspx?pr.x=38&pr.y=13&sy=2011&ey=2018&scsm=1&ssd=1&sort=country&ds=.&br=1&c=534&s=NGDP_RPCH%2CNGDPD%2CNGDPDPC%2CPPPGDP%2CPPPPC&grp=0&a (Accessed December 24, 2013).
33. Ministry of Mines Report, at http://(mines.nic.in/writereaddata/Contentlinks/1ed4a15b370646d7be2c6defb2ecf6c9.pdf (Accessed December 24, 2013).
34. Indian Ministry of Mines Annual Report 2012-13, at http://mines.gov.in/annual2013E.pdf (Accessed December 24, 2013).
35. US Geological Survey Report 2011-12.
36. **Open Cast mining** is a method in which minerals are extracted from earth by their removal from an open pit or borrow. It is done in situations where the minerals or rocks are available for extraction near the earth's surface.
37. Ministry of Mines Annual Report 2011-12.
38. "Annexure 3.6", Ministry of Mines, at http://mines.gov.in/annual201112/3.6.pdf (Accessed December 24, 2013).
39. "Industry", India Mining 2013, at http://www.india-mining.in/industry.html (Accessed on March 26, 2014).
40. Ibid.
41. "Foreign trade data", Indian Bureau of Mines, at http://ibm.nic.in/IMYB2011_Foreign%20Trade.pdf (Accessed December 24, 2013).
42. "Boron Mineral", Indian Bureau of Mines, at http://ibm.nic.in/IMYB%202011_Boron%20Minerals.pdf (Accessed December 24, 2013).
43. **UNFC system** is the international term defined by the UN for geological assessments on the basis of Geological Assessment, Feasibility Assessment and Economic Viability as a three-dimensional system. For further details, http://ibm.gov.in/unfc.pdf.

44. *Indian Bureau of Mines Mineral Year Book2011.*
45. "Fluorite", Indian Bureau of Mines, at http://ibm.nic.in/imyb2010_fluorite.pdf (Accessed December 24, 2013).
46. "Molybdenum", Indian Bureau of Mines, at http://ibm.nic.in/imyb2010_molybdenum.pdf) (Accessed December 24, 2013).
47. "DLA Strategic Materials", Global Security, at http://www.globalsecurity.org/military/agency/dod/dnsc.htm (Accessed December 24, 2013).
48. "Strategic Materials: Technologies to Reduce U.S. Import Vulnerability", United States Office of Technology Assessment, Congress, 1987.
49. Dr. Kent HugHes Butts, Mr. Brent BanKus, 2nD Lieutenant aDaMnorris. "Strategic Minerals Is China's Consumption a Threat to United States Security?" Center For Strategic Leadership and Development, 2013, at http://www.csl.army.mil/usacsl/publications/IP7_11.pdf (Accessed December 24, 2013).
50. "US Chromium Imports", *US Geological Survey Mineral Year Book 2012.*
51. "U.S. Reported Consumption and Stocks of Chromium Products", Index Mundi - Country Facts, at http://www.indexmundi.com/en/commodities/minerals/chromium/chromium_t2.html (Accessed December 24, 2013).
52. Government stockpile inventory reported by DLA and Brazil Geological Survey Report, 2012.

REFERENCES

*World Mineral Statistics 2012,*MineralsUK, BGS, at http://www.bgs.ac.uk/downloads/start.cfm?id=2701(Last Accessed March 2014).

International Minerals Statistics and Information, Country Profiles, USGS, at http://minerals.usgs.gov/minerals/pubs/country/(Last Accessed March 2014).

Indian Minerals Year Book 2012, Indian Bureau of Mines, at http://ibm.nic.in/imyb2012.htm (Last Accessed March 2014).

International Trade And Market Access Data, *WTO Trade Statistics,* World Trade Organization, at http://www.wto.org/english/res_e/statis_e/statis_e.htm (Last Accessed March 2014).

Publications and Data, Geoscience Australia, Australian Government, at http://www.ga.gov.au/ (Last Accessed March 2014).

4

Risk Assessment of India

Policies on strategic minerals are decided based on geopolitical factors, which arise from the interplay of geography and politics at various levels—from national to global.[1] The geographical locations of various minerals in the Earth's crust, locations of current material production units, knowledge about the existing material reserves and their owners and the political stability of such locations are required to be factored in for undertaking any risk assessment of the states.

Owing to an increase in demand for minerals because of rapid industrialisation at the global level, risk assessment must be conducted on a routine basis. There have been various risk methodologies identified, and all of them have their own advantages as well as limitations too.

Various states use specific models to identify the risk to supplies. A simplistic but effective model has been adopted by the British Geological Survey.[2] It has devised a ranking system based on a few criteria. Further, these criteria are given indicative scores, and a scale based on high and low risk indicators is decided. Subsequently, by taking mathematical averages, gradation is done. The criteria identified are as follows:

- Scarcity
- Production concentration
- Reserve distribution
- Recycling rate
- Substitutability
- Governance (top producing nation)
- Governance (top reserve-hosting nation)

There are a few other models that broadly cover the similar criteria as mentioned above. It could said that depending on the needs for individual nations and their geopolitical standings the indicators in the risk models could differ, but by and large the criteria for risk identification remain the same. Figure 4.1[3] could be viewed as a broad representation for Risk Assessment Model for Strategic Minerals.

Figure 4.1: A Representative Risk Assessment Model for Strategic Minerals

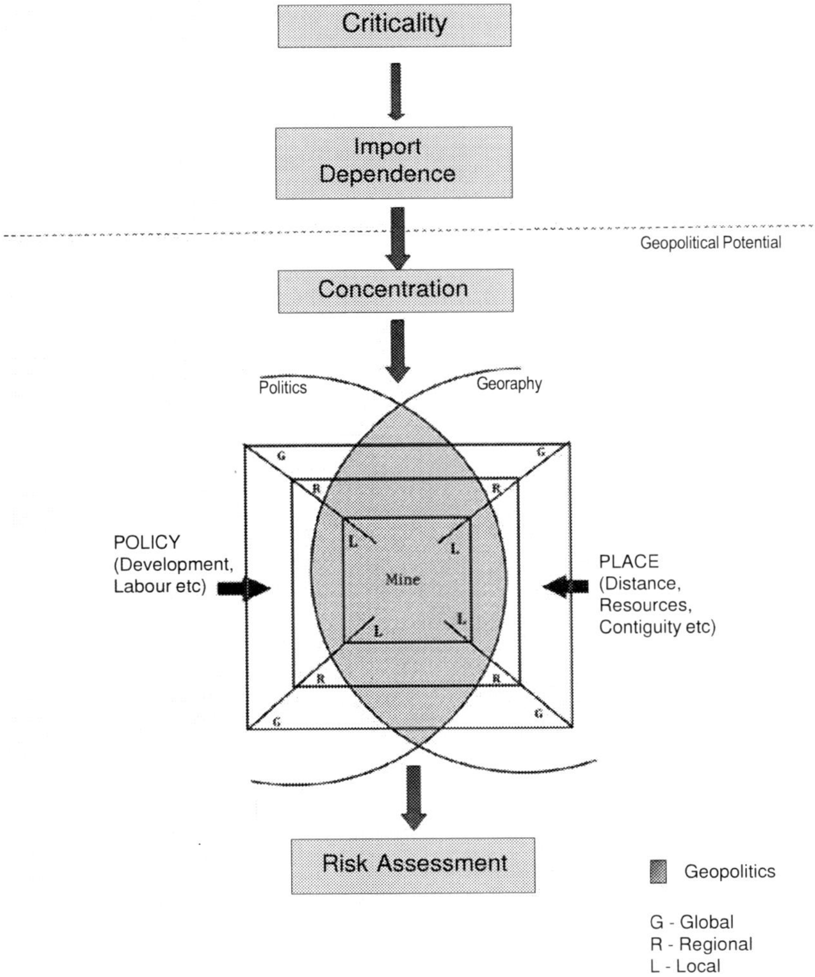

Source: Ewan W. Anderson, *Strategic Minerals.*

India's Strategic Materials 'Resource Management' Assessment

India needs to factor in the following issues when making policies concerning mineral resources:

1. Various nations in the world are consuming mineral resources at an exponential rate, placing demands on limited resources and escalating the prices for these raw materials.
2. It is becoming difficult to access untapped mineral resources within India due to social, political and security compulsions. At the same time, environmental consciousness is on increase, and unchecked mining at the cost of environment is in nobody's interest.
3. States having mineral surplus have realised its worth and are now cautiously trading in this sector. Moreover, on various occasions, the developed states, being financially and technologically superior, are managing their own supplies from outside and keeping their own reserve capacity intact.

There are no direct answers to various questions concerning strategic materials in India. Based on information available about the administration of minerals in the country and technological requirements of a few strategic sectors, a broad estimation in regards to the strategic materials required could be made. However, exactly which materials are strategic to India is not known. It is also important to estimate the level of dependence of India's industry on strategic materials. In addition, the knowledge is essential in regards to the nature of the supply route of such materials and about the level of dependence on foreign agencies.

No specific answers are available (or obtainable) for the above queries; therefore, in this chapter, an attempt has been made to undertake a macro-analysis of this subject based on available and derived information. This could also assist in providing some clues for developing future policy options.

The Indian State faces wider security challenges than most other states in the world. India is the only country in the world which shares major portion of its borders with two nuclear weapon states with whom India has fought wars in the past. India is itself a nuclear weapons state. Unfortunately, India is also a victim of international terrorism and also faces unrest within (in limited areas).

Geographically, India is a unique state in the world, as it covers every imaginable terrain such as rain forests, deserts and snow-capped mountainous ridges. Moreover, peninsular India is surrounded by disaster-prone Himalayan mountain ranges to its North and the Northeast. India has a land frontier of 15,200 km, a coastline of 7,516.6 km and an exclusive economic zone of 2.2

million sq. km, as well as island territories, vital offshore installations and airspace to defend.[4] The Indian Forces, therefore, have to remain prepared and address various security challenges. They also have to play an important role in the management of various natural disasters. India is amongst the world's top countries in terms of defence expenditure and imports significant amount (approximately 70 per cent) of defence hardware. India proposes to spend around US$ 45 billion on defence in 2013-14. There are few reports indicating that this amount be increased to US$ 66-67 billion by 2020.

The Defence Research and Development Organisation (DRDO) is the key organisation with a vast network of 52 laboratories, and is involved in various areas from aeronautics, combat engineering to life sciences. It is responsible for India's missile programme. Defence Public Sector Units (DPSUs) arena integral part of India's defence production architecture and account for more than 65 per cent of the total output. Per year value of their production is around US$ 4 billion. The private sector also plays a significant role in the defence industry as sub-contractors and ancillary industry. In various cases, they are the suppliers of raw materials, semi-finished products, parts and components to DPSUs, ordnance factories (which provide the production base), base workshops of the army, base repair depots of the air force, the dockyards of the navy, etc. Foreign companies account for the majority of procurement from the private sector in India, with approximately 70 per cent of Indian defence procurement coming from overseas sources.[5] However, it is important to mention that this figure is disputed by people working in the system; as per them, the import dependence is much less than what is being projected in certain reports. Recently, India has permitted 49 per cent Foreign Direct Investment (FDI) in its defence sector.

The above backdrop signifies that even though India imports majority of its defence hardware, still there is appreciable dependence on the local industry (both public and private). Moreover, it assists in appreciating the importance of strategic materials to India's defence, space, missiles, energy and other strategic sectors.

Every industry has certain key drivers that influence the supply of strategic materials. Such drivers have socio-political, geographical, economical, and technological and aspects, and may vary from material to material. Broadly, they could be analysed at structural and domestic levels. At the structural level, they could relate to the changing global balance of power and growing competition and cooperation amongst nations and policies of the states to keep the export/import of strategic under control. While at the domestic level, the internal political dynamics, various socioeconomic factors, mining polices, state of industry, technological development aspects and environmental issues are of significance. Any analysis of this subject needs to cater for uncertainties and risks too.

Globally, some systematic studies in respect of Probabilistic Mineral Resource Assessments to estimate the amount of undiscovered resources have been undertaken, and mathematical models like deposit density models or ore-deposit-types models are also available. Further, in some cases, Quantitative National Mineral Resource Assessments have been undertaken. However, the information identifying the probable needs of the industry (for a particular state) concerning strategic materials during 'no-war' and 'war' situations is not available, at least not in the open domain. Here the purpose is to build up a context to demonstrate the need for developing an India-centric model.

For this purpose, it would be useful to focus on the following questions that are essential to conduct a review:

1. How strategic materials are defined in the Indian context? How identification of strategic materials is assessed?
2. What is the approximate volume of strategic material required presently as well as the future projections?
3. How are strategic materials needs satisfied? What are the types and amount of strategic materials locally available, and what are the import needs?
4. What is India's technological competence in this field? What is India's nature of dependence on outside agencies for technological assistance?
5. What is the pattern of export/import of the materials required for the strategic purposes? Which states are dependent on us for the supply and what is our dependency? Are we exporting any strategic materials which are also required for internal usage?
6. What are the economic policies and compulsions in respect of export/ import of such materials?
7. What is the nature of international agreements by Indian agencies with the agencies from other states?
8. What is the nature of dependence on outside agencies for the supply of such materials? What alternatives are available if such supply stops suddenly?
9. Which are the states on which India is dependent for the supply of strategic materials? What is the nature of political stability in those states? What the chances that these supplies could be diverted to other states due to geopolitical and economic reasons? Would these states be pressured by India's adversaries to stop/reduce such supplies?

10. What are the possible indicators that the supply chain (both internal and external) of strategic material to Indian industry could get disrupted (natural reasons like disasters or otherwise)?
11. What are the procedures and possibilities in regards to substitutions?
12. What are the social and environmental challenges faced by a state regarding its mineral deposits?

The following sections discuss two models—Porters Five Forces Analysis and Likert Scale Analysis—to put in perspective how India is positioned in regards to its strategic minerals needs.

Model 1: Porters Five Forces Analysis

In 1979, a young associate professor called Michael Porter at Harvard Business School published his first article for *Harvard Business Review* (*HBR*). The article was titled "How Competitive Forces Shape Strategy". In the following years, Michael Porter's explication of the five forces that determine the long-run profitability of any industry shaped a generation of academic research and business practice. His model presents five forces that determine the competitive intensity and, therefore, attractiveness of a market. He explains why a fast-growing industry is not always profitable, how government policies play a role by changing the relative strength of the forces and how to use the forces to understand complements. He also shows how a company can influence the key forces in the industry to create a more favourable structure for itself or to expand the pie altogether. In some total, it could be argued that the model essentially talks about the health of the industry and reveals why industry profitability is what it is.[6]

The fundamental objective to apply Porter's model in strategic mining industry is to learn more about its health in general and understand its strengths. This could also enhance the knowledge about India's mining industry. Based on Porter's model, a profile of India's mining industry has been created for better appreciation of the industry status.[7] Porter's five forces are as follows, and their diagrammatic representation is also in Figure 4.2:[8]

1. Bargaining power of buyers/customers
2. Power of suppliers
3. Threat of substitute products (including technology change)
4. Threat of new market entrants
5. Existing competitive rivalry between suppliers

Porter is also known to have presented a simple identification of five generic descriptions of industries as follows:

Figure 4.2: Porters Five Force Model

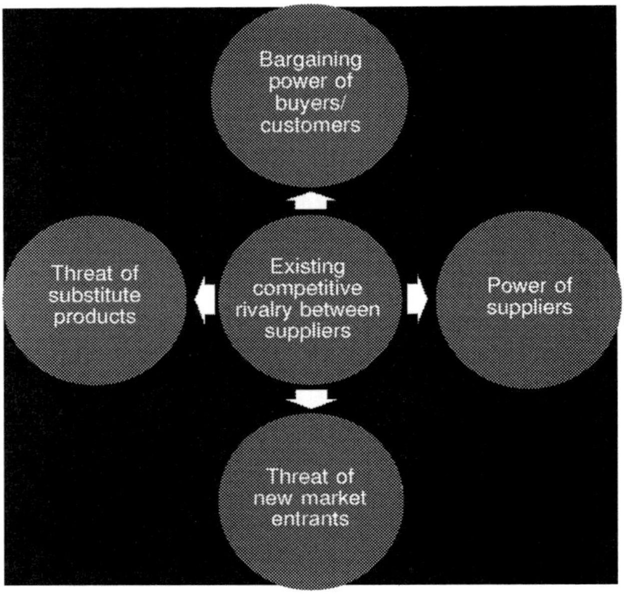

Source: Harvard Business Review.

- **Fragmented** (e.g., shoe repairs, gift shops)
- **Emerging** (e.g., space travel)
- **Mature** (e.g., automotive)
- **Declining** (e.g., solid fuels)
- **Global** (e.g., micro-processors)

Broadly, the strategic minerals industry could be directly and/or indirectly associated with some of the above generic descriptions like global and both emerging as well as mature.

Force 1: Bargaining Power of Buyers/Customers

The customer in this case would be the section of India's strategic industry which depends on the purchase of strategic materials. Such purchase could be undertaken via domestic purchase or dependence on imports.

For the purpose of this assessment, only information in regards to exports is important. The important questions here are: What is the nature of exporters that the Indian industry is depending on? What are the bargaining powers (if any) available with India?

Table 4.1 represents the present percentage dependence of each mineral on a particular country for the imports of both ores and concentrates as well as alloys and scrap. Higher dependence on a particular country decreases the bargaining power of the customer, as bargaining power has direct correlation with potential supplier/exporters present in the market. Higher number of alternatives assures that no single supplier shall have the bargaining leverage. The table also represents the alternative countries which can supply these minerals in order to increase the bargaining power.

Table 4.1: Percentage Dependency of Imports on Various Countries

Minerals	Countries		Percentage		Alternative countries
	Ores n Conc.	Alloys & Scrap	Ores n Conc.	Alloys & Scrap	
1	2	3	4	5	6
Antimony	South Africa	China	92.8	90	Bolivia
	Italy		2.0		Russia
	France		2.5		Australia
	Others		2.5		
Boron	Turkey	Turkey	43	55	Chile
	US	US	25	34	Russia
	Bolivia		15		
	Argentina		8		
Cobalt	Democratic Rep. of Congo	Congo	74	16	Australia
	People's Rep. of Congo	Zambia	22	15	Brazil
	Others[9]	US	4	11	Russia
		Canada		11	Zambia
		Belgium		10	
Fluorite	China		83		South Africa
	Kenya		12		Mongolia
					Mexico
Germanium	US		34.6		
	Australia		23.3		
	China		16		
	South Africa		11.23		
Molybdenum	US	China	21	63	Peru
	Chile	Austria	37	19	Russia
	Netherland		14		
	Canada		9		
Nickel	Canada	Australia	45	26	Brazil
	US	Russia	42	23	South Africa
	Uganda	Norway	9	8	Cuba
	Russia	Finland	2	7	

1	2	3	4	5	6
Selenium	Japan	NA	32	NA	Canada
	China		22		Chile
	Korea		14		Peru
	Belgium		13		
	Germany		10		
Tin	People's Rep. of Congo	Malaysia	41	46	
	South Africa	Indonesia	40	17	
	China	Belgium	13	10	
		Singapore		8	
Tungsten	NA	China	NA	44	Russia
		Germany		15	Canada
		Rep. of Korea		11	Chile
		US		8	

Source: Compiled from US Geological Survey, Export-Import Data, Ministry of Commerce, Indian Federation of Mines and Indian Bureau of Mines.

From Table 4.1, it is clear that for a few minerals such as antimony, cobalt, fluorite, nickel and molybdenum, the bargaining power is very less, as our dependency on countries like China, South Africa, Australia and Congo is on the higher side. While for other minerals, the bargaining power is moderate, as the existing dependency is reasonable. The future probable demand for some of these minerals such as cobalt, nickel molybdenum and tungsten is expected to grow exponentially for two specific reasons. First, there is a higher global demand as the world investment in high-end technology is following an increasing trend. Second, countries like China, South Africa and Singapore are developing rapidly, and hence, their domestic demand is also increasing. Therefore, at present, India needs to come up with highly focused policies, engage in various bilateral and multilateral engagements at high level and undertake long-term collaborations with 'potential alternative countries' in order to increase the bargaining power.

Force 2: Power of Suppliers/Bargaining Power of Suppliers

As strategic minerals are used in high-end technologies in strategic industries such as defence, nuclear and aerospace, the demand for the minerals is high while the supply for most of them is limited due to high global and domestic demands. Fewer supplier choices increase its dependency and reduce the bargaining power.

For strategic minerals, the leverage is low, even though for a few minerals, the reserves are available, but the resources to extract them is either limited or economically not feasible for the country. Some suppliers also enjoy high bargaining power for particular minerals because globally they are only available within the geographical territory of their country.

Table 4.2 shows the percentage of world production of some of the strategic minerals. The idea here is to demonstrate the bargaining power of these countries and the high bargaining power of suppliers from these countries. (Table 4.2 contains only a few minerals which dominate or have higher percentage of world production.)

Table 4.2: World Mineral Monopoly

Minerals	Country	Percentage of World Production
Antimony	China	53
	Russia	19
	Bolivia	17
Bismuth	China	52 (the only country which produces Bismuth from Bismuth ore)
	Belgium	36
Beryllium	US	65 (65 per cent of these resources is in non-pegmatite form)
Cobalt	Democratic Rep. of Congo (DRC)	56
Germanium[10]	China	Approx. 68
Lithium	Australia	Aprox. 35
	Chile	35
Nickel	Australia	Approx. 40
Tungsten	China	64
Tin	China	44

Source: Compiled using US Geological Survey, Indian Bureau of Mines and UK Geological Survey.

World production for the most of the minerals as shown in Table 4.2 is dominated by China, but it also has some of the highest world consumption of such materials. The general imports trend for India appears more to be from both developed as well as underdeveloped countries like Russia, South Africa, Bolivia, Chile, Congo and Zambia as their domestic demand is low. Even though the investments to these countries is significant, it also assures probable long-term supply of most of these minerals. Hence, the bargaining power of suppliers is either low or moderate for India. The future bargaining power for India will depend on the stability of governments in some of these countries.

Force 3: Threat of Substitute Products (Including Technology Change)

In strategic mineral industry, substitutes indeed have more positive impact than threats. The potential alternatives reduce the risk of dependence on specific states for mineral supply imports. However, it important to note that for the production of key technologies, the quality requirements and technical specifications in respect of strategic materials are very stringent. Hence, alternatives are not accepted readily. This makes it difficult to find exact alternative materials (substitutes) the stringent technical requirements and hence imprecise substitutes are not possible. Moreover, some of the strategic minerals have substitutes which are also not readily available because they also belong to the strategic minerals category.

Table 4.3 demonstrates the potential substitutes of some of the strategically important minerals. (The portions in bold refer to some of the challenges associated with the substitutes.)

Table 4.3: Potential Substitutes

Minerals	Substitutes
Antimony	• Compounds of chromium, tin, titanium, zinc and zirconium substitute for antimony chemicals in paint, pigments and enamels.
Beryllium	• Copper alloys containing nickel and silicon, tin, titanium, or other alloying elements or phosphor bronze alloys (copper-tin-phosphorus) may be substituted for beryllium-copper alloys, but these substitutions can result in substantially reduced performance. • Aluminium nitride or boron nitride may be substituted for beryllium oxide in some applications. **However, in this case, the process (technical) of application becomes more complex.**
Bismuth	• Indium can replace bismuth in low temperature solders. • Resins can replace bismuth alloys for holding metal shapes during machining. • Free-machining alloys can contain lead, selenium or tellurium as a replacement for bismuth.
Boron	• Some enamels can use other glass-producing substances, such as phosphates. • Insulation substitutes include cellulose, foams and mineral wools
Cobalt	• **In some applications, substitution for cobalt would result in a loss in product performance.** • Potential substitutes include barium or strontium ferrites, neodymium-iron-boron or nickel-iron alloys in magnets. • Iron-cobalt-nickel, nickel, cermets or ceramics in cutting and wear-resistant materials • Nickel-based alloys or ceramics in jet engines; rhodium in hydroformylation catalysts.
Gallium	• Liquid crystals made from organic compounds are used in visual displays as substitutes for Light Emitting Diodes (LEDs). • Indium phosphide components can be substituted for GaAs-based infrared laser diodes in some specific-wavelength applications, • Silicon is the principal competitor with GaAs in solar-cell applications. • GaAs-based ICs are used in many defence-related applications because of their unique properties, **and there are no effective substitutes.**

Minerals	Substitutes
Germanium	• Silicon can be a less-expensive substitute for germanium in certain electronic applications, **but effectiveness is not guaranteed.** • Some metallic compounds can be substituted in high-frequency electronics applications and in some LED applications. • Zinc selenide and germanium glass substitute for germanium metal in infrared applications **systems but often at the expense of performance.** • Titanium has the potential to be a substitute as a polymerisation catalyst.
Indium	• Indium's recent price volatility and various supply concerns associated with the metal have accelerated the development of ITO substitutes. • Antimony tin oxide coatings, which are deposited by an ink-jetting process. • Carbon nanotube coatings, applied by wet-processing techniques, have been developed as an alternative to ITO coatings in flexible displays, solar cells and touch screens, but **they are expensive to use.** • Researchers have recently developed a more adhesive zinc oxide and powder to replace ITO in LCDs. • **The technology is estimated to be commercially available in coming few years.** • Gallium arsenide can substitute for indium phosphide in solar cells and in many semiconductor applications.
Lithium	• Substitution for lithium compounds is possible in batteries, ceramics, greases and manufactured glass. • Zinc as anode material in primary batteries; and sodic and potassic fluxes in ceramics and glass manufacture. • Lithium carbonate is not considered to be an essential ingredient in aluminium potlines. • Substitutes for aluminium lithium alloys in structural materials are composite materials consisting of boron, glass or polymer fibres in resins.
Molybdenum	• **Substitution is difficult for molybdenum in its major application as an alloying element in steels and cast irons.** • In fact, because of the availability and versatility of molybdenum, industry has sought to develop new materials that benefit from the alloying properties of the metal. • Potential substitutes for molybdenum include chromium, vanadium, niobium (columbium) and boron in alloy steels; • **Tungsten** in tool steels; graphite, tungsten and tantalum for refractory materials in high-temperature electric furnaces; and chrome-orange.
Nickel	• **Nickel is hard to substitute for applications** like ultrahigh-chromium stainless steels for austenitic grades in construction applications. • Nickel-free specialty steels are sometimes used in place of stainless steel within the power-generating and petrochemical industries. • Titanium alloys can substitute for nickel metal or nickel-based alloys in corrosive chemical environments. • Use of **nickel in light and high efficient batteries is difficult to substitute** for its critical applications such as in defence and solar batteries.
Niobium	• The following materials can be substituted for niobium, **but a performance or cost penalty may ensue.**

Minerals	Substitutes
	• Molybdenum and vanadium, as alloying elements in high-strength low-alloy steels; tantalum and titanium, as alloying elements in stainless and high-strength steels. • Use of niobium in high temperature applications used in aerospace industry **vital and properties are hard to be substituted.**
Selenium	• Silicon is also the major substitute for selenium in low- and medium-voltage rectifiers and solar photovoltaic cells. • Sulphur dioxide can be used as a replacement for selenium dioxide in the production of electrolytic manganese metal **but is avoided due to environmental constraint.**
Tantalum	• The following materials can be substituted for tantalum, **but usually with less effectiveness:** niobium in carbides; aluminium and ceramics in electronic capacitors. • Hafnium, iridium, molybdenum, niobium, rhenium, and tungsten in High temperature applications.
Tin	• Aluminium, glass, paper, plastic or tin-free steel substitute for tin cans and containers. • Other materials that substitute for tin are epoxy resins for solder; aluminium alloys, copper-base alloys and plastics for bronze.
Tungsten	• Potential substitutes for cemented tungsten carbides include cemented carbides based on molybdenum carbide and titanium carbide. • Potential substitutes for other applications are as follows: molybdenum for certain tungsten mill products; molybdenum steels for tungsten steels. • Depleted uranium or lead for tungsten or tungsten alloys in applications **requiring high-density** or the ability to shield radiation; and depleted uranium alloys or hardened steel for cemented tungsten carbides or tungsten alloys in armour-piercing projectiles. • **In some applications, substitution would result in increased cost or a loss in product performance.**

Source: Compiled using US Geological Survey, Indian Bureau of Mines and UK Geological Survey.

Force 4: Threat of New Competitors

The competitors, on a global scale, are the countries which could replace the existing supplier states. However, broadly, the global geological mapping of materials has already been done, and there is a clarity in respect of the mineral-rich geographical areas, typically, regarding the states they belong to. Hence, the possibility of the entry of new competitors is minimal. Only if major breakthroughs in extracting the minerals from the seas are realised, there exists a possibility of new competitors entering this field.

As mentioned in the Table 4.1, already some knowledge about the states which could offer the alternatives is available. However, only the geographical availability of the minerals is not sufficient because the process of extraction and processing is technologically challenging and costly. This demands a high level of bilateral and multilateral engagements. So, in order to increase the competitive rivalry, which will indeed have a positive effect in future, it is essential for countries to invest in developing countries to exploit their resources and increase the supply of minerals in the market. For states like India, it would be essential to undertake the cost-benefit analysis for making any such investments in order to look for alternative suppliers for imports.

Force 5: Competitive Rivalry

Few competitors mean fewer firms are competing for the same customers and resources. Fewer suppliers for specific materials indicate monopoly, but at the same time if there are fewer buyers, then the supplier also has limited options. If demand is high but the suppliers are limited, then obviously there is likely to be the so called 'resource war for minerals'.

Currently, the need for strategic materials is significant globally. The Chinese mineral industry's domination in this field, and the dependence of many states in the world on it amply demonstrate this fact. For example, China has significant investments in the developing and resource-rich countries of Africa. It is also planning to setup multibillion-dollar mines in Afghanistan and Pakistan. China has built bilateral as well as multi-lateral relations with Central Asian countries.[11] All this would allow China lead position in the global strategic materials market (presently, too, it is the leader). China also has a geographical advantage in this field. At the same time, as seen from Table 1, there are few states like Russia and Australia which could offer some competition to China. India must ensure that there are multiple options regarding the import of the strategic materials so that there is no overdependence on one country.

Broad Evaluation

The Five Forces Analysis provides an overall idea about the competitive strength and attractiveness of the strategic materials market. Porter himself calls these forces as the micro-environment. However, in this particular case, the information presented above to describe and discuss various forces does provide an understanding about the overall environment. Each force individually and all forces collectively would have implications for every country depending on its policies and requirements about the strategic materials. For a state like India, the challenges are twofold: one, as a producer of the strategic materials and the other as a user of strategic materials. India's minerals and mining industry need to factor in the outcomes of the Porter method analysis for the assessment of their position in the global market and to plan for the future. India's industry, which is dependent on imports of strategic materials, could draw its conclusions based on the model output, whereas Indian policymakers should factor in various aspects highlighted by this model in order to develop a long-term policy where the dependence on overall imports could be reduced.

Drawbacks and Inapplicability of Porter's Five Forces

It is also important to mention that this model has some limitations which are as follows:

- It offers only qualitative analysis of the market, and hence, the results of this model cannot be deemed conclusive.
- Many aspects of the model (buyer, supplier, etc.) are not of any relevance when it comes to matters of national security.
- We currently function in a highly dynamic and relatively volatile environment. Hence, any analysis done is only short-lived and may not hold true for the future.
- The model is based on the idea of 'competition' – which is not the bone of contention in this given scenario or any matter of national security.

The above-mentioned limitations indicate that the strict usage of this model could be possible only in imitated cases and under stringent boundary conductions. However, the strength of the model lies in the fact that even the structured presentation of data under five different forces identified by this model allows a methodological valuation of the problem under discussion.

The Indian mining industry could be said to have come into existence with the establishment of Indian Bureau of Mines (IBM) in 1948.The Indian mining industry has limited foreign investors and is dominated by local players. India is the world's largest producer of mica blocks and mica splitting in the world. India also contributes significantly towards the global production of chromite, iron ore, bauxite, limestone, manganese, etc. Contribution by the Indian mining industry was 2.63 per cent of the GDP, and contributed revenues of approximately over US$ 45 billion in 2011. However, it is difficult to find the exact contribution of strategic materials to the total contributed revenue. The other model presented in this chapter offers a clearer picture about India's actual dependence on strategic materials.

Here the purpose has not been to use Porter's Five Forces Analysis in a classic sense, like to use it for understanding the profitability and the dynamics of competitive structure of the mining industry in India. The purpose has been to put in broad context the five forces of this model in respect of India's strategic mining industry with a view to appreciate the strengths and limitations of this industry and to have a better understanding of the overall dynamics of this industry. The strategic minerals industry is actually a secondary portion of the materials industry. Practically, it is difficult to isolate a section of mining industry and analyse only that sector as a separate unit. Such assessment becomes further difficult because of the strategic connotations associated with this industry. Here, the five forces model is essentially about assessing the micro-environment. Such analysis is essential to know few basic realities like the bargaining power of buyers and suppliers, the competitive rivalry in the industry, nature of substitute's options, etc. Thus, Porter's five forces are discussed herein the context of India's need for strategic materials (minerals) and its dependence on the global strategic materials industry.

Here, the model has not been used to study the strengths and limitations of India's strategic materials industry. Also, no attempt has been made to recognise the exact financial effectiveness of this industry. The basic idea behind using this methodology is to develop a reasonable understanding of the global strategic materials industry and broadly ascertain India's dependence on the global supply of such material. There could be some amount of subjectivity, implicit variability and uncertainty in assumptions while doing this appraisal. However, to bring in objectivity in assessment, as far as possible, empirical analysis has been attempted.

Model 2: Assessment Using Likert Scale

There is a general perception that if the knowledge of the occurrence of some likely event exists, then there are no surprises, and hence, there is no risk attached to it. Should there be an element of uncertainty surrounding the occurrence of any event, then the risk exists.[12] However, the idea of risk should not be associated only with the improbability of the event. Risk is more about possible threats and opportunities. It is about the probable impact on the ability of a group, society, industry or country to meet their goals. In short, risk could be associated with both the challenges and the opportunities. Hence, effective risk identification is essential for managing the present and future in the most cost-effective way. Social science researchers have identified various composite measures to assess concept that is too complex to be analysed simply. Scale is one such type of composite measure and various scales like Staple Scale, Semantic Differential Scale and Likert Scale have been devised to undertake such analyses. Here, Likert Scale has been used to analyse the exact nature of risk India faces in respect of strategic materials.

This risk assessment model for strategic materials is a weighted average model based on a few important parameters which are commonly considered as significant contributors towards risk. The degree of parameters is measured using Likert Scale. The value of each parameter derived using the Likert Scale becomes an input for weighted average computations. Each risk factor (parameter) is given an equal weight in the model, thereby making it robust for comparative analysis of various strategic materials.

The Likert Scale is a psychometric[13] scale and commonly involves conducting surveys, questionnaires and also engages mechanisms to "measure constructs such as attitudes, images and opinions".[14] This scale expects the respondents to indicate preferences or degree of agreement or disagreement with each of a series of statements about the stimulus objects. Likert Scale is a non-comparative scaling technique and is one-dimensional (only measures a single trait) in nature. Respondents are expected to indicate their level of agreement with a given statement by way of an ordinal scale. This scale in its most common forms comprises a five-point scale ranging from "Strongly Disagree" on one end to "Strongly Agree" on the other with neither "Neither Agree nor Disagree" in the middle.

Figure 4.3: Likert's Five-point Scale

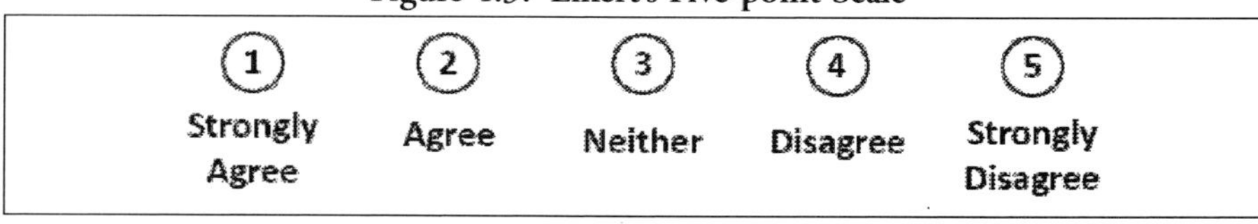

Some practitioners also advocate the use of seven- and nine-point scales which add additional granularity. Sometimes a four-point (or other even-numbered) scale is used where no indifferent option is available. Each level on the scale is assigned a numeric value or coding as shown in Figure 4.3. The analysis could be conducted on an item-by-item basis (profile analysis), or a total (summated) score can be calculated.[15]

For this particular study, a four-point scale has been used. Such a scale is basically used to facilitate data analysis, by assigning an integer value on the scale. The details are as follows:

Figure 4.4: Risk Factors Assigned on Likert Scale

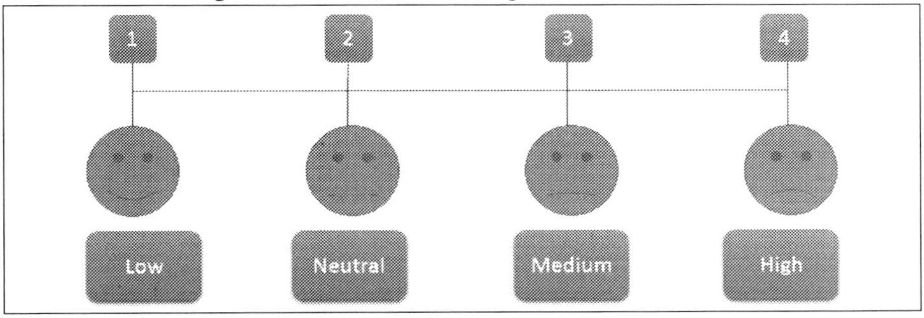

The traditional way to use Likert Scale is to sum the values of each selected option and create a score. This method is commonly known as 'arithmetic mean'. There is another form of mean considered as a more accurate process called Weighted Average Mean. Here "instead of data contributing equally to the final average, some data points contribute more than others".[16]

The mathematically Weighted Average Means is represented as follows:

$$\underline{x} = \sum_{i=1}^{n} \frac{w_i x_i}{w_i}$$

Where w_i represents the value assigned on the Likert Scale, and x_i is the weighted percentage value assigned to each factor. Risk value assigned to the factor on Likert Scale varies from 1-4, where minimal value 1 represents low risk, while 4 represents high risk (see Figure 4.4).

The factors to be introduced on Likert Scale for analysis have been considered on the basis of probable causes which might affect the supply of minerals in future. Availability of risk factor involves the possibility of imports from other countries, diversifying the risk. When some countries hold the monopoly of certain material in terms of production and reserve, the risk become higher. The other factor involves import dependency of particular country which resembles the risk. The future probable demand directly or indirectly impacts the imports as higher global demand might raise the international price which indeed might effects the amount of imports. There is an additional factor of substitution which is not included in the analysis above due to complications involved in giving the integer value for risk. The substitution factor becomes intricate as substitutes might be already in the list of critical minerals, or some of them might have the advantage of reusability and could be extracted from alloys and scraps.

In this particular case, for the purposes of broad understanding, maintenance of same 'Datum level' for every mineral assessed and ease of calculation the 'contribution' of every risk factor has been assumed to be same.

Hence, the entire process of calculation is analogous to arithmetic averages. However, the Weighted Average Mean method has been used to indicate that for a precise and critical analysis the contribution of every factor needs to be given special attention because it could have varied impact on the overall risk. Tables 4.4 to 4.16 compute the risk factors for some strategic minerals.

Table 4.4: Computation of Risk Factor for Antimony (Sb)

Factors/Scale	Low	Neutral	Medium	High	Percent
Availability risk			X		25
Import dependency on particular country				X	25
Imports			X		25
Probable future demand		X			25

$$\underline{x} = \sum_{i=1}^{n} \frac{w_i x_i}{w_i}$$

$$\underline{x} = \sum_{i=1}^{n} \frac{3\times0.25 + 4\times0.25+3\times0.25+2\times0.25}{0.25+0.25+0.25+0.25} = 3.0$$

Risk Factor - 3.0/4.0

Similarly, computation of risk factor is done for all other minerals as tabulated below:

Table 4.5: Computation of Risk Factor for Boron (B)

Factors/Scale	Low	Neutral	Medium	High	Percent
Availability risk	X				25
Import dependency on particular country			X		25
Imports		X			25
Probable future demand			X		25

Risk Factor- 2.25/4.0

Table 4.6: Computation of Risk Factor for Cobalt (Co)

Factors/Scale	Low	Neutral	Medium	High	Percent
Availability risk			X		25
Import dependency on particular country				X	25
Imports				X	25
Probable future demand				X	25

Risk Factor- 3.75/4.0

Table 4.7: Computation of Risk Factor for Fluorite (CF_2)

Factors/Scale	Low	Neutral	Medium	High	Percent
Availability risk			X		25
Import dependency on particular country				X	25
Imports			X		25
Probable future demand			X		25

Risk Factor- 3.25/4.0

Table 4.8: Computation of Risk Factor for Gallium (Ga)

Factors/Scale	Low	Neutral	Medium	High	Percent
Availability risk	X				25
Import dependency on particular country	X				25
Imports	X				25
Probable future demand			X		25

Risk Factor- 1.5/4.0

Table 4.9: Computation of Risk Factor for Germanium (Ge)

Factors/Scale	Low	Neutral	Medium	High	Percent
Availability risk				X	25
Import dependency on particular country				X	25
Imports			X		25
Probable future demand				X	25

Risk Factor- 3.75/4.0

Table 4.10: Computation of Risk Factor for Lithium (Li)

Factors/Scale	Low	Neutral	Medium	High	Percent
Availability risk		X			25
Import dependency on particular country				X	25
Imports				X	25
Probable future demand			X		25

Risk Factor- 3.25/4.0

Table 4.11: Computation of Risk Factor for Molybdenum (Mo)

Factors/Scale	Low	Neutral	Medium	High	Percent
Availability risk			X		25
Import dependency on particular country			X		25
Imports				X	25
Probable future demand				X	25

Risk Factor- 3.5/4.0

Table 4.12: Computation of Risk Factor for Nickel (Ni)

Factors/Scale	Low	Neutral	Medium	High	Percent
Import dependency on particular country			X		25
Imports			X		25
Probable future demand				X	25
Availability risk		X			25

Risk Factor- 3.0/4.0

Table 4.13: Computation of Risk Factor for Niobium (Nb)

Factors/Scale	Low	Neutral	Medium	High	Percent
Import dependency on particular country				X	25
Imports			X		25
Probable future demand		X			25
Availability risk				X	25

Risk Factor- 3.25/4.0

Table 4.14: Computation of Risk Factor for Selenium (Se)

Factors/Scale	Low	Neutral	Medium	High	Percent
Import dependency on particular country			X		25
Imports			X		25
Probable future demand			X		25
Availability risk		X			25

Risk Factor- 2.75/4.0

Table 4.15: Computation of Risk Factor for Tin (Sn)

Factors/Scale	Low	Neutral	Medium	High	Percent
Availability risk		X			25
Import dependency on particular country			X		25
Imports				X	25
Probable future demand				X	25

Risk Factor- 3.25/4.0

Table 4.16: Computation of Risk Factor for Tungsten (W)

Factors/Scale	Low	Neutral	Medium	High	Percent
Availability risk				X	25
Import dependency on particular country			X		25
Imports				X	25
Probable future demand				X	25

Risk Factor- 3.75/4.0

Finally, Table 4.17 lists the risk factors for the above-mentioned strategic minerals.

Table 4.17: Risk Factor for Various Minerals

Minerals	Risk Factor out of 4
Antimony	3.0
Bismuth	-
Beryllium	-
Boron	2.25
Cobalt	3.75
Fluorite	3.25
Gallium	1.5
Germanium	3.75
Indium	-
Lithium	3.25
Molybdenum	3.5
Nickel	3.0
Niobium	3.25
Selenium	2.75
Tantalum	-
Tin	3.25
Tungsten	3.75

Analysis

The above methodology indicates the overall risk factor associated with each strategic mineral on the basis of four vital factors. The above analysis also gives a comparative risk factor which varies from 1.5 at one end (lower) of the scale to 3.75 at other (higher). It is observed that out of 13 materials, 30 per cent of the minerals lie in the bracket of higher risk, while more than 50 per cent lie in the medium risk bracket. The strategic minerals which are in higher risk bracket are mainly cobalt, germanium, molybdenum and tungsten.

A detailed examination of these minerals mainly from supply-demand perspective is as follows:

Cobalt (Co)

Cobalt is mainly used in high-end technology such as production of superalloys, gas turbine blades and cutting tools.

I. The Democratic Republic of Congo (DRC) holds the monopoly in total reserves and is one of the principal producers contributing about 55 per cent, followed by Zambia (9 per cent), Australia (8 per cent) and Russia (5 per cent).
II. India's 74 per cent of cobalt imports are from DRC followed by Zambia with 22 per cent. This indicates that India's almost 96 per cent of total imports are only from two sources.
III. India does not have any primary source of cobalt; hence it imports large amount of cobalt in terms ores and concentrates and alloys and scraps.
IV. India's demand of cobalt is expected to rise in the future with the expansion of aerospace industry in the country. Overall, there would be increasing usage of cobalt-based superalloys in civil and military aviation sectors. Also, the usage would be as a catalyst for gas-to-liquid production of rechargeable batteries for hybrid electric vehicles and cellular telephones. The use in aerospace and energy generation industries which use cobalt-bearing superalloy for the production of gas turbine engine parts is likely to grow in the future; hence, the global demand is expected to increase multi-fold.[17]

Due to the specialised nature of applications and requirement of high-quality cobalt, there is a difficulty in substitution; hence, options are limited. Cobalt has the advantage of reusability, but due to high consumption, the domestic demand is mainly met by high imports of both ores and concentrates and in form of alloys and scraps.

Germanium (Ge)

Germanium is the sole element used in the electronic industry apart from its other applications.

I. China is one of the major producers of germanium. China's refinery production was about 70 per cent of the world's total production in 2012. Other producers include the US, Russia and Australia. Though almost 30 per cent of the total germanium consumed worldwide is produced from recycled materials, still to meet the increasing global demand, the existing ores and concentrates deposits are not enough.
II. About half of India's total imports of germanium come from China followed by the US and Australia.
III. India has limited primary resource of germanium ores and concentrates; however, the consumption is likely to increase in future. Naturally, the dependency on imports is likely to increase.
IV. India has a rapidly expanding electronics and communication equipment production industry. Also, India is keen towards achieving maximum indigenisation of its military industry which includes development and production of sophisticated military electronic equipment. All this indicates that the demand for germanium is likely to increase in future.

Silicon can be used as a less expensive element to substitute germanium in the electronic industry to an extent. Zinc selenite is used as a substitute for germanium in infrared applications systems, but often at the expense of performance.

Molybdenum (Mo)

Iron and steel industry and superalloy consumption accounted for about 81 per cent of the molybdenum consumed in 2011.

I. Global availability of Molybdenum reserves and also the maximum production of mineral have the Chinese footprint (38 per cent). The US (31 per cent), Chile (13 per cent) and Canada (5 per cent) are sources for procurement. Overall, the availability is risk is 'medium' for this mineral.
II. India's imports are mainly from Chile contributing 37 per cent of total imports, followed by the US (22 per cent), Netherlands (14 per cent) and Canada (9 per cent). Though India's dependency on Chile for imports is comparatively high, but the flexibility for diversification exists.

III. India is geographically not blessed with any molybdenum deposits. This mineral has metallurgical applications, such as alloys, and is used by structural steel and stainless steel production industries. India has become the world's fourth-largest producer of crude steel and is slated to become the second-largest steel producer by 2015. The total market value of the steel sector in India stood at US$ 57.8 billion in 2011 and is expected to touch US$ 95.3 billion by 2016.[18]

IV. A strong growth in steel and superalloys sector in India is expected in the near future; hence, probable future demand for molybdenum is expected to be high.

V. Molybdenum has unique properties which make it as an important alloying element in steels and cast iron production. It is difficult to get a substitute for this mineral. Some available substitutes include chromium, vanadium and niobium, which are also in the list of strategic minerals for India.

Tungsten (W)

Tungsten is a vital mineral of strategic importance. It acts as an important mineral for making special alloys used in various strategic industries. It is exceedingly used as filament for electric bulbs and in the making of high-speed tools. This material belongs to the high risk bracket due to following reasons:

I. China holds more than half of world production and reserves contributing about 60 per cent followed by Russia (9 per cent), Canada (4 per cent) and the US (5 per cent).

II. Interestingly, India's imports are not from countries having major deposits of tungsten. India mainly imports tungsten from two countries, Democratic Republic of Congo (41 per cent) and South Africa (40 per cent); hence, India's import dependency is not on a single source, and for India, the risk belongs to 'medium' category. At the same time, it is also important to note that there is no indigenous production of tungsten concentrates in India;[19] hence, there is total dependence onimports.

III. Due to the increasing demand of superalloys in high-end technological industries, the dependence of this mineral is expected to increase in future.

IV. Tungsten can be reused; therefore, the scrap also becomes an important source of raw material for the tungsten industry. Other substitutes are mainly titanium carbide, ceramics, ceramic-metallic composites and molybdenum. In general, due to quality concerns, availability factor and cost issues, various available substitutes are generally not considered as efficient options.

Tables 4.18 and 4.19 list the imports and exports of cobalt, molybdenum, germanium and tungsten in 2010-2011.

Table 4.18: Percentage Imports in 2011

Material	Countries	Percentage Imports (2011)
Cobalt	DRC	74
	Zambia	22
Molybdenum	Chile	37
	US	22
	Netherland	14
	Canada	9
Germanium	China	44
	US	19
	Australia	16
Tungsten	DRC	41
	South Africa	40

Source: Indian Bureau of Mines and Ministry of Commerce (Import-Export Databank).

Table 4.19: Imports and Exports of Minerals in 2010-2011 (data in metric tonnes)

Materials		Imports	Exports
Cobalt	Ores and Conc.	5,041	51
	Alloys and Scraps	726	264
Molybdenum	Ores and Conc.	4,382	938
	Scrap	412	15
Tungsten	Ores and Conc.	27	32
	Alloys and Scraps	404,654	432,709
Germanium	Oxides	2,855.27	14.08

Source: Indian Bureau of Mines and Ministry of Commerce (Import-Export Databank).

In closing

India is one of the emerging economies in the world, and its needs for mineral resources to sustain growth are significant. This chapter has tried to put in context India's requirements and the sources available to satisfy its needs. In order to understand this, two models were studied, both having different approaches to address the issue. However, when viewed together, they provide a broad idea about the current as well as future risks that India could face. The above analysis denotes the percentage dependency of India on various countries for the supply of strategic minerals.

It has been observed that India has significant dependence on countries like China and Africa in respect of imports of strategic minerals. Any internal or external factors that could influence the supplies from these states significantly increases the risk of supply. Today, the African region in general faces significant security challenges, and naturally, the internal situation in that region could impact the supply of the strategic minerals to the outside world. Chinese monopoly in respect of various strategic minerals could be a cause of concern not only for India and also for many other states. It is also important to note that China also has a larger control over African mineral production. Overall, India's dependency apart from the geopolitical factors would also be influenced by other factors such as cost, logistics and investment opportunities.

NOTES

1. Ewan W. Anderson, *Strategic Minerals*, Praeger, New York, 1988, p.55.
2. "Risk List 2012", Geoscience Centre, British Geological Survey (BGS), at http://www.bgs.ac.uk/downloads/start.cfm?id=2643 (Accessed July 19, 2013).
3. Ewan W. Anderson, p.57, No. 1.
4. "Defence: Sector Overview," Invest India, at http://www.investindia.gov.in/?q=defence-sector (Accessed July 19, 2013).
5. Ibid. "A Brief Report on Defence Sector in India", August 2012, Report Prepared by ASA and Associates, New Delhi, at http://www.asa.in/pdfs/surveys-reports/Defence-Sector-in-India.pdf (Accessed July 20, 2013).
6. "The Five Competitive Forces That Shape Strategy", *Harvard Business Review*, at http://hbr.org/2008/01/the-five-competitive-forces-that-shape-strategy/ (Accessed July 19, 2013).
7. Two specific works are available which evaluate Russia's and China's mining industry based on Porters Five Forces Analysis. Please refer:
   "Mining Industry in Russia: Porters Five Forces Analysis", *Research and Markets*, at http://www.researchandmarkets.com/reports/2299504/mining_industry_in_russia_porters_five_forces (Accessed July 19, 2013).
8. "Michael Porter's Five Forces Competition Theory Model", *Business balls*, at http://www.businessballs.com/portersfiveforcesofcompetition.htm (Accessed September 10, 2013).
9. Others countries include the US, Canada and Belgium.
10. "Material Handbook Germanium", UK Energy Research Centre, at http://www.ukerc.ac.uk/support/tiki-download_file.php?fileId=3011 (Accessed September 19, 2013).
11. Arvind Gupta, "India and Central Asia: Need for a Pro-active Approach", Institute for Defence Studies and Analyses, at http://www.idsa.in/policybrief/IndiaandCentralAsia_agupta_141013 (Accessed September 11, 2013).
12. *A Guide to Risk Management*, Queensland Treasury and Trade, 2011, Queensland Government, at http://www.treasury.qld.gov.au/office/knowledge/docs/risk-management-guide/guide-to-risk-management.pdf (Accessed September 11, 2013).
13. Psychological measurements like the measurement of knowledge, abilities, attitudes and personality.
14. "How to Use the Likert Scale in Statistical Analysis", *Applied Statistics*, at http://statisticscafe.blogspot.in/2011/05/how-to-use-likert-scale-in-statistical.html (Accessed September 20, 2013).

15. Bertram, Dane, "Likert Scale", http://poincare.matf.bg.ac.rs/~kristina/topic-dane-likert.pdf (Accessed September 21, 2013).
16. "Weighted mean", Princeton University, at http://www.princeton.edu/~achaney/tmve/wiki100k/docs/Weighted_mean.html (Accessed September 21, 2013).
17. "Cobalt", Report of Indian Bureau of Mines, 2011.
18. http://www.ibef.org/industry/steel.aspx (Accessed December 7, 2013).
19. "Tungsten", Indian federation of Mines.

5

India's Import Dependency

Import dependency is not unusual either for India or for various other nation-states. The Indian State is dependent in various fields either partially or fully on imports. India's growing dependence on imported energy is well known. Coal and oil are two sectors where India has significant dependency on imports. Further, there are a few other areas where the dependence on imports is significant, and strategic minerals is one such area. Overall, dependency management is a significant (and serious) business for strategic decision-makers globally. In the Indian context, it is essential for the policy-makers to identify and implement sustainable solutions for reducing the disadvantages it has in the arena of strategic materials. The Government of India's Planning Commission has published a very detailed report during May 2012 titled "Sustainable Development: Emerging Issues in India's Mineral Sector", which has identified specific areas of concerns including import dependence. Various other reports have analysed mineral dependence and its impact on country's economic and institutional development for various countries.[1] Thus, such reports highlight the fact that handling import dependencies is an important aspect in planning for existing and future needs of strategic materials.

This chapter discusses the larger geopolitical aspects of India's mineral dependency. The purpose is to factor foreign policy and economic diplomacy related issues to understand how India is positioned in regards to continuing with its present import structure. Chapter IV broadly identified that India's dependence on imports is mainly on states like China, Brazil, Democratic Republic of Congo, Russia, Australia and the US. The mineral deposits and production capabilities of these states are already discussed elsewhere in this book. This chapter deliberates on India's relationships with these states and takes a broad overview of political and industrial dynamics of these states.

It is difficult to isolate the exact influence of India's bilateral relationships with mineral relevant states supplying strategic materials. However, a broad understanding about India's overall relationships with these states could be an indicator for judgement. Amongst the states identified, India has had excellent relationship with Russia for many decades. Because of India's nuclear policies, the Indo-US relationship has witnessed various ups and downs in the past. India has fought a war with China in 1962; however, during last few years, a significant amount to harmonisation in the relationship has been witnessed. Following paragraphs present a backdrop of India's bilateral relationships with various major strategic mineral exporters to India.

Amongst the six states, namely China, Democratic Republic of Congo (DRC), Russia, Brazil, Australia and the US, on which India is significantly dependent on procuring minerals, India is most dependent on DRC. Unfortunately, DRC is one country with maximum political turbulence, and the African region as such has witnessed various civil wars. Hence, when debating bilateral relations of India, specifically in the case of DRC, the internal situation in a country also needs to be discussed, because unsettled political conditions and an ongoing bloody conflict in any state would obviously impact the exports from that state. While discussing India's geopolitical relationship with these states, this chapter also presents information in regards to important bilateral agreements undertaken by Government of India with these states in the field of minerals.

DRC

India always had a cordial and friendly relationship with the Democratic Republic of Congo (DRC). India was among the first countries to establish a diplomatic mission in Kinshasa, the capital and the largest city of the DRC. India sent its Ghurkha troops to DRC during 1960-62, under United Nations Operation in the Congo (Opération des Nations Unies au Congo, or ONUC),[2] for countering the rebellion in Katanga. At present, more than 3,000 Indian troops are deployed under the largest ever UN Peacekeeping operation in the country, United Nations Organisation Stabilisation Mission in the Democratic Republic of the Congo (MONUSCO). In general, trade and commercial linkages between both countries are limited. But, there are a few Indian companies engaged in the mining of copper, cobalt and diamond in DRC. A large portion of DRC's pharmaceutical imports are sourced from India. An Indo-Congolese Chamber of Commerce and Industry has been in existence from pre-civil war days, but has not been active.[3]

Figure 5.1: DRC Map

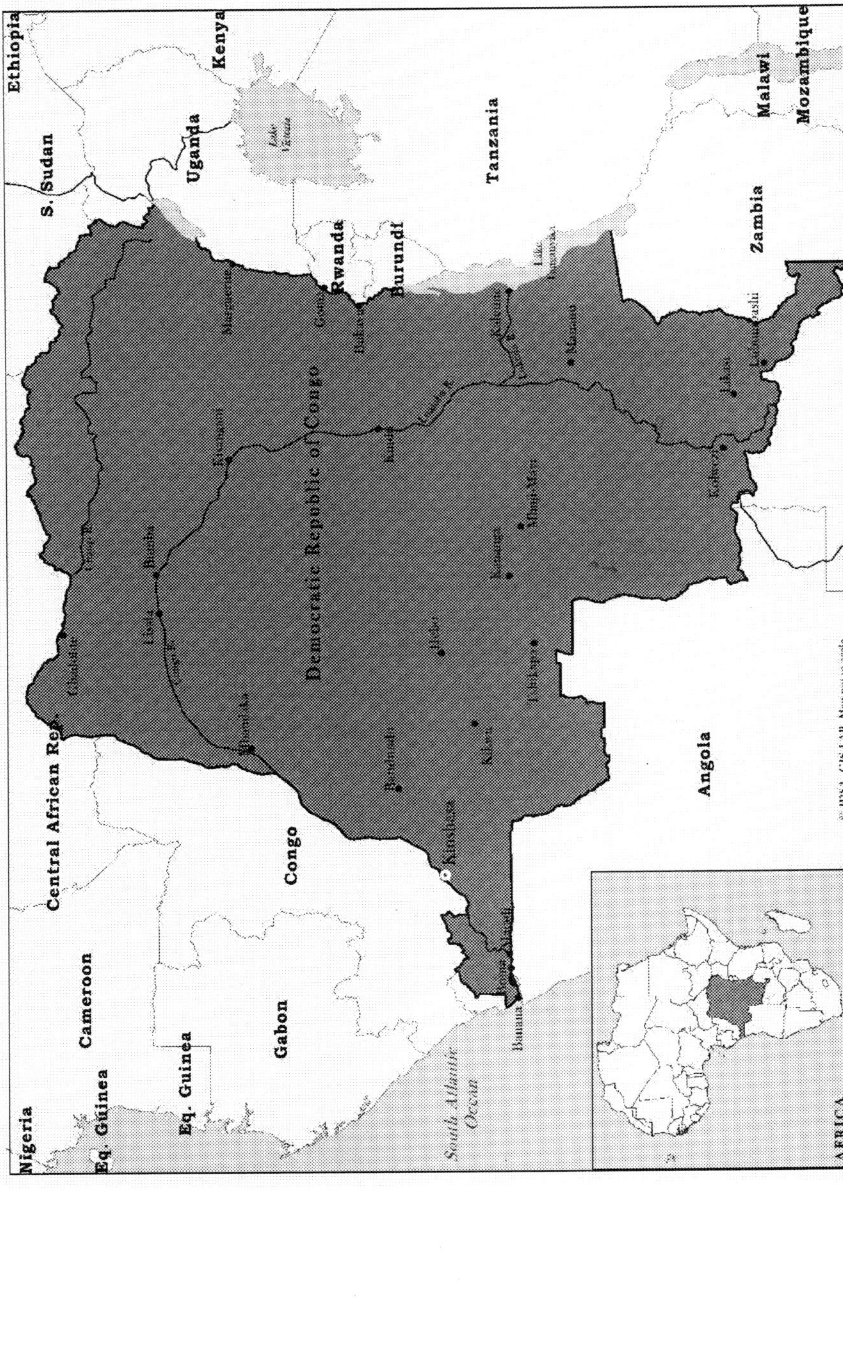

Source: Diplomacy in action, US Department of State.

DRC is known to be the richest country in the world regarding natural resources. For India, it is important to factor in the internal situation in DRC while planning its production cycle. DRC has a long history of civil wars and political instability.

DRC is a big country in the centre of the African continent (see Figure 5.1). DRC (formerly known as Zaire) is bordered by nations with whom it has had conflicts. It is second largest country in Africa in terms of area. It has witnessed an extreme bloody stage of conflict since the outbreak of fighting in August 1998 (the Second Congo War). Some 5.4 million people have died in both violent and non-violent (diseases like malaria, etc. and malnutrition) situations.[4]

Presently, uncertainty and near-war situation continues to exist in DRC. Regional blocs as well as the UN are making all efforts to find a lasting solution to the security crisis in the DRC.[5] It is important to note that along with political instability, issues like natural disasters and hunger are impacting the social fabric of the many states in Africa including DRC. There have been a number of complex reasons, including conflicts over basic resources such as water, access and control over rich minerals and other resources as well as various political agendas. Various armed groups like M23 and local militias are operating in that state bringing in significant amount of instability.[6] Since the beginning of 2012, ethnic tensions and inequitable access to land have led to renewed violence in the east and north-east of the DRC. This has resulted in the displacement of more than 2.2 million people inside the country. In addition, almost 70,000 people have crossed the border into neighbouring Rwanda and Uganda. At the same time, some earlier refugees from the DRC have started returning home too.[7] Normally, the minerals produced in DRC are considered as Conflict Minerals because they are mined in the areas of armed conflicts and human rights abuses.

It has been observed that all the actors involved in finding the solution to crisis in the region also are aware that the authority of the state would need to be restored, and diplomacy has limited relevance; so, there has been a need to use force for bringing normalcy.

In spite of having unsettled conditions and a politically fractured system, DRC is conscious of the fact that it needs to exploit its 'mineral power' to support its economy. It is aware that the global growth in demand for scarce raw materials owing to industrial surges in countries like China, India, Russia and Brazil makes their nation an extremely important player in respect of global strategic mineral business. It is expected that more economic and strategic initiatives (some are ongoing) to bringing more security to DRC would be undertaken by the rest of the world.

The economic and political engagement of India with the African continent is as such growing. However, India's association with DRC could be viewed as a bit uneven, despite India being the largest contributor in the UN mission underway to restore normalcy in the region. There have been some reports that the DRC Government has been particularly aggrieved because some Indian UN troops have at times grown too familiar with the rebel militia they are supposed to oppose. However, various informal discussions with various Indian and other officials indicate that these are mere perceptions, and in reality, all activities on ground happen in accordance with the UN guidelines. Indian had been involved with DRC for decades in various mining, construction, finance and telecommunications operations. Unfortunately, not much support has been received by Indian companies operating over there in terms of banks loans, etc. from the Indian government, and that could be one of the reasons for limited Indian investment. There are some misgivings about the nature of wage structure offered by some Indian companies, too. As the same time, there are some shining examples like the Bharti industrial group, which is respected for its business activities and ethics.[8]

India's Bilateral Agreements with Africa

(a) In the arena of mining, India has an old relationship with Africa. One of the important agreements titled "Indo-South African Cooperation" was initiated in August 18, 1998 in Cape Town. Under this agreement, six projects for mutual cooperation were signed highlighting the following issues:[9]

   I. Establishment of a detailed correlation on a formation level between the Karoo sequences in Southern Africa and the Gondwana sequences in India.
   II. Identification of offshore diamond deposit near Indian costal region; geoscience mapping was established.
   III. Development of a Pre-Gondwana Precambrian crustal evolution and metallogenic map for India and Southern Africa.
   IV. Evaluation of stability of underground mine workings through micro-seismic techniques.
   V. Hydro-fracturing for street measurement.
   VI. Characterisation and processing of gold, diamond and platinum group of metal ores and evolution of suitable beneficiation processes.

(b) Within one year after the establishment of this cooperation in a meeting at New Delhi, the progress on earlier project was evaluated while agreement was made for eight new projects, seven of which are enlisted as follows:[10]

I. Bacterial Leaching of Low Grade Gold Ores.
II. Development of suitable underground mining methods for exploitation of chromite deposits of Sukinda, Orissa.
III. Retreatment of Tailings at K.G.F. (Kolar Gold Fields).
IV. Setting up of a pilot training-cum-production centre in South Africa for cutting and polishing of precious and semi-precious stones.
V. Investigations to develop and economically viable flow-sheet for extraction of gold from the gold ore of Bhukia Jagpura Deposit, near Banswara, Rajasthan.
VI. Development of National Institute of Miner's Health, Kolar.
VII. Application of Ground Penetration Radar of Exploration and Location of Abandoned Galleries and Water Bodies in mines.

There has been a series of talks over this cooperation agreement subsequently too, in the form of various meetings held in New Delhi as well as Cape Town till 2005. Further, after a gap of several years, the Ministry of Mines participated in the Annual Mining Indaba at Cape Town held during February, 1-4, 2010.

(c) In 2002, India signed a Memorandum of Understanding (MoU) with Morocco in the field of geology and mineral exploration. The MoU was signed to promote mineral exploration, provide training to the personnel, facilities and labs for Morocco scientists in field of geological and geophysical mapping, mining environment and mining regulations.[11]

(d) Republic of Namibia and Ministry of mines signed a MoU on August 31, 2009 in New Delhi for cooperation in the field of geology and mining.[12]

(e) India-Malawi Joint Working Group on Mineral Resources Development, a protocol was signed for future course of action in cooperation for mineral exploration on 17th October, 2011 in New Delhi.

(f) India has signed a MoU with Mali on high level cooperation in the field of Geology and Mineral Resources on January 11, 2012. The MoU includes investment in Research and Development (R&D) in the country; encouraging transfer of technology; training personnel; development of geological and mineral resources; exploring prospects for mining exploration; visits of expert teams; public and private sector investments to develop mining activities in Mali; information exchange on new sources and mining; cooperation on mining laws and policies; joint ventures to promote geological studies and development of mineral deposits and efficient methods for processing of minerals.[13]

(g) India has also signed a MoU with Mozambique in a first Meeting of the Joint Working Group, held on March 1-2, 2012 at Maputo, Mozambique, in the field of Mineral Resources to list the course of action to be taken in mineral exploration.[14]

Australia

Australia views itself as part of India's extended neighbourhood. India and Australia have several commonalities, which serve as a foundation for closer cooperation and multifaceted interaction, on lines similar to what India has developed with other Western countries. Both states are strong, vibrant, secular and multicultural democracies. They both have a free press and an independent judicial system; the English language is also an important link. Cricket and now the large numbers of Indian students coming to Australia for education are also significant elements in the awareness at the popular level. Over the years, this relationship has grown in strength and importance since India's economic reforms in the 90s and has made rapid strides in all areas—trade, energy and mining, science & technology, information technology, education and defence.

India is Australia's largest export market for gold and chickpeas, second largest market for coal and copper ores and third largest market for lead and wool. Four products—coal, non-monetary gold, copper ores & concentrates and petroleum—accounted for over 80 percent of India's imports from Australia, with coal and gold being the dominant imports in 2011-12.

The trade amongst both these states is growing exponentially since the last few years. From US$ 5.79 billion in 2003-04, trade in goods and services between India and Australia reached US$ 19.16 billion in 2011-12. India's exports to Australia were US$ 3.45 billion, while India's imports from Australia were US$ 15.73 billion. India's export of goods to Australia in 2011-12 was US$ 2.60 billion and India's import of goods US$ 13.71 billion. India's export of services was US$ 0.84 billion and import of services was US$ 1.68 billion.[15]

India's Bilateral Agreements with Australia

a) In 2001, "India-Australia Joint Working Group on energy and minerals" got established to share knowledge. Australia is recognised as having advanced geological concepts and technology with a vast geo-scientific knowledge base. India is keen to explore the new mining techniques and to take advantage of the innovation in mining industries by Australia. The first meet for the same working group was held in Sydney, Australia on April 10, 2000. Australia has agreed to assist India with mineral processing technologies and utilisations techniques.[16]

b) In January 2003, a meeting for "India-Australia Joint Working Group on Energy and Minerals" was held in Canberra. New projects were purposed in the field of petroleum and natural gas, non-conventional energy resources and mining by developing a collaborative approach.
c) On May 25, 2005, Ministry of Environment and Forest, Ministry of Mines, signed a MoU for environmental governance and mine rehabilitation.
d) On February 2, 2006, the Joint Working Group met for the enhancement of agreement made in 2000. In addition, Federation of Indian Mining Industries (FIMI) and Mineral Council of Australia (MCA) established a MoU for expansion of Indian investment in processing and production of mining sector in Australia. The agreement also highlights development of the bilateral environmental policies.
e) On October13, 2009, Geological Survey of Western Australia had a meeting with Geological Survey of India to enhance knowledge capability by exchanging scientists in earth science activities and mineral exploration.

Brazil

Traditionally, India's relationships with the Latin American States have been friendly, and it has close interactions with them both at bilateral and multilateral levels. Particularly, for last few years, India-Brazil bilateral relations have been in a state of upswing. Communication revolution of the 20th and 21st century has made the geographical divide between these two states irrelevant. These states share various cultural and political values. Overcoming the limitations of distance and language, both the states have been strengthening their bilateral relationship in various fields. Both the states are being viewed as rising powers, both regionally and globally. The states are also engaging with each other at various important multilateral forums and playing their role towards evolving a global order.

The states have strong trade and economic ties; moreover, their relationship is maturing as a response to economic realities. There has been two-way investment between India and Brazil with the Brazilian companies investing in automobiles, IT, mining, energy, biofuels, footwear sectors, and Indian companies investing in IT, Pharmaceutical, Energy, agri-business, mining, engineering/auto sectors.[17] Both the states have decided to work towards achieving a target of $10 billion bilateral trade over the next few years from the US$ 7.73 billion in 2010.[18] Also, in recent past, both the states decided to develop defence co-operation, and an announcement setting up of an India-Brazil joint defence committee was made in April 2010.[19]

On the ideological front, Brazil and India share a core set of values—democracy, market economy and a strong urge to emerge as a major power in the world by imbibing the best practices for development. They understand that their relationship has great geopolitical importance and are likely to remain in the centre stage of global politics in the coming years. This relationship has geopolitical, economic and strategic dimensions.

India and Brazil, in many ways, represent Asia's and Latin America's foremost developing states keenly watched by many in the world for their economic and technological developments. India has recorded sustained high economic growth rate in the past few years, and same is the case with Brazil. Both the states have developed an extensive infrastructure for Science and Technology (S&T) which encompasses agencies of central and regional government as well as public and private organisations. They signed an agreement on cooperation in the fields of S&T at New Delhi on July 22, 1985. This agreement came into force on January 24, 1990 according to the Contracting Parties with respect to constitutional procedures (in accordance with Article X).[20] Over the years, it has been observed that the major areas of collaboration in the S&T arena include climate research, biotechnology, bioinformatics, human health, renewable energy, marine sciences and new materials.

India's Bilateral Agreements with Brazil

India and Brazil signed a MoU in the Sixth Brazil-India Joint Commission Meeting that was held in Brasilia on October14-15, 2013. The MoU is a next step in agreement reached during November 2012 for Cooperation in the field of Geology and Mineral Resources between Geological Survey of India (GSI) and Geological Survey of Brazil (Companhia de Pesquisa de Recursos Mineirais, or CPRM). A letter of intent was also signed between Brazil Ministry of Mines and Indian Ministry of Steel enhancing cooperation in mineral industry special focus on steel in February 2013 in Brasilia.

Presently, India's main cooperation with Brazil is mainly in the gas and energy sector; however, there are good prospects that a collaboration in the future could happen towards the import of minerals like Cobalt, Nickel, Tin and Tungsten from Brazil.

China

It has become predictable wisdom that China is the post-Cold War world's emerging great power that poses the most intricate questions for the future of international security.[21] The last half-a-decade has shown a substantial growth in China's global power status. This has essentially happened because of the current and 'projected' economic transformation of China. The economic growth in China has accelerated along with increased integration with the global economy.[22] Since opening up of its economy in 1978, China has averaged around 9.4 percent annual GDP growth, one of the top growth rates in the world. The last three decades of economic liberalisation have also shown the world the magnitude of China's labour force, creativity and purchasing power; its commitment to development and its degree of national cohesion.[23] Today, 'Rise of China' (the term coined in 2003 by China's political establishment was Peaceful Rise of China[24]) has become a part of a lexicon, and the global community understands that China has arrived and will increasingly shape even global future, not just its own. To a large extent this has become possible because of the correct strategic choices made by China regarding economic liberalisation.

India has fought one war with China during 1962. This 1962 border clash saw bilateral relations enter the abyss. However, over a period of time, now, the relationship has significantly improved. Presently, these relations have reached a level where these states have even conducted a few joint military exercises. Both the states understand their increasing importance in global geopolitics. However, in spite of this new found bonhomie, still, some amount of distrust exists. The border issue is far from resolved, both the states continue to have different perceptions about the demarcation of borders and various misgivings about the intentions of both the states do exist.

India-China bilateral trade which was as low as US$ 2.92 billion in 2000 reached US$ 70 billion in 2012,[25] making China India's largest goods trading partner. India's imported goods worth US$ 40.88 billion (+38%) from China, resulting in an adverse balance of trade of US$ 20 billion in 2011. India's total exports to China were US$ 15.68 billion (+7.37%), and China's exports to India reached US$ 32.49 billion (+26.33%).[26] During the visit of Chinese Premier Wen to India in December 2010, both countries committed to have bilateral trade target of US$ 100 billion for 2015. However, it appears as a very ambitions figure, and the situation on ground is indicative that the business may not be as vibrant as expected.

India's Bilateral Agreements with China

A MoU was signed on September 15, 2005 between Ministry of Mines and the Ministry of Land & Resources of the People's Republic of China to promote joint ventures in both countries, undertake research, technical assistance and training programmes for metallic and non-metallic minerals. The agreement also highlights the cooperation between Geological Survey of India (GSI) and the Chinese Academy of Geological Sciences (CAGS).[27]

Russia

India's bilateral ties with Russia (and earlier with the erstwhile USSR) have been a key pillar of India's foreign policy for many decades. India sees Russia as a longstanding and time-tested friend that has played a significant role in its economic development and security. Since the signing of the "Declaration on the India-Russia Strategic Partnership" in October 2000, India-Russia ties have acquired a qualitatively new character with enhanced levels of cooperation taking place in almost all areas of the bilateral relationship including political, security, trade and economy, defence, science and technology and culture. Under the Declaration of Strategic Partnership, several institutionalised dialogue mechanisms have been put in place that operate at the political and official levels, and ensure regular interaction and follow up on cooperation activities. In 2010, this idea of strategic partnership has been further elevated to the level of a "special and privileged strategic partnership". India and Russia have been collaborating in several high-technology projects in the fields of nuclear energy, defence technology and space. Apart from this, these states are collaborating on various other areas including pharmaceuticals, information technology, steel, hydrocarbons, diamonds and food products. Bilateral trade between India and Russia has been growing steadily. Trade in 2009 was US$ 7.5 billion, in 2010, US$ 8.5 billion and in 2011, it reached US$ 8.9 billion. In 2011, Russian exports to India amounted to US$ 6.1 billion, and imports from India to Russia amounted to US$ 2.8 billion. Bilateral trade between both countries in 2012 grew by over 30 per cent. The two-way investment between the two countries stands at approximately US$ 7.8 billion.[28]

India's Bilateral Agreements with Russia

In November 2001, both countries held the seventh session on "Indo-Russia Working Group" for metallurgy and mining sector in Moscow. A detailed agreement was signed for cooperation on transfer of technology in ferrous and non-ferrous metallurgical sector.[29]

United States

Indo-US relations have undergone unprecedented transformation since the beginning of the 21st century. In May 1998, the US had imposed sanctions on India for its nuclear tests, but a decade later, following difficult bilateral and complex multilateral negotiations, both countries completed an historic cooperation agreement with India on civil nuclear energy (July 2005). This deal could be viewed as a result of shift of the centre of economic gravity to the east. The US understood the importance of India as an emerging as a key player in global business. This new relationship rests on a convergence of US and Indian national, global and commercial interests, and never in the history have they been so closely aligned. On the ideological front, the US and India share a core set of values—democracy, unity in diversity and strong but civilian-controlled militaries—all these ideas also have great geopolitical importance and are likely to remain in the centre stage of global politics in the coming years.

It is also important to note that since the finalisation of the deal, actually making it work on the ground has been a difficult proposal for both the states. As such the Indo-US nuclear deal has gone through many upheavals since 2005. It took the US more than five years to review various sanctions and export control restrictions put on different India establishments particularly the agencies dealing with the defence and space technologies. Only by 2010-2011, various restrictions were eased out and transfer of technology became possible. At the same time, particularly, in the nuclear energy sector, both the states are finding difficulties due to differing perceptions in regards to the safety and security aspects.

On the trade front, both the states have established a reasonable and progressive association. Total bilateral trade between both countries in goods touched US$ 62.8 billion in 2012. India trade surplus reached US$ 18 billion, as Indian exports accounted for US$ 40.5 billion. Total trade in service was US$ 45.9 billion.

NOTES

1. "Blessing or Curse? The Rise of Mineral Dependence among Low- and Middle-Income Countries", Oxford Policy Management, at http://eiti.org/files/2011-12-19-OPM-Blessing-or-curse.pdf (Accessed December 12, 2013).
2. The United Nations Operation in the Congo (Opération des Nations Unies au Congo, or ONUC), which took place in the Republic of the Congo from July 1960 until June 1964.
3. "India – Democratic Republic of Congo Relations", Embassy of India, Kinshasa, at http://www.eoikinshasa.nic.in/pdfs/DRC-relations.pdf (Accessed December 12, 2013).
4. "Global Issues: Social, Political, Economic and Environmental Issues", The Democratic Republic of Congo, at http://www.globalissues.org/print/article/87 (Accessed December 17, 2013).
5. "African Leaders to Meet Over DRC Security Situation", *Voice of America*, November 3, 2013, at http://http://www.voanews.com/content/african-leaders-to-meet-over-drc-security-situation/1782477.html (Accessed December 18, 2013).
6. "Congo Kinshasa: After North Kivu, UN and DRC Forces Set Sights on Orientale—Norwegian Council for Africa", Fellesrådet for Afrika, at http://www.afrika.no/Detailed/24642.html (Accessed December 19, 2013).
7. "2014 UNHCR Country Operations Profile", UNHCR, Democratic Republic of the Congo, at http://www.unhcr.org/pages/49e45c366.html (Accessed December 18, 2013).
8. Gregory Mthembu-Salter, "Goodwill and Hard Bargains: The DRC, China and India", SAIIA Occasional Paper No. 14, March 2012, at http://dspace.cigilibrary.org/jspui/bitstream/123456789/32882/1/saia_sop_114_mthembu_salter _20120328.pdf?1 (Accessed December 15, 2013).
9. Ministry of Mines. Annual Report, Government of India, 2001, at http://mines.nic.in/writereaddata/Filelinks/ee2c7565_aneng-2001.pdf (Accessed December 15, 2013).
10. Ibid.
11. Ibid.
12. "Chapter 7", Annual Report 2009-10, Ministry of Mines, "Annual Report 2001-02" http://mines.nic.in/index.aspx?lid=318&level=2&chk=24dfe45y5edf5e3) (Accessed December 25, 2013).

    And Annual Report 2001-02, Ministry of Mines, at http://mines.nic.in/index.aspx?lid=318&level=2&chk=24dfe45y5edf5e3 (Accessed December 25, 2013).
13. "International Cooperation", Ministry of Mines, at http://mines.gov.in/writereaddata/Contentlinks/743df104c7624aa399728b4360d668b2.pdf (Accessed December 25, 2013).
14. Press Information Bureau Releases, Ministry of Commerce & Industry, at http://pib.nic.in/newsite/erelease.aspx?relid=81130 (Accessed December 24, 2013).
15. "India-Australia Relations", Ministry of External Affairs. Government of India, n.d., at http://mea.gov.in/Portal/ForeignRelation/India-Australia_Relations.pdf (Accessed December 27, 2013).
16. *Ministry of Mines Annual Report*, Government of India, 2001, at http://mines.nic.in/writereaddata/Filelinks/ee2c7565_aneng-2001.pdf.
17. "India-Brazil Relations", Ministry of External Affairs, Embassy of India, at http://www.indianembassy.org.br/eng/bilateral_relations/brazil.pdf (Accessed Sep 12,2011).
18. Sujay Mehdudia, "India-Brazil Bilateral Trade to Touch $10 billion", *The Hindu*, New Delhi, Mar 8,2011.
19. K.P. Nayar, "In Brazil, A Goal for India", *The Telegraph*, Calcutta, Apr 17, 2010.
20. United Nations—Office of Legal Affairs, at http://untreaty.un.org/unts/120001_144071/19/6/00015778.pdf (Accessed September 19, 2013).
21. Avery Goldstein, "Great Expectations", in Michael Brown, et al. (eds), *The Rise of China*, The MIT Press, London, 2000, p.3.

22. Ronaldo Munck, *Globalisation and Contestation*, Routledge, New York, 2007.
23. Zheng Bijian, "China's 'Peaceful Rise' to Great-Power Status", *Foreign Affairs*, September/ October 2005, pp.18-19.
24. Zheng Bijian developed his influential thesis of China's "peaceful rise" in 2003. For details, please refer:
    Zheng Bijian, *China's Peaceful Rise: Speeches of Zheng Bijian 1997-2005,* Brookings Institution Press, Washington, DC, 2005.
25. "India and China: Old Ties, New Horizons", Ministry of External Affairs, Government of India, at http://www.mea.gov.in/in-focus-article.htm?22360/India+and+China+Old+Ties+ New+Horizons (Accessed December 25, 2013).
26. "India-United States of America Relations", Ministry of External Affairs, Government of India, at http://meaindia.nic.in/meaxpsite/foreignrelation/china.pdf (Accessed December 25, 2013).
27. "Chapter VIII", Annual Report 2005-2006, Ministry of Mines, at http://mines.nic.in/ index.aspx?lid=320&level=2&chk=24dfe45y5edf5e3 (Accessed December 25, 2013).
28. "India-Russia Relations", Ministry of External Affairs, Government of India, at http:// www.mea.gov.in/Portal/ForeignRelation/Russia_-DEC_2012.pdf.
    "India, Russia sign pacts to boost investments", *The Hindu Business Line*, New Delhi, December 24, 2012, at http://http://www.thehindubusinessline.com/industry-and-economy/ economy/india-and-russia-sign-mou-envisage-investments-upto-2-b/ article4234685.ece?homepage=true&ref=wl_home (Accessed December 25, 2013).
29. Ministry of Mines Annual Report, Government of India, 2001, at http://mines.nic.in/ writereaddata/Filelinks/ee2c7565_aneng-2001.pdf (Accessed December 25, 2013).

6

Challenges for the Indian Mining Sector

In the Indian context, there are various issues in regards to management of mining industry (as a whole) which if not addressed properly could have a significant impact on its suitability. Mostly, these issues are of environmental relevance or social relevance. Obviously, the solutions to such problems would be political in nature. However, the purpose here is not to debate the politics behind such issues but to highlight the presence of these issues and elucidate the possible limitations in regards to the management of domestic materials industry.

It is common knowledge that there is an ever-increasing demand for minerals, particularly, in a country like India which is highly overpopulated and has significant need for infrastructure development. Increasing industrialisation, with cumulative emphasis on the strategic industry, demands timely and sufficient availability of 'raw material'. Within the country, the ore deposits are not evenly distributed, and from mining perspective, some of these locations are not convenient either socially or geographically.

Environmental Impacts of Mining

The process of extraction of minerals form the earth's surface creates various imbalances which harmfully impact the surrounding environment. Globally, the impact of the mining industry on environment has been a major public concern. Over the years, many environmentalists have played an important role towards making humans aware about the nature of degradation unscientific mining methods bring in. Depending on the nature of site and activity undertaken, the mining operations could leave a temporary or permanent impact on the surrounding environment. The impact could be of varying nature, namely water pollution, damage to flora and fauna, adverse effects on agriculture (e.g., infertile soil), air pollution leading to respiratory diseases in humans and affecting the existence of wildlife.

The environmental impact of mining is not limited only to the existing mining operations. Mining residues and scars at old mining sites also add to the misery of the environment in general. The majority of air emissions associated with the mining industry include dust and oxides of nitrogen, sulphur dioxide and carbon monoxide. Some of these come from mining vehicles and on-site plant machinery. Further, water quality may be affected by:

1. ***Acid mine drainage***: When large quantities of excavated rock containing sulphide minerals interact with water and oxygen they create sulphuric acid.
2. ***Heavy metal contamination and leaching:*** Heavy metals occur naturally in many ores, and are often released in the mineral extraction process. Metals (i.e., arsenic, cobalt, copper, cadmium, lead, silver and zinc) contained in an excavated or exposed rock may be reached out and carried downstream by the flowing water.
3. ***Processing chemical pollution:*** Spilling, leaking or leaching of chemical agents (i.e., cyanide or sulphuric acid) from the mine site into nearby water bodies.
4. ***Erosion and sedimentation:*** Erosion of cleared land surface and dumped waste material resulting in sediment loadings into the adjacent water bodies, particularly during rainfall.[1]

Overall environmental challenges bring various other issues to the fore like management, rehabilitation, and legislation on environment, particularly, environment protection and biodiversity conservation, and issues related to human rights violations, controls on excessive usage of water in various mining activities, etc.

India has huge mineral resources and a very active mining industry. There is a significant amount of private and some amount of foreign investment into this sector. Indian Government has to keep this industry thriving since the growth engine of the country is significantly dependent upon the performance of this industry. This sector in India is facing various challenges, chief among them are listed as follows:

- Massive investment in exploration and up-gradation of technology.
- Mitigation of environmental degradation due to mining
- Adoption of environmental friendly technologies
- Handling social issues
- Rehabilitation of closed and abandoned mine sites

Impacts of Open Pit Mining

The environmental issue related to methods of mining sector in India has been a major concern for many years. India has a very high percentage of open pit mining. For instance, the total coal mining in India is more than 70 per cent of open pit mining.[2] Opencast or open pit mining is a method in which extraction of a mineral is done near the surface of earth, creating large open pits. The most lucrative reason for using such mining methodology is its relatively low cost-extraction ratio. Unlike underground mining methods, opencast mining does not require costly structural supports and extraction technologies. It's a comparatively safer method too; therefore, companies save cost of expensive insurance premiums. However, such activity presents huge social and environmental challenges. Removal of overburden contributes to soil erosion, land degradation and removal of natural habitat. Chemicals used in extraction mixed with water during rainy season end up polluting the underground water reserves. Contaminants mixing into the soil leads to land degradation. The dust generated during mining activity and the chemicals used lead to chronic human health issues and also leaves a lasting impact on biodiversity.

There are many sustainable methods of mining. However, such methods require huge capital investments. Furthermore, mining operations are finite economic activities sustaining on the availability of material deposits (such deposits are finite in nature), that is, they remain financially viable for only a limited time period. The governments usually lay down guidelines for "Final Mines Closure Plan" highlighting the "rehabilitation process as an ongoing programme designed to restore physical, chemical and biological quality disturbed by the mining to a level acceptable to all concerned. It must aim at leaving the area in such a way that rehabilitation does not become a burden to the society after mining operation is over. It must also aim to create as self-sustained ecosystem."[3] Due to major social issues combined with inadequate transparency and accountability, the rate of illegal mining in India is almost double that of legal mining; hence the issues relating to opencast mining become more complex and challenging.

The Indian Government is trying to deal with all such environmental and other related challenges upfront, and various legal mechanisms have been formulated. However, the country is facing multiple challenges. The biggest environmental challenge is about the mines which are no longer in use. Also, there are various visible and not so visible impacts on environment.[4] In respect of environmental issues related to the mining industry, people expect greater public accountability. Unfortunately, these issues which have wider social impact also suffer from the prospects of wrong and intentional misinformation campaigns. Such campaigns at times stall the progress of industry.

Threat from Naxalism

One of the most significant internal threats faced by the Indian State is the threat from Naxalism, which has been prevalent since 1967. It is a violent movement based on Maoist ideology. For many years, these 'left wing' groups have been operating in different parts of India under different organisational casings. This movement has some of its roots located within the country's social and economic inequalities as well as in environmental degradation.[5] Over the years, it has been observed that the face-off with Naxalites is hurting India's industry. There are some mineral-rich areas which are under the control of the Naxalites.[6] All this does have a certain impact on the mining industry. Also, at places due to the threat posed by the Naxal groups, including kidnapping and killings carried out by them, the staff working in the mineral industry is not very keen to work on various projects undertaken in the Naxal-dominated areas. Figure 6.1 is a superposition of Naxal-prone areas on the areas rich with minerals and related deposits. It gives a broad indication about the regions where this problem is prevalent.

It is evident from Figure that various deposits of materials which are strategic in nature for India are found in Naxal-affected areas. The Indian state would need to decide their policies in regards to excavation of minerals like tungsten, manganese, etc. by factoring in threat from Naxalism.

Illegal Mining

Underground mineral resources area property of nation-states. However, there are many cartels involved in stealing these resources. Illegal mining has been a global curse for many decades and is prevalent in various parts of the world in some form or the other. This form of mining can be operated on the surface or underground. Broadly, illegal mining is the absence of land rights, mining license, exploration or mineral transportation permit or of any document that could legitimate the on-going operations. In general, most illegal mining takes place in low-grade areas or abandoned mining sites. Low productivity and limited production could be considered as main characteristics of illegal mining. However, there could be some exceptions to this, and as per some estimates, 70 to 80 million tons of coal is illegally produced in India annually in addition to the official production figure of about 350 million tons. Also, there are cases like Blood Diamonds (in Africa) which come from illegal mining activities.[7]

Figure 6.1: Map of India Highlighting Naxal-affected States

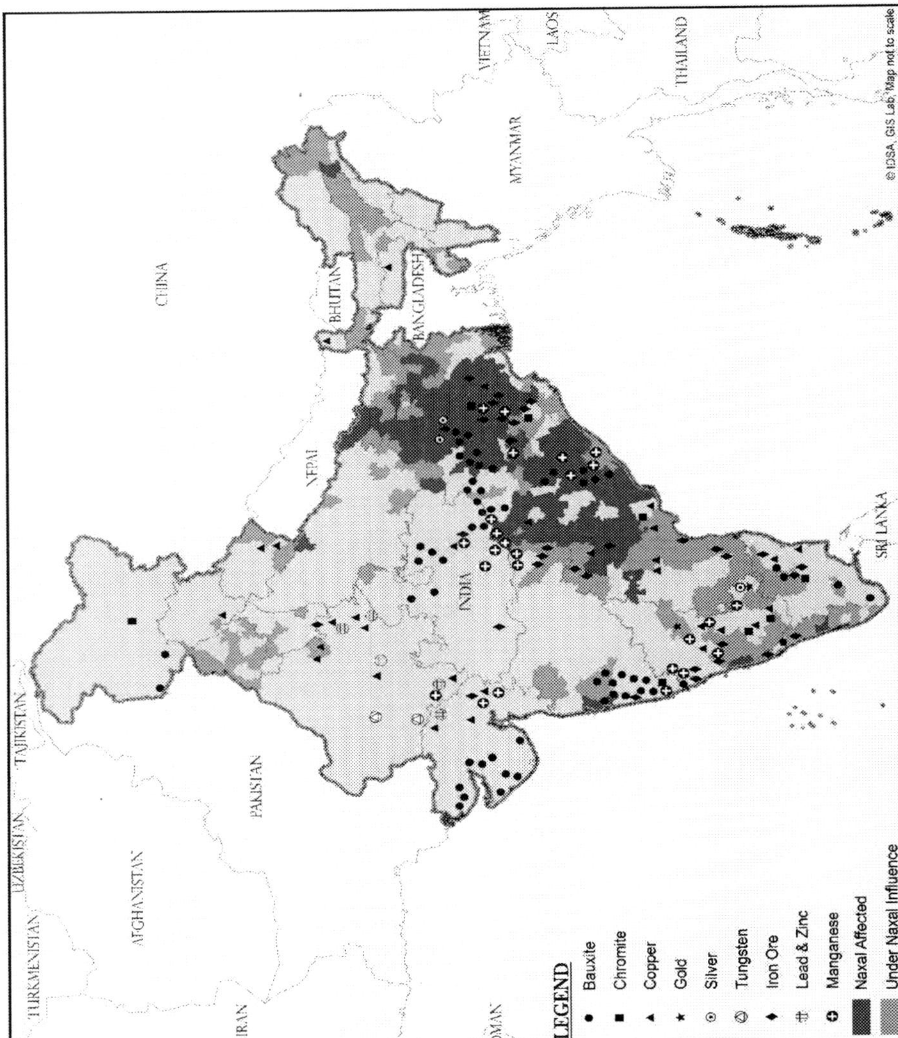

Source: Compiled by using GIS maps.

Particularly, in various developing economies, the mining sector has been found most vulnerable to denigration; therefore, for sustainable mining, good governance and administration is a prerequisite. Lack of effective governance and apathy towards implementation of legal provisions contribute towards the growth of illegal mining. This eventually disturbs the social fabric of the society in the region, leads to government loosing revenue, raises environmental concerns and also discourages the private sector from making investments. Presently, in countries like India, in certain areas, illegal mining has made significant impact. There are multiple problems: from illegal land acquisition to issues related to mining licensing system, ambiguity about legal requirements for environmental clearances and issues related to the transportation of material from the site to factory. Various such problems adversely affect the governance, ecology, internal and social security of a state.

According to the Government of India, any violation of relevant provision of mining law under MMDR Act, 1957,[8] the Forest Conservation Act, 1980 and the Environment (Protection) Act, 1986 comes under illegal mining. Table 6.1 indicates the number of illegal mining cases in the recent past.

Table 6.1: Illegal Mining Cases and State-wise Loss to the Country

Sr. No.	State	2010-11	2011-12	2012-13	2013-14 (up to June 13)	Fine realised by State govt. (million $)
1	Andaman & Nicobar	0	3	0	N. A.	10
2	Andhra Pradesh	13,939	19,913	16,592	2,024	19.795
3	Assam	0	0	0	N. A.	0
4	Chhattisgarh	2,017	2,946	3,238	846	4.927
5	Goa	13	1	0	N.A.	0.003
6	Gujarat	2,184	3,485	6,023	1,054	85.2838
7	Haryana	3,446	2,022	3,517	N. A.	2.2961
8	Himachal Pradesh	1,213	1,289	0	N. A.	0.144
9	Jharkhand	199	364	663	250	0.4528
10	Karnataka	6,476	6,691	6,677	1,827	11.804
11	Kerala	2,028	3,175	4,550	1,224	2.465
12	Madhya Pradesh	4,245	7,147	7,169	1,484	19.9036
13	Maharashtra	34,265	40,642	42,918	7,248	27.703
14	Mizoram	0	2	16	4	0.00161
15	Odisha	420	309	314	76	6.823
16	Punjab	754	314	19	N. A.	0.2896
17	Rajasthan	1,833	1,201	2,861	654	4.231
18	Tamilnadu	277	123	295	23	7.09
19	Uttar Pradesh	4,641	4,708	3,266	N.A.	4.866
20	West Bengal	239	269	479	N. A.	0
	Grand Total	7,8189	94,604	98,597	16,714	197.787

Source: Answer to Lok Sabha Question No. 294, Parliamentary Proceeding, May 2012.

From Table 6.1, it is observed that there has been rise of about 30 per cent in the number of cases since 2011. The above figures are cases declared by the federal governments to the central government. It is highly probable that the number of unregistered cases are significant.

Numerous factors could be attributed to the rise in such cases. In the report submitted to the planning commission by Institute for Studies in Industrial Development (ISID), the major reason highlighted was the issue of irregularities in the implication of MMDR Act, 1957.[9] According to this Act, mines are granted only to applicants who have infrastructure and capital to carry out mining by sustainable means. There has been many cases of violation to this law. According to Rules 37 and 46 of the Mineral Concession Rules, 1960, transfer of mining or operational rights, directly or indirectly to any other body is prohibited without the consensus of government. In a case study, in Karnataka, it was highlighted that many companies enter into the so-called "rising contract" according to which companies or private contractors are given responsibilities for mining of minor minerals. These contractors sell them under the payment of consideration or premium to the company. In effect, the contractor who may not come under the provision or law of mining has maximum control. These are done without the consideration of government approvals. These bodies make maximum profits by bribing the politicians and local authorities.

In remote and unreachable areas, local people and tribes with the help of some contractors are involved in illegal mining. The mining method used in such cases is open cast mining on uncultivated private land or by cutting down forests. Often, it is the local mafia taking the land from local people by threating.

Mining companies even under the supervision of government often use illegal mining methods such as mining beyond the area of lease or by cutting down the forest for roads or dumbing wastes on non-leased land. In spite of Forest Conservation Act 1980 where "no-objection certificate" is a requirement for mining, it has been reported that many companies take these documents by bribing the forest officials without the verification of the official records.

The illegally extracted minerals are then transported, and either sold to mining companies or are exported illegally. Since 2011, 157,579 vehicles have been seized for transporting minerals under fake or forged documents. In various case, even the required permits from forest and state authorities for the transportation of minerals are obtained by bribing the respective officials.

Apart from aforementioned companies, there are many small and medium companies under lease. In a draft document of Sustainable Development

Framework for the Mining Sector by Ministry of Mines claims that under the current capacity Indian Bureau of Mines (IBM) can only regulate 2,500 leases,[10] while there are approximately 7,000 leases and 5,000 operational mines in the country. Therefore, regulation checks for major mines happen only once, and small-scale mining is let unregulated.

Realising the criticality of illegal mining, the matter has been raised many times in parliamentary proceedings. A question to this effect in the Indian Parliament could be viewed as a case in point. In the lower house of the Indian parliament (Lok Sabha), a question (number 294) was asked on December 6, 2013 in regards to illegal mining activities and loss of revenue to the government.[11] All this indicates that there is awareness amongst the population and the political class concerning issues related to illegal mining.

The government has been aware about this menace and has taken some specific steps to address this issue. To raise the bar for transparent implementation, the Mines and Minerals (Development and Regulation) Bill, 2011 (MMDR Bill) was introduced in the Lok Sabha on December 12, 2011 to modify the previous 1957 version. The bill includes the following provisions, with special focus on regulation and steps towards prevention of illegal mining:[12]

- It provides for establishment of a National Mining Regulatory Authority, which consists of a Chairperson and not more than nine members to advise the Government on rates of royalty, dead rent, benefit sharing with District Mineral Foundation, quality standards and also conduct investigation and launch prosecution in cases of large scale illegal mining.
- It provides for establishment of State Mining Regulatory Authority consisting of such persons as may be prescribed by the State Government to exercise the powers and functions in respect of minor minerals.
- It provides for establishment of a National Mining Tribunal and State Mining Tribunals to exercise jurisdiction, powers and authority conferred on it under the proposed legislation.
- It empowers the State Governments to constitute Special Courts for the purpose of providing speedy trial of the offences relating to illegal mining.
- It empowers the Central Government to intervene in the cases of illegal mining, where the concerned State Government fails to take action against illegal mining.
- It provides for stringent punishments for contravention of certain provisions of the proposed legislation.

Other than above-mentioned bill, the government has taken many other steps in coordination with regional administrations, and some important provisions are mentioned as follows:[13]

- In 2005, Centre advised the regional administrations to develop task forces which can regulate the illegal mining. It was reported that 23 regions so far have setup the task forces; however, the effectiveness of such forces remains questionable.
- To have regional level Coordination-cum-Empowered Committee (SCEC) in coordination to railways and ports to look into related aspects of illegal mining. It was reported that 13 regional governments have implemented the committee so far.
- To step up special cell, marketing intelligence, remote sensing, etc. and develop a joint plan of action.
- A Central Coordination-cum-Empowered Committee set up under Secretary (Mines) which form a coordination system between regional governments and centre while passing critical issues to the centre.
- Custom authorities are advised to share export figures with state government.
- Government has notified amendment in Rule 45 of Mineral Conservation and Development Rules, 1988, on February 9, 2011 making it mandatory for all miners, traders, stockiest, exporters and end-users to register with IBM and report their transaction in minerals on monthly basis for a proper end-to-end accounting of minerals.
- Task force setup by IBM to have satellite inputs to take action against illegal mining.

Indian Government is well aware about illegal mining and has made various legal provisions to address this issue. However, regional imbalances, economic disparities and political compulsions some of the challenges. Therefore, it is important to establish a strong and result-oriented implementing body to ensure that the legal architecture functions properly.

Along with the above challenges, there are also Techno-Commercial and Regulatory Issues which merit attention. The entire procedure of mining is a complex task and involves multiple processes. Various technical and commercial components involve issues related to survey, geology, mining techniques and technologies, life-cycle costs, production and processing methods, processes and practices in respect of surface and underground mining and few other challenges involving business practices. Similarly, there are various regulatory issues like different legal mechanisms, mining industry guidelines, safety and inspection guidelines, export and import licensing procedures, environmental clearances, etc. It is imperative that India's mining sector remains prepared to address all such challenges.

NOTES

1. "Mining and the Environment", Australian Bureau of Statistics, at http://www.abs.gov.au/ausstats/abs@.nsf/46d1bc47ac9d0c7bca256c470025ff87/ce28d7fbe5faa308ca256cae0015da32!OpenDocument (Accessed December 29, 2013).
2. A K Debnath and S K Dubey, "Strategy for Stepping up Coal Production in CIL", India Energy Forum, atindiaenergyforum.org/4th-coal-summit/presentations/.../ak-debnath.doc (Accessed December 30, 2013).
3. "Guidelines for Preparation of Mine Closure Plan", Indian Bureau of Mines, at http://ibm.nic.in/mineclosuregl.pdf. (Accessed December 30, 2013).
4. Pradeep S M, "The Indian Mining Sector: Effects on the Environment and FDI Inflows", at http://www.oecd.org/env/1830307.pdf (Accessed August 4, 2013).
5. Lennart Bendfeldt, "Naxalism: The Maoist Challenge to the Indian State", at http://www.in.boell.org/web/52-764.html (Accessed Sep 5, 2013).
6. "Companies Bleed in Naxalites Bloodbath", *Business Standard*, Delhi, April 8, 2010, at http://business.rediff.com/report/2010/apr/08/companies-bleed-in-naxalite-bloodbath.htm (Accessed Aug 30, 2013).
7. "What is Illegal Mining?" at http://mining.about.com/od/OperationsManagement/a/What-Is-Illegal-Mining.htm) (Accessed on January 03, 2014).
8. *Mines and Minerals (Development and Regulation) Act, 1957 (No. 67 of 1957)*,Controller General, Nagpur, Maharashtra, Indian Bureau of Mines, Ministry of Mines, Government of India,2012, at http://mines.nic.in/writereaddata/Filelinks/e342d686_MMDR%20Act%201957.pdf (Accessed December 31, 2012).
9. For the text of this Act (as amended up to May 10, 2012), please visit: http://mines.nic.in/writereaddata/Filelinks/e342d686_MMDR%20Act%201957.pdf (Accessed January 3, 2014).
10. "Sustainable Development Framework for the Mining Sector for the Ministry of Mines (GoI)", EMR, Ministry of Mines, at http://mines.nic.in/writereaddata/filelinks/2155afeb_FINAL%20REPORT%20SDF%2029Nov11.pdf (Accessed January 1, 2014).
11. Lok Sabha Unstarred Question No. 294 on Illegal Mining, 2013, at http://mines.nic.in/writereaddata%5CContentlinks%5Cce87bcf98ad14fa595a93ee60d91cba6.pdf (Accessed December 30, 2013).
12. *MMDR Bill*, Press Information Bureau, Ministry of Mines, Government of India, 2013, at http://pib.nic.in/newsite/PrintRelease.aspx?relid=98580 (Accessed January 1, 2014).

13 Lok Sabha Unstarred Question No. 294 on Illegal Mining, No. 11.

7

Rare Earth Materials

The previous chapters in this book have discussed various aspects of strategic materials. However, the issues concerning Rare Earth Elements (REEs) or Rare Earth Materials (REMs) have not been discussed. In literature on minerals, generally, REEs are discussed as a separate category because of their importance and because all such elements under consideration have specific relevance or usages.

Particularly, since the beginning of the 21st century, the supply of some critical REEs has increasingly become more problematic because of various reasons including the monopoly of China in regards to its natural deposits. It has been identified by various sources that around 95 per cent to 97 per cent of global supply of REEs is controlled by China. Various countries have their own apprehensions regarding the availability of such materials, and some of them are trying to find alternative mechanisms to satisfy their industry requirements for such materials. This chapter takes a broad overview of the existing state of affairs in respect of REEs.

What are REEs?

Rare earths are a set of 17 elements at the bottom of the periodic table used in a variety of renewable energy and defence applications, including precision-guided munitions, wind turbines, unmanned aerial vehicles, hybrid vehicles and tactical wheeled vehicles.[1] REEs are mainly used in many new electronic and advanced components, such as fuel cells, mobile phones, displays, hi-capacity batteries, permanent magnets and green energy devices.[2] According to the 2013 Worldwide Threat Assessment of the National Intelligence Office of the US, REEs are essential to civilian and military technologies, and a major portion of to the 21st century global economic growth is dependent on them. The textbook definition of REEs is as follows:

> ...those elements that are part of the family of lanthanides on the periodic table with atomic numbers 57-71. Scandium (atomic number 21) and Yttrium (atomic number 39) are grouped with the lanthanide family because of their similar properties. Rare earth elements are separated into two categories, light rare earths and heavy rare earths. The light rare earth elements are Lanthanum, Cerium, Praseodymium, Neodymium, and Samarium (atomic numbers 57-62), and they are more abundant than heavy ones. The heavy rare earth elements (atomic numbers 64-71 plus yttrium, atomic number 39) are not as predominant as light rare earths and are generally used in high tech applications. For example: Erbium is used for fibre [*sic*] optics in communications. Europium and Terbium are used as phosphors. Gadolinium is used for in MRIs.[3]

The REE group of 17 chemical (metallic) elements consists of the 15 lanthanide elements along with Yttrium and Scandium. They share many similar properties, which is why they occur together in geological deposits. The 17 REEs are found in all REE deposits, but their distribution and concentrations vary. They are referred to as 'rare' because it is not common to find them in commercially viable concentrations. REEs generally fall into one of two categories: Light Rare Earth Elements (LREEs) and Heavy Rare Earth Elements (HREEs), with varying levels of uses and demand. REE mineral deposits are usually rich in either LREEs or HREEs, but rarely contain both in significant quantities.[4]

Heavy Rare Earths

- Europium (Eu)
- Gadolinium (Gd)
- Terbium (Tb)
- Dysprosium (Dy)
- Holmium (Ho)
- Erbium (Er)
- Thulium (Tm)
- Ytterbium (Yb)
- Lutetium (Lu)
- Yttrium (Y)

Light Rare Earths

- Lanthanum (La)
- Cerium (Ce)
- Praseodymium (Pr)
- Neodymium (Nd)
- Samarium (Sm)

It may be noted that Yttrium is lighter than the LREEs, but included in the HREE group because of its chemical and physical associations with HREEs in natural deposits.

REEs are an integral part of various modern technologies. As mentioned above, many such technologies have relevance in the areas of defence, energy, etc. Particularly, for the electronic components used in computers and televisions, REEs are of considerable use. They are important for manufacturing small-sized products like cell phones and laptops. In the defence arena, they are important for the production of cruise missiles, precision-guided munitions and reactive armours. They also are useful in making radar systems. They have utility for the production of almost all modern warfare related hardware—from platforms like fighter jets, drones to the technologies required for the development network warfare-centric capabilities. Further, REEs are finding increasing utility in the production of various green technologies, for example, in contemporary wind turbines and plug-in hybrid vehicles. In oil refineries, REEs are used as catalysts.

Explicit REE Significance

In order to appreciate the relevance of REEs for modern day industry, it is important to discuss the specific applicability of individual REEs.

One of the essential components of the cellular telephone include ceramic magnetic switches that contain REEs and indium and the base stations for the cell phone networks that also use the element indium, as well as tantalum. Each of these minerals has specific properties important to the function of the given component for which substitution of other minerals or their derived materials is difficult.[5]

Cerium is being used for the purposes of polishing various types of mirrors and lenses. Europium provides the red colour in displays used in all modern tablets and smart phones. Technologists and chemists are yet to find alternatives for these elements. Fibre-optic cables use erbium to boost the signal carried over long distances. Other REEs such as gadolinium are used for the miniature, high-performance magnets[6] employed in portable disc drives, popularly known as memory sticks. While super-strong neodymium-iron-boron magnets are needed for military weapons systems, samarium-cobalt magnets are vital to precision-guided missiles, smart bombs and aircraft.

Interestingly, REEs are actually not as rare as the name suggests. They are found in various rock formations. The average concentration of REEs in the Earth's crust ranges from 150 to 220 parts per million. In comparison, with new other commonly used metals this concentration is much higher. For example, copper (55 parts per million) and zinc (70 parts per million). An REE like Cerium is more abundant than copper or lead. All the REEs except promethium are more abundant than silver or mercury. Even the rarest, terbium and lutetium, are nearly 200 times more common than gold.

Global REE Deposits and Mining Processes

Presently, China holds half of the world's deposits of REEs, 55 megatons (Mt), while the US holds the next largest national reserves with approximately 13 Mt. India has about 3.1 Mt of estimated reserves. Not enough information is available in regards to holdings of the Commonwealth of Independent States (CIS).[7] In addition, the natural reserves of rare earths are also concentrated in a few more countries like Brazil, Malaysia, Russia and Democratic Republic of Congo. Due to such unequal distribution of sources, the REEs have become a very vital strategic resource.

The known geological sources in regards to presence of these elements are concentrated in specific regions, and this offers a few states a major advantage. The major challenge is the economics of mining. This is because separating REEs from ores is a very complex and costly proposal. REEs often occur in multiple minerals, each of which requires a different separation process. This leads to a situation where every mining facility requires custom-made producers and technologies for excavation in respect of the nature of material it has to deal with. Occasionally, REEs are found in ores along with radioactive elements such as uranium, thorium and radium, making them difficult and expensive to handle safely.[8]

In general, REEs are principally found in carbonates, which are igneous rocks comprising more than 50 per cent carbonate minerals. Less important sources are secondary deposits which form when rare earth and heavy minerals are concentrated by the physical weathering of primary mineralisation.

Most REE mines produce only REEs, although there are a few where REEs are produced as a by-product. Most use large-scale techniques, involving drilling, blasting and hauling as part of the production process. Separation of the ore from the waste can be carried out in a variety of ways. The production process is quite complex as one rare earth mineral may contain up to 17 different elements which must be separated from one another. Figure 7.1 summarises the basic steps of mining and processing an REE.[9]

China has a monopoly on REEs, and it being the main stakeholder in respect of REEs, the knowledge of Chinese investments practically paints the total picture of global REE activities.

Figure 7.1: Basic Steps of Mining and Processing an REE

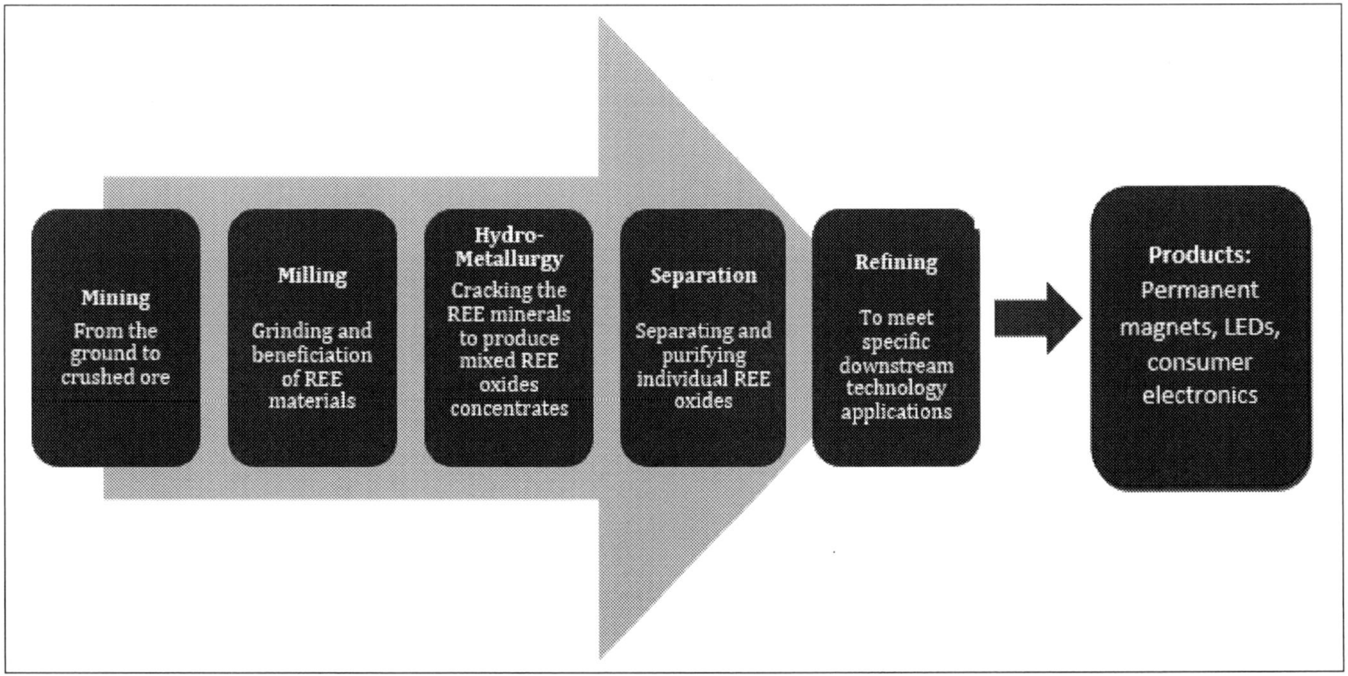

REEs and China

China fully understands the geostrategic importance of REEs and has been making sustained efforts to maintain its monopoly in this field. One of their most powerful leaders during 1970-90s, Deng Xiaoping was quoted as: "There is oil in the Middle East; there are rare earths in China".[10] During 1992, he had called for developing the rare earth industry. Deng's call to invest in this new area and preserve monopoly has been carried out nearly flawlessly. China dominates the world market, and in recent months, has taken control of mines in Brazil and Australia, thereby eliminating potential competitors. It is poised to do with rare earths what the Organization of Petroleum Exporting Countries has done with oil: make the world dependent.[11]

Mainly, due to unequal distribution of sources, the REEs and techno-economic challenges associated with the mining of these elements have become vital strategic resources. Unfortunately, all these years, only China has made sustained investments in this sector, and only very recently some other states in the world having appreciated the importance of REEs and the disadvantages of overdependence on China have started making both technological and financial investments in this sector.

On its part, China also understands that its total monopoly is held sacred by other states. In order to bring in more clarity about its actions in this field, China published a White Paper titled "Situation and Policies of China's Rare Earth Industry" during June 2012.[12]

According to this White Paper, "China can produce over 400 varieties of rare earth products in more than 1,000 specifications. In 2011, China produced 96,900 tonnes of rare earth smelting products, accounting for 90% of global output. The nation holds 23 per cent of the world's total rare earth reserves."[13] But disputing this, some analysts claim that China has only 36 per cent of REE reserves. Be that as it may, whether it is alumina or zinc, China is presently the leading producer of at least 38 minerals while South Africa and Russia are leading producers of six minerals each and the US of five minerals.[14]

While the White Paper (referred above) states that China's REE industry is showing growth (market value US$ 15.8 billion), some reports indicate that China's REE exports quota has fallen dramatically between 2006 (61,560 metric tonnes) and 2011 (30,246 metric tonnes); for 2012, the current estimates are 31,438 metric tons.[15] Japan has primarily been the major importer of China's REE. The US was once self-sufficient in domestically produced REEs, but over the past 15 years has become 100 per cent dependent on imports, primarily from China because of lower-cost operations.[16]

China offers major support to its mining industry in the form of subsidies; the industry has, at its disposal, cheap labour as well. The Chinese have realised a complete monopoly in this field by manipulating the economics of business: they have made products available at very cheap rates in the international market, which has indirectly led to other countries losing interest in the business. Now, with the major market share in hand, the Chinese can afford to control the market as per their resolve.

China has successfully controlled the global REE market for many years. However, it is only now that the Chinese have felt the need to bring out a White Paper on this subject. This clearly indicates that since their monopoly is being debated internationally, they want the rest of the world to know about their policies and ethics. They are using the route of White Paper to inform others that they have various regulations in place and have plans to improve existing legal structures further. The Chinese are also keen to cooperate internationally on export mechanisms and the development of new REE-related technologies. However, the REEs' strategic relevance is far greater than their economic importance, and China's core interests in this business cannot be commercial alone. It appears to have made investments in this business both for economic and strategic purposes.

Sensing its importance in the REE market, China had, in early 2012, announced new restrictions on rare earth exports to the US and other countries. (Earlier, in 2010, it had temporarily stopped shipments to Japan due to a territorial dispute over fishing rights.) As a result, the US, Japan and the European Union made an official complaint to the World Trade Organisation (WTO) about China's restrictive export policies. They are of the opinion that China is using its near-monopoly "to subsidize [*sic*] domestic manufacturers and to force foreign manufacturers to move their operations there."[17] China appears to be intentionally choking-off global exports to derive benefits domestically. In early July 2012, China formally rejected the request by the US, Japan and the EU for a WTO panel to arbitrate (as per the rules, only one such blocking of a proposal is permitted). On March 13, 2012, the EU requested consultations with China with respect to China's restrictions on the export of various forms of rare earths, tungsten and molybdenum. Subsequently, in agreement with China, states like Canada, Japan and the US had to join the consultations. Finally, on September 12, 2012, the US, the EU and Japan requested the Director-General to compose the panel. On 24 September 2012, the Director-General has composed the panel.[18] Subsequently, the first written submission was made by the EU on October 30, 2012.[19] One year after this, on October 30, 2013, WTO gave a ruling against China.[20]

Largely, China has been found manipulating the REE prices as per its convenience, probably, since it does not have any competitors. A vast difference in pricing has been found in pre-2010 and post-2010 period. "REE prices spiked after China enacted a 40 per cent export quota cut in July 2010, peaking at record highs in mid-2011". Some decrease has been observed as on December 2012, but "the prices still remained at least 80 per cent, and as much as 600 per cent...above pre-July 2010 levels". China's monopoly in this sector has continued for many years, but now it seems to be taking advantage of the situation. It deliberately ceased production of these rare metals during 2012, in what was almost certainly an effort to drive up world prices. China also restricts exports of REEs effectively forcing large commercial electronics companies that need such rare metals in their devices to build within China.[21]

It is important to note that the state-run labs in China have consistently been involved in research and development of REEs for over 50 years. Prompted by economic growth and increased consumer demand, China is engaging in the increased production of wind turbines, consumer electronics and other sectors. All this is increasing the domestic demand for REEs. It is expected that this increased domestic demand along with the increased awareness about the safety and environmental issues may eventually increase the costs of operations in China's rare earth industry. REE manufacturing is set to power China's surging demand for consumer electronics—cell phones, laptops and green energy technologies.[22] Hence, China is unlikely to make any compromises with its REE policies.

Challenging the Chinese Monopoly

Over the last few years, realising the dangers of Chinese monopoly, countries like India, Japan and Vietnam have started collaborating in REEs. North American countries are also planning to increase their investments. It is expected that more than 15 per cent to 20 per cent of rare earth minerals could be mined outside of China by the end of this decade. Vietnam is known to have significant rare earth reserves and—by collaborating with Japan—is expected to make significant inroads in this field. However, till date all these states as well as the powers like the US and the EU have been unable to produce viable alternatives to rare earths. Apart from investing in the REE sector, there is also a need to revisit the aspect of overdependence and look for alternatives. For many of these materials, there is a need to look for some effective substitutes and also there is a need to invest into recycling.

It's interesting to note that one of the biggest REE consumers and responsive and technological superior industrial power like the US has also misjudged the importance of REEs. Before 1990, the US was largely self-sufficient in this field. But increasingly stringent environmental regulations and growing competition from low-cost producers in China with access to high-quality deposits led to a collapse in domestic production. By 2000, the US developed 100 per cent dependency on the imports of REEs. It's more surprising that all this happened in spite of the US being fully aware about the dependence of its defence industry on REEs and of its overdependence on China, a politically difficult state to handle. Now, the US has restarted its domestic production and resumed mining at Mountain Pass in California's Mojave Desert, which was earlier suspended in 2002. New supplies are also becoming available from Mount Weld in Australia. It is expected that at present around 10 per cent of the global needs of REEs could be taken care of without China's assistance.[23]

The US Department of Energy proposes to spend more than US$ 100 million to create a new organisation designed to look at new methods to produce REEs. Researchers in Japan during 2013 have discovered large deposits of rare earth materials useful for various commercial and military weapons systems. The rare metals that Japan found off the country's Pacific coast appear to be both abundant and cheap to mine. However, Japan plans to explore and study these deposits from the seabed in the Pacific for two more years and would subsequently start mining them.[24] It is expected that it could take minimum five years for the REE industry to get developed outside China. Again financial compulsions are also expected to override the necessity felt to outdo Chinese monopoly. It has been reported that Australian companies[25] are planning to delay the development of few facilities owing to the weakening prices for the minerals.

India and REEs

For a rapidly developing economy like India with significant investments in strategic sectors like aerospace and defence, the dependence on REEs is obvious. India has no significant presence in this sector and depends mostly on imports. However, understanding the necessity to reduce the import dependency, India has been taking steps to reduce this dependence. Interestingly, till about 2004, India was making investments towards building its REE infrastructure; however, the plan was deferred because it seemed economically unviable to compete with Chinese prices.

India is planning to increase its output three times over by 2017. Interestingly, India was one of the early investors in the arena of REE. Immediately after the country got its independence from the British colonial rule, the Indian Rare Earths Ltd. (1950) was established. This organisation has four production plants and is presently a profit-making organisation.[26] However, due to limited natural availability of the deposits of the REEs, India could not achieve much in this field. During the last few decades with increasing imputes on industrialisation and growth of domestic defence industry, India has started realising the increasing necessity of REEs. Having understood the politics of REE, India is making more investments to build on this sector.

Rare earth deposits in India are of two major types: endogenic and exogenic. The endogenic deposits include some carbonatites, pegmatitic rocks (found at a place called Chhotonagpur), metamorphic-metasomatic veins, and the Exogenic deposits comprise coastal or beach placer, inland placer and offshore placer. Endogenic deposits do not appear to be very attractive from the exploitation point of view. Mainly beach placers are mined in India at present. Monazite is the principal ore mineral for REE in India, although xenotime holds out some prospect for the future. Of India's estimated reserve of 5 million tonnes of monazite, 70-75 per cent occurs in beach placer and the rest in the inland and offshore varieties. Monazite-content of beach sands may be up to 11 wt per cent. Inland placers contain either monazite or xenotime as the principal REE-bearing mineral. Of late, work on inland placer has started for xenotime. Factors controlling placer formation are: (1) provenance, (2) physico-chemical properties of the minerals in the placer, (3) physico-chemical ambience, and the source rocks/earlier deposits are exposed to, and (4) physical process of concentration. In the development of India's beach placer deposits, granites, granitic pegmatites, migmatites, gneisses, charnockites, leptynites and khondalites provided the necessary source and the tropical climate with heavy rainfall and strong wave action was especially conducive to the concentration of the placer-minerals in suitable locales.[27] It may be noted that the following map constitutes of few elements which are not the 'classical REEs'. However, it has been noticed that the geological survey of India do consider them under the REE category.

Based on its preliminary surveys, during the second half of 2012, Geological Survey of India (GSI) set in motion an ambitious five-year project for geo-chemical mapping to identify reserves of rare earths and other strategic minerals across India (see Figure 7.2). A major primary source of REEs has been discovered in Rajasthan and presently its capacity is under assessment. However, to find the geographical location of the source is only the first step. It is important to have adequate and requisite infrastructure to undertake further processing. India has plans to engage private laboratories along with

Figure 7.2: Location of India's REEs

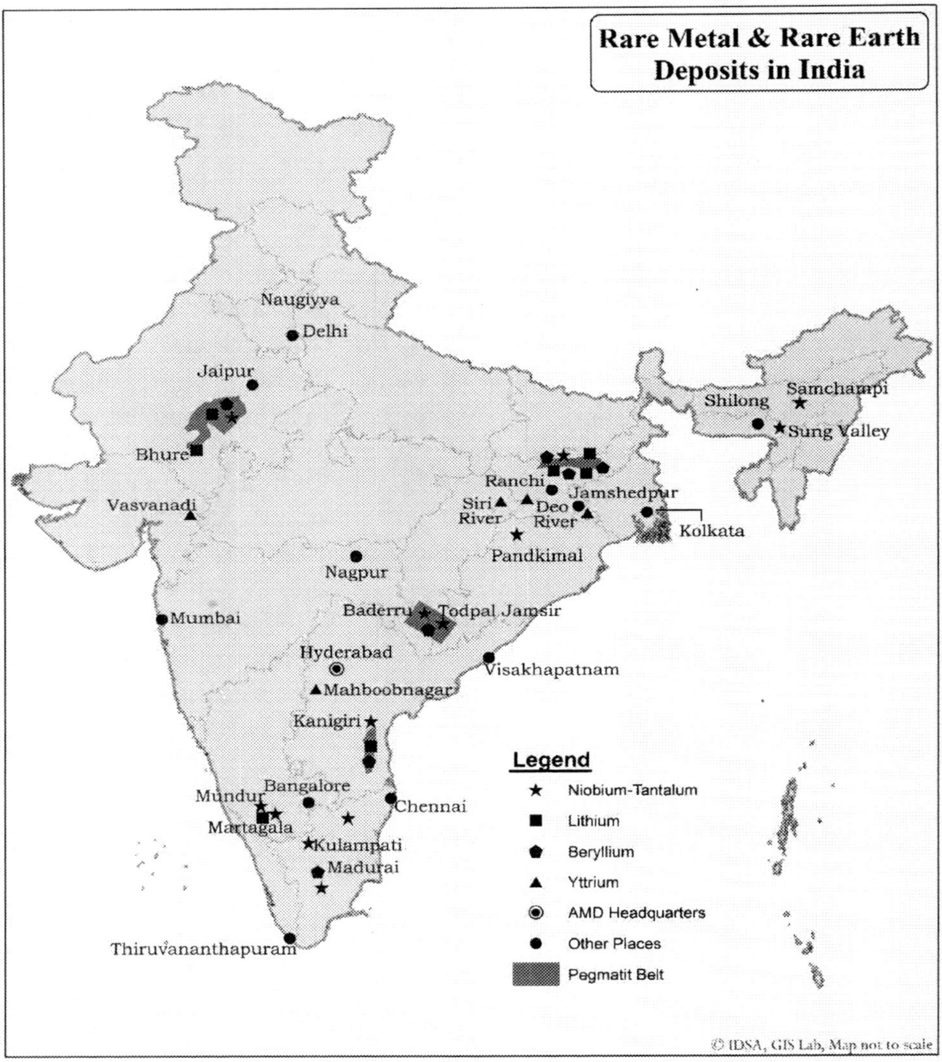

Source: Geological Survey of India (GSI).

government laboratories for undertaking chemical analysis. This becomes essential due to the voluminous nature of the requirement.

This mammoth project by GSI is first of its kind one-sweep attempt to identify potential RE and strategic minerals reserves in the country. The project covers India's Obvious Geological Potential (OGP) area—around 8 lakh sq. km—in the next four-five years. India's total area is around 36 lakh sq. km from which Deccan plateau and some other areas are removed to arrive at OGP. It may be noted that India has, so far, only surveyed 2,200 km of its 7,500 km length coastline for Monazite's. Electric and Hybrid Vehicles—that use lanthanum, neodymium, dysprosium, terbium and cerium—are expected to reach the 1 million vehicle mark. All this essentially indicates the need of REEs for India[28].

The Indian Rare Earth Limited and the Department of Atomic Energy are keen to undertake rare earth mining along the east cost of Indian peninsula at Bramhagiri in Odisha's Puri district after huge deposits of rare earth minerals were found there. Also, India has announced that it is keen to explore and develop deep-sea mining for REEs.[29]

For a state like India, it is important to develop a micro-level understanding of all important REE requirements. The priority values chains for defence and economic sectors need to be specifically identified.[30] There is a need to evolve a mechanism where private industry partnership are welcomed and international partners identified for technology collaboration.

REEs on the Critical List

Like any other mineral source, 'finiteness' is an issue with the REEs too. Due to significant increase in demand mainly due to the rapid growth being witnessed in the energy and high-tech sectors, some REEs find themselves on the critical list. The criticality will remain dynamic essentially depending on the end application demand pattern. It's difficult to have a correct forecast in regards to supply and demand needs for the future. However, some extrapolation of the existing pattern and possible nature of demand in the future could give abroad idea about the rare earths that would be in short supply and the one in surplus. The fastest-growing market segments are permanent magnets, rechargeable batteries and phosphors, particularly given their application in the fast growing green energy and high-tech segments. In 2010, the US Department of Energy classified the five REEs critical to these markets to be in short supply. Four of these are the HREEs. China's Ministry of Commerce has indicated that China's HREEs could be depleted in the next 15-20 years (see Table 7.1).[31]

Table 7.1: REE List, Application and Annual Growth

	REE on the critical list	Applications	Estimated compound annual growth rate 2010-2015 (in per cent)
Light	Neodymium	Permanent magnets, auto catalysts, petroleum refining, lasers	16
Heavy	Dysprosium	Permanent magnets, hybrid engines	16
	Europium	Phosphors, fuel cells, neutron absorbers	27
	Terbium	Phosphors, permanent magnets	30
	Yttrium	Red phosphor, fluorescent lamps, ceramics, metal alloys	30

Source: IMCOA and CIBC World Markets and Dundee Capital Markets.

These minerals, with the exclusion of Yttrium, are likely to be in short supply over the next 10 years. The magnitude and duration of these shortages will mainly depend on the success of REE exploration projects. Understating the need, some states have begun to develop strategies to safeguard their REE supplies in order to overcome the future supply problems. Also, a few private companies are establishing joint ventures with mining companies. Today, essentially this situation has emerged because of shortage of supplies, China's monopoly and skewed export policies, economic un-viability of the sector, etc. It is important to ensure serious shortages are averted in the long term. Figure 7.3 illustrates the widening gap between the supply from China and the demand from the rest of the world.

Figure 7.3: Widening Gap Between the Supply from China and the Demand from the Rest of the World

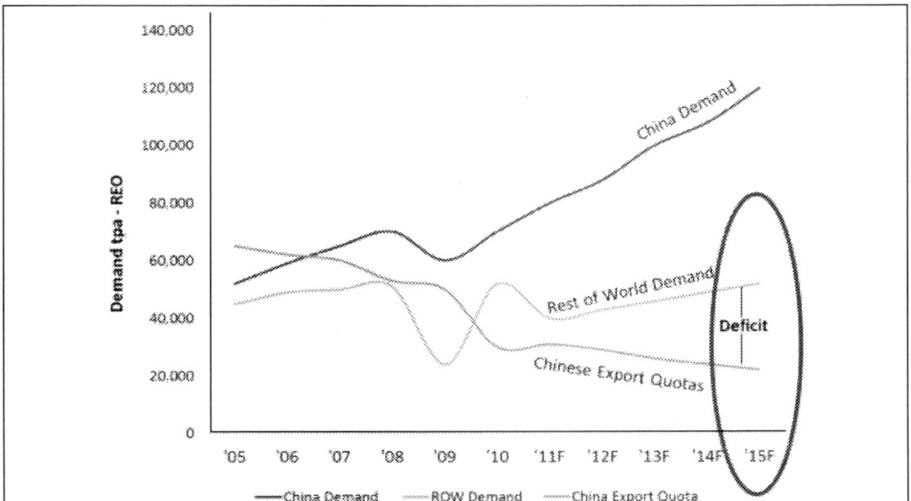

Source: Rare Earth Material 101 IAMGOLD Corporation.[32]

Wrapping up

Presently, China is the global leader in the REE sector and could continue to be in the forefront in the near future too. Fortunately, both industrially developed and developing states have understood the necessity to break the Chinese monopoly in this sector. It is important for states like India to make appropriate investments in this sector because it offers various commercial, strategic and diplomatic advantages. Also, there is a need for scientists and technologists to find correct alternatives to REEs to reduce the world's overdependence on REEs.

NOTES

1. "Rare Earth Elements 101", IAM Gold Corporation, at http://www.iamgold.com/files/REE101_April_2012.pdf (Accessed July 22, 2013).
2. Stefania Massari and Marcello Ruberti, "Rare Earth Elements as Critical Raw Materials: Focus on International Markets and Future Strategies", *Resources Policy*, 38 (1), March 2013, pp.36-43.
3. Cindy Hurst, "China's Rare Earth Elements Industry: What Can the West Learn?" March 2010, Institute for the Analysis of Global Security (IAGS), at http://fmso.leavenworth.army.mil/documents/rareearth.pdf (Accessed March 12, 2012).
4. http://www.iamgold.com/files/REE101_April_2012.pdf (Accessed Jul 22, 2013).
5. *Minerals, Critical Minerals, and the US Economy*, A US Committee Report, The National Academies Press, Washington, 2007, p.14.
6. "Rare Earth Elements", Strategic Materials Advisory Council, at http://www.strategicmaterials.org/rare-earth-elements-2/ (Accessed March 26, 2014).
7. Elliot Brennan, "The Next Oil? Rare Earth Metals", January 10, 2013, at http://thediplomat.com/2013/01/10/the-new-prize-china-and-indias-rare-earth-scramble/ (Accessed on Aug 6, 2013).
8. John Kemp, "News Analysis: Phoenix Rises from Ashes to Mine Rare Earths after a Decade", *Business Day*, August 2, 2013, at http://www.bdlive.co.za/world/americas/2013/08/02/news-analysis-phoenix-rises-from-ashes-to-mine-rare-earths-after-a-decade (Accessed September 22, 2013).
9. IamGold "Rare Earth Elements 101", No. 1. at www.iamgold.com/files/ree101_april_2012.pdf?
10. As quoted by: Paul Krugman, "Rare and Foolish", *New York Times*, October 17, 2010, at http://www.nytimes.com/2010/10/18/opinion/18krugman.html (Accessed June 24, 2012).
11. Kent Garber, "America's New Energy Dependency: China's Metals", *US News*, July 1, 2009, at http://www.usnews.com/news/national/articles/2009/07/01/americas-new-energy-dependency-chinas-metals (Accessed Aug 4, 2013).
12. "Situation and Policies of China's Rare Earth Industry", White Paper, Information Office of State Council. People's Republic of China, 2012, at http://www.miit.gov.cn/n11293472/n11293832/n12771663/n14676956.files/n14675980.pdf (Accessed Aug 2, 2013).
13. Dorothy Kosich, "Chinese Govt. White Paper Pledges International REE Cooperation", June 20, 2012, at http://www.mineweb.com/mineweb/view/mineweb/en/page72068?oid=153603&sn=D... (Accessed on July 16, 2012).
14. Gus Lubin, Noah Plaue and Shlomo Sprung, "A Shocking Number of Minerals Are Controlled by China", July 11, 2012, at http://www.businessinsider.com/china-leads-production-in-dozens-of-miner... (Accessed July 16, 2012).
15. A. Greer Meisels, "The Rare Earth Race", June 26, 2012, at http://nationalinterest.org/

commentary/the-race-rare-earth-elements-7120 (Accessed July 10, 2012).
16. Marc Humphries, *Rare Earth Elements: The Global Supply Chain*, CRS Report for Congress, at http://www.fas.org/sgp/crs/natsec/R41347.pdf (Accessed July 12, 2012).
17. "Chinese Official Defends Country's Rare Earth Export Policies." China Mining, at http://www.chinamining.org/News/2012-03-15/1331775278d55250.html (Accessed July 16, 2012).
18. "China – Measures Related to the Exportation of Rare Earths, Tungsten and Molybdenum", Dispute Settlement: Dispute DS432, World Trade Organization, at http://www.wto.org/english/tratop_e/dispu_e/cases_e/ds432_e.htm, (Accessed Aug 7, 2013).
19. "China – Measures Related to the Exportation of Rare Earths, Tungsten and Molybdenum" (WT/DS432), First Written Submission by the European Union, at http://trade.ec.europa.eu/doclib/docs/2013/april/tradoc_150806.pdf (Accessed December 20, 2012).
20. Cecilia Jamasmie, "WTO Tells China to Drop Restrictions on Rare Earths Exports", October 30, 2013, at http://www.mining.com/wto-tells-china-to-drop-restrictions-on-rare-earths-exports-75613/ (Accessed November 12, 2013).
21. Jeff Nesbit, "China's Continuing Monopoly over Rare Earth Minerals", *US News*, April 2, 2011, at http://www.usnews.com/news/blogs/at-the-edge/2013/04/02/chinas-continuing-monopoly-over-rare-earth-minerals (Accessed July 28, 2013).
22. Marc Humphries, No. 16.
23. John Kemp, "More Mines Open, Making Rare Earths Less Rare", Aug 1, 2013, at http://in.reuters.com/article/2013/08/01/column-rare-earths-idINL6N0G224I20130801 (Accessed Aug 5, 2013).For a detail assessment in regards to the ups and downs in the US REE industry sector and how China has intelligently cultivated the REE industry, please see: Jeff Nesbit, No. 21.
24. Jeff Nesbit, No. 21.
25. Dow Jones, "Lynas Delays Rare-Earths Plan", *The Australian*, August 1, 2013, at http://www.theaustralian.com.au/business/mining-energy/lynas-delays-rare-earths-plan/story-e6frg9df-1226689090691# (Accessed on Aug 7, 2013).
26. Balance sheets and other information available on: http://www.irel.gov.in/ (Accessed July 12, 2012).
27. "Geology Rare Earth Elements", Geological Survey of India (GSI), Ministry of Mines, Government of India, at http://www.portal.gsi.gov.in/portal/page?_pageid=127,719655&_dad=portal&_schema=PORTAL (Accessed Aug 2, 2013).
28. "DNA Special: New Project to Tap Country's Minerals", *DNA*, New Delhi, September 9, 2012, at http://www.dnaindia.com/india/report-dna-special-new-project-to-tap-country-s-minerals-1738620.
29. "IREL Keen to Mine Rare Earth at Bramhagiri", *Business Standard*, Kolkata/ Berhampur, August 20, 2012, at http://www.business-standard.com/article/companies/irel-keen-to-mine-rare-earth-at-bramhagiri-112082000036_1.html (Accessed January 4, 2014).
Adam Currie, "India Revisits Rare Earth Potential", September 17, 2012.
30. For a detailed study on this subject, please refer: Chandrasekhar, S. "Does India Need a National Strategy for Rare Earths?" International Strategic and Security Studies Programmed, NIAS, India, at http://isssp.in/does-india-need-a-national-strategy-for-rare-earths/.
31. "Rare Earth Elements 101", No. 1.
32. Ibid.

8

Emerging Materials

For any work on strategic materials there always could be a temptation to include a segment on advanced or new materials with a view to argue that modern technology does not restrict nation-states to depend only on conventional minerals, and there is scope for the usage of new or advanced materials as a replacement to the existing strategic materials. However, there exists a possibility that debating new materials could divert the key focus of this study; at the same time, absence of debate on this subject would amount to avoiding to deliberate on the future. It is unlikely that the importance of existing strategic materials and rare earth elements is going to reduce anytime in the near future, but at the same time, new materials are expected to make significant impact in years to come.

It is not the purpose here to get into the details of the basis of Material Science which essentially involves relating the properties and performance of a material (in a particular application) to the structure of the atoms. It is a known fact that the present level of technology is not capable of manufacturing a perfect crystal of any material, and scientists are essentially involved to manipulate the defects in the crystalline materials. Presently, various research activities are happening in respect of all experimental and theoretical aspects of advanced materials in the fields of science, engineering and medicine including synthesis, fabrication, processing, spectroscopic characterisation, physical properties and applications of all kinds of inorganic and organic materials, metals, semiconductors, superconductors, ceramics, glasses, ferroelectrics, low and high-k dielectrics, sol-gel materials, liquid crystals, biomaterials, organics and polymers, polymer-based electronics, optics, photonics and biological devices.[1]

Advanced materials in some form or the other have been debated and researched in the realm of Material Science for many years. Globally, many research labs are developing new materials for various industrial applications and also finding its relevance for societal use. Particularly, various breakthroughs in the field of micro and nanotechnology are found impacting some aspects of modern research in Material Sciences significantly. From strategic materials perspective, various developments in the arena of the new materials are being observed with great interest particularly to solve the challenges of substitution. It is likely that in some cases the development of new materials could actually depend on supply of existing strategic materials as the raw materials.

Biomaterials, electronic and magnetic materials, forensic engineering, glass science, metallurgy, etc. are the sub-disciplines of Material Science. Any focused debate on various aspects of new materials and its relevance for various branches of Material Science is beyond the scope of this work. With a purpose to highlight few important contributions of advances in science and technology, which could impact the present strategic materials architecture, few new materials/ideas are discussed in the following sections.

Graphene

Graphene is a new material that is expected to be more solid than steel and a better conductor than copper. As its name indicates, graphene is extracted from graphite, the material used in pencils. Like graphite, graphene is entirely composed of carbon atoms and 1mm of graphite contains some 3 million layers of graphene. Whereas graphite is a three-dimensional crystalline arrangement, graphene is a two-dimensional crystal, only an atom thick. Graphene conducts electricity better than copper. It is 200 times stronger than steel, but six times lighter. It is almost perfectly transparent since it only absorbs 2 per cent of light. It impermeable to gases, even those as light as hydrogen or helium, and chemical components can be added to its surface to alter its properties. The isolation of graphene has successfully been demonstrated in laboratory, and the scientists won the 2010 Nobel Prize in Physics for this success.

Being transparent as well as a good conductor, graphene could replace the electrodes in the indium used in touch screens. Since it is light, graphene could be integrated into composite materials to eliminate the impact of lightning on aircraft fuselages. It is also waterproof and would be perfect to use in hydrogen reservoirs. The major challenge for the Information and Communications Technology (ICT) industry is to find alternatives for information processing and storage beyond the limits of existing Complementary Metal–Oxide–Semiconductor (CMOS). There are good indications that graphene is a prime candidate for “Beyond CMOS” components, and is, despite its revolutionary nature, complementary to conventional CMOS technologies. Presently, further research and experimentation is underway on this subject to make this idea feasible for usage in industrial sectors like electronics, energy, health and construction. Typically, it takes about 40 years for a new material to move from an academic laboratory into a consumer product. However, in case of grapheme, within 10 years, it has jumped from laboratory into industrial laboratory, and now even pilot products are available. As per some forecasts, the future of graphene market could be worth US$ 1.5 bn in 2015 and US$ 7.5 bn in 2025.[2]

In this context, it is important to mention the present status of graphite because it is going to be the raw material for grapheme. In the Indian context, this work has not identified graphite as a strategic material. However, graphite has been named a “supply critical mineral” and a “strategic mineral” by the US and the European Union. Like in the case of various other materials, China has a tight grip on the worldwide graphite supply too, controlling over 70 per cent of it (Figure 8.1).

Figure 8.1: Share of Graphite Producing Countries in World

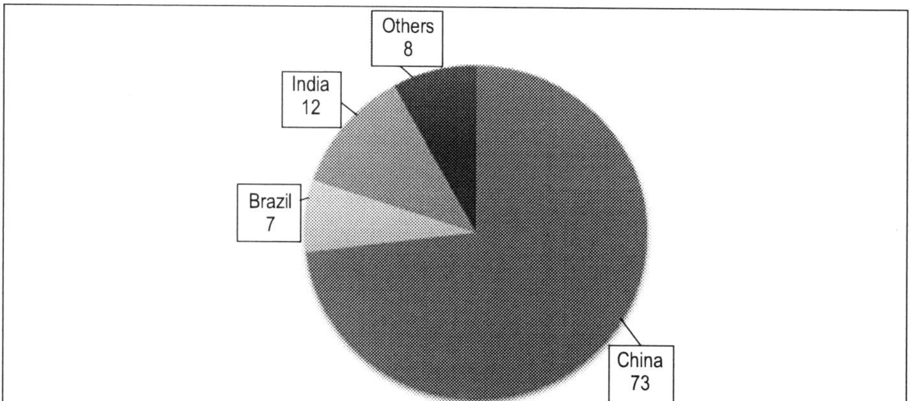

Source: US Geological Survey.

Further, China has been limiting graphite exports with quotas causing graphite prices to rise. Also, owing to environmental concerns, China recently ordered restrictions on any further graphite mines in two of its largest graphite-producing regions.[3] Naturally, this opens an opportunity for others to enter this market in a big way. Figure 8.2 indicates how the supply/demand

Figure 8.2: Natural Graphite Supply and Demand

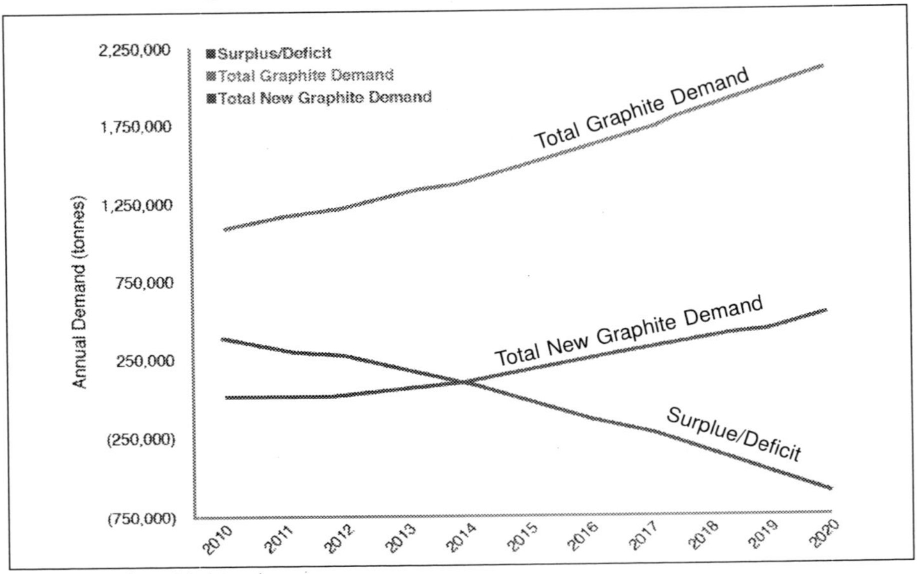

Source: Angle Publishing.[4]

imbalances in the coming years could become problematic for many states in the world.

In recent years, the graphite prices have already started showing a steep rise. Any major technical breakthroughs in respect of grapheme will put more pressure on the graphite pricing policy. Hence, it is important to ensure that no manipulation and cartelisation of graphite business takes place.

Germanane

Scientists have developed a new method[5] of depositing germanium in atomically thin layers, boosting its performance 10-times over silicon-making it an easier-to-fabricate alternative over other next-generation materials like graphene. It can be used in producing next generation of fast and compact computing chips and making power-efficient processors resulting in cheaper mass-produced chips. It has also been claimed that this material would be suitable for optical applications too. This material could be useful in fabricating next-generation optoelectronic devices and advanced sensors. Besides being based on germanium instead of carbon like graphene, the biggest difference between the materials is that germanane has the potential to be more easily grown using conventional semiconductor fabrication equipment than graphane.

Stanene

Scientists have been trying to develop room-temperature superconductors—materials that conduct electrons with zero resistance, and do so without cumbersome, energy-sucking super cooling—for more than three decades. Now researchers predict that a new material called stanene (a combination of the Latin word for tin (stannum) and the suffix found in the word grapheme), composed of a one-atom-thick sheet of tin, could act much like a room-temperature superconductor, leading to faster, more efficient microchips.

This new material has not yet been fabricated, but has raised many expectations. Stanene was discovered by researchers from the US Department of Energy's (DOE), SLAC National Accelerator Laboratory and Stanford University and is predicted to revolutionise computing by replacing the copper wires still used in modern computer chips. It could increase the speed and lower the power needs of future generations of computer chips. If present predictions by scientists are confirmed by experiments that are underway in several laboratories around the world, then this material could change the face of ITC technologies in particular.[6] Presently, there are many technological obstacles standing between stanene and converting it as a final usable product. It would require a few more years of research to prove the actual worth of this material.

Metamaterials

These are exotic composite materials that display properties beyond those available in naturally occurring materials. Instead of constructing materials at the chemical level, as is ordinarily done, these are constructed with two or more materials at the macroscopic level. One of their defining characteristics is that the electromagnetic response results from combining two or more distinct materials in a specified way which extends the range of electromagnetic patterns because they are not found in nature. Scientists have studied the application of metamaterials for more than 60 years, albeit without using the term itself, with research dating back to the 1940s.

Metamaterials are defined as macroscopic composites having a manmade, three-dimensional, periodic cellular architecture designed to produce an optimised combination, not available in nature, of two or more responses to specific excitation.[7] Subsequently, the idea of Metamaterials has evolved further, and now it is considered as a new class of ordered composites that exhibit exceptional properties not readily observed in nature. "While the original metamaterials definition encompassed many more material properties, most of the subsequent scientific activity has centred on the electromagnetic properties of metamaterials gains its properties from its structure rather than directly from its composition."[8]

Researchers are currently exploring the best possible ways to use this artificial type of matter. With metamaterials, the sum of the parts, not the parts themselves, determines how the material behaves. Researchers have found that by using certain materials—like gold and copper arranged in certain patterns and shapes—they can combine the properties of those materials. In other words, unlike natural matter, metamaterials' behaviour depends on the properties of the materials that make it up and the way the materials are put together.

For more than a decade (since early 2000s), various attempts are been made to commercialise the application of this technology. Presently, satellite antennas built using metamaterials technology are opening doors to new markets for the satellite communications industry and ushering in a new era of mobility. The technology is expected to provide new communications solutions previously impossible with traditional satellite antennas. Few scientists are even found discussing (theoretical) possibilities of using such material for making an entire aircraft or battle tank invisible.[9] As per present state of prediction, metamaterials could bolster the satellite communications industry too.

3D Printing Technology

3D printing is the new technological revolution waiting to find its spot in the future. From medical science to sophisticated arenas like defence and space, the printer is expected to redefine methods of manufacturing by reduction of cost, labour and time. 3D printing is similar to 2D printing where the print evolves putting ink layer by layer. Unlike 2D printers, 3D printing do the same job in 3D form, replacing ink of printer with desired material considering strength and utility.[10] A computer model is created using 3D Computer Aided Design (CAD) by scanning the model to be replicated. This model is then printed in Selective Laser Sintering (SLS) where a material is melted and extruded in layers, one upon the other. For instance, Lockheed Martin has already deployed 3D[11] printing machines to manufacture parts of satellite and aircraft using material such as titanium. The material is heated and then applied in successive layers to create almost any shape saving cost and reduction in cycle time and material waste.[12] Taking the possibility of using 3D printers to the next level, it was reported in recent months that National Aeronautics and Space Administration (NASA) is planning to launch

3D printers at the international space station in order to manufacture spare parts and tools in zero gravity. The wide possibility and seamless transition of manufacturing on 3D printers could the demand of strategic minerals in future.[13] Also, over a period of time, the materials which could be put in use for 3D printing would be specifically identified as 'strategic materials'.

Molybdenum disulphide (MoS2)[14]

MoS2 is a novel two-dimensional semiconductor with potential applications in electronic and optoelectronic devices.[15] It is an inorganic compound, a silvery black solid that occurs as the mineral molybdenite, the principal ore for molybdenum and is relatively unreactive.[16] This material is being used in industries and is also finding some utility for 3D printing. Molybdenum is composed of two sulphur atoms. Scientists have been studying and experimenting to enhance its properties as it gives benefits of graphene without modification to make electronic materials such as transistors (consume 100,000 times less energy in standby state that traditional silicon material) and rectifiers.[17] Besides electronics, it can be used in lubricants as it gives more shear strength due to low coefficient of friction (as low as 0.02). It also could be used to make varieties of catalyst and chemicals which are much more efficient than its previous counterparts.

New Solar Cells

Solar cells is one of the most 'emphasised' areas of research in the present scenario. It has been argued that due to environmental reasons there is an immediate necessity for a shift to using green methods of energy production. The demand for green and efficient technology has already surged in recent years. Energy production from solar power is one of the central choices for obvious reasons. Presently, globally, various research ideas are in the pipeline to make solar cells much more efficient. Some researchers have developed[18] semiconductors made of alloys incorporating indium, gallium, and nitrogen.[19] This technology can "convert virtually the full spectrum of sunlight-from the near infrared to the far ultraviolet-to electrical current".[20] In this particular case, the strategic mineral put in use is indium. From this case, a broad conclusion be drawn that strategic materials could have relevance for green technologies too.

Shape Memory Alloys[21]

Like the name suggests, shape memory alloys are metals which remember their shapes. Atoms in every metal arrange themselves in specific pattern known as 'phase'. Any alteration in the pattern of arrangement is called 'phase change'. In general, metals do not possess tendency of rapid phase change; however, in shape memory materials, rapid phase change is possible depending on the environment in which these materials are deployed. Unlike existing metals, these metals have the capability to change shape tens of thousands of times when heated and cooled without degrading their original properties. When a metal is in its initial phase, the atoms are organised in a specific arrangement called 'monoclinic arrangement' or 'martensite'. When the metal is heated, the atoms moves in columns, a phase called 'austenite' by switching seamlessly amongst each other. For this reason, they are called 'shape memory' metals.[22]

Their remarkable ability to remember their shape and return to their original stage make them potential materials to be used in strategic industries in future. They have numerous applications ranging from electronics, automotive, aerospace, biomedical, space vehicles to jet engines. For instance, currently, martensite metals are made of an alloyed mixture of nickel and titanium, also called 'Nitinol'. Due to its significant mechanical and electrical properties, it can be used in making actuators. A Nitinol wire of 0.020 inches in diameter can lift as much as 16 pounds and can sustain 50,000 psi restoration stress. When electricity is passed through this wire, internal heat is generated causing transformational phase change.[23] According to one study, it can be used in space applications such as solar panel and windshield wiper of mars rovers. In Mars rovers, they could be used in metals holding solar panels which will move when electrically heated giving maximum surface area to the panel.[24]

So far, this material has been successfully deployed by Boeing in its Dreamliner 787 in form of 'chevrons'[25] at trailing edge of engine to reduce noise in airport. Also, it has been used in medical science as super elasticstents to support arteries and vessels.[26] There are possibilities to alloy this material with a mixture of zinc, gold and copper which may transform this metal into more 'active materials' by enhancing its retractable characteristics. There are endless possibilities of using such materials in numerous applications on further research.

Self-Healing Artificial Material

Inspired by nature and biological systems, self-healing material is a class of materials with the ability to self-heal (repair/recover) in case of any wear and tear. It is the process of re-forming broken molecular bonds to at least partially restore any mechanical properties the material had before the damage. Some self-healing materials require the input of a catalyst, an outside agent that helps the healing process along, making it favourable in general conditions.[27]

The basic material classes include plastics, metals, ceramics, concrete and polymers. The chemical engineering department of Stanford University has created a self-healing artificial material which is also pressure sensitive. This material is a mixture of plastic and nickel nanoparticles.[28] While plastics induce long fibre chains fused together by hydrogen bond, nickel increases the mechanical strength as well as induce pressure sensitive properties. The result is a material which, when sliced, could be pressed back together to regain the material. The material will be able to heal to its original strength up to 75 per cent in matter of few seconds while 100 per cent in 30 minutes. The material is expected to have prodigious advantages in future. It can be used in prostheses, coating of electronics and many defence equipment. The full potential usage of such material is still to be exploited; however, foreseeable reality is that such materials will revolutionise Material Science.

Boron, Aluminium and Magnesium (BAM) 'Ceramic' Alloy[29]

BAM is typically a ceramic alloy made up of boron, aluminium and magnesium (AlMgB14) with titanium boride (TiB2). It was accidently discovered in 1999 by the US Department of Energy Ames Laboratory in Iowa when a research for efficient electric substance was in its nascent stage. Harder than diamond, BAM is one of the hardest materials known till today. While diamond has simple, regular and symmetrical crystalline structure, BAM's structure is complex, has low symmetry and often has a few atoms missing.

BAM is slipperier than Teflon, inducing the property of self-lubrication. Researchers believe that its self-lubricant properties would be a great aid to cutting tools which are made of diamond. Because of its hardness and self-lubricating properties, it can be used in making cutting tools, moving components in machines, gears, etc. as it will boost energy efficiency and longevity by reducing friction.[30] The coefficient of friction of BAM is about 0.02; therefore, it can be used in making engine housing. BAM + titanium boride can be potentially used as a coating for the blades of pumps which will decrease the energy consumed and increase efficiency. It is also possible this material could find potential use in medical implants such as artificial knee and hip replacement joints. The material has potential application in aerospace and defence, mainly in areas like production of rifle barrels, armour blade, jet nozzles and munitions.[31]

Ceramic Matrix Composites (CMC)[32]

Ceramics are known as inorganic and non-metallic materials that have utility in our daily lifestyle. Such materials includes tiles, bricks, plates, glass, etc. Ceramics have wider applicability from being used as an electrically conductive materials to airplanes and space shuttles. They also have utility in products like watches (quartz tuning forks-the time keeping devices in watches), snow skies (piezoelectric-ceramics that stress when a voltage is applied to them), automobiles (sparkplugs and ceramic engine parts found in race cars) and phone lines. They can also be found on space shuttles, appliances (enamel coatings) and airplanes (nose cones). Ceramics can be dense or lightweight depending on the requirements.

Advanced ceramic materials make various incredible applications possible today due to various technological developments in this field. These materials are actually value-added technical ceramic, which are ceramics exhibiting a high degree of industrial efficiency. Ceramic materials used as technical ceramics or advanced ceramics in technical applications are required to satisfy extremely high demands in terms of their properties. The property spectrum ranges from wear and heat resistance, temperature and corrosion resistance all the way to biocompatibility and food compatibility. Because of such diverse properties, they significant amount of utility in various strategic industries too.

However, such ceramics made-up of alumina, silicon carbide, aluminium nitrate, etc. are easily fractured under mechanical or thermo-mechanical loads. To overcome this difficulty, Ceramic Matrix Composites (CMCs) are introduced. Generally, CMCs include a combination of type of fibre/type of matrix. CMC materials are found being used for the preparation of the heat shield in space vehicles, as components for high-temperature gas turbines, etc.

Qingsongite

Qingsongite[33] is a recently christened mineral and has an atomic structure similar to diamond; it has high density and is also nearly as hard as diamond. Qingsongite was first created in the laboratory in 1957, and geologists first found natural qingsongite, which is a cubic boron nitride, in chromium-rich rocks in Tibet in 2009. Even though the original discovery of this mineral was made in 2009; still, it got official approval by the International Mineralogical Association only in August 2013. This mineral is the first boron mineral found to be formed at extreme conditions in deep earth. Otherwise, all other known boron minerals are found at Earth's surface. This mineral was found in the southern Tibetan mountains of China. Interestingly, cubic boron nitride was created first in the laboratory in 1957, and since then is being recognised as an important technological material with wider applicability in strategic industries because of its specific properties.

NOTES

1. "Science of Advanced Materials", American Scientific Publishers—New Titles at the forefront of Nanotechnology, at http://www.aspbs.com/sam/ (Accessed January 1, 2014).
2. "Graphene—The New Wonder Material", *The Guardian*, November 22, 2013, at http://www.theguardian.com/science/2013/nov/26/graphene-molecule-potential-wonder-material.
   "Graphene: Wonder Material for Electronics, Computers and Beyond", November 15, 2013, at http://phys.org/print303720717.html.
   "Graphene: 'Miracle Material' Will Be in Your Home Sooner Than You Think", at http://cacm.acm.org/opinion/interviews/168536-graphene-miracle-material-will-be-in-your-home-sooner-than-you-think/fulltext (Accessed December 28, 2013).
   K.S. Novoselov et al:, "A Roadmap for Graphene", *Nature*, 490, October 11, 2012, pp. 192–200.
3. "Graphene, An Advanced Strategic High Tech Material", Global Research, at http://www.globalresearch.ca/graphene-an-advanced-strategic-rare-earth-material/5341866 (Accessed December 20, 2013).
4. "Natural Graphite supply/demand" Angle publications at https://images.angelpub.com/2013/15/18919/ea-graphite-chart1.png (Accessed December 20, 2013).
5. R. Colin Johnson, "Germanane Beats Graphene", *EE Times*, November 4, 2013, at http://www.eetimes.com/document.asp?doc_id=1263163 (Accessed January 7, 2014).
6. Charles Q Choi, "Could Atomically Thin Tin Transform Electronics?" Dec 4, 2013, at http://www.scientificamerican.com/article.cfm?id=could-atomically-thin-tin-transform-electronics.
   James Vincent, "New Wonder Material 'Stanene' Could Replace Graphene with 100% Electrical Conductivity", November 27, 2013, at http://www.independent.co.uk/news/science/new-wonder-material-stanene-could-replace-graphene-with-100-electrical-conductivity-8967573.html (Accessed January 2, 2014).
7. Rodger M. Walser, University of Texas at Austin, 1999.
8. "Metamaterials", at http://phys.org/tags/metamaterials/.
9. Ibid.
   Josh Clark, "Is the Army Testing an Invisible Tank?" at http://www.howstuffworks.com/invisible-tank1.htm.
   VernFotheringham, "Metamaterials: Transformative Technology for The Satellite Communications Industry", *Sat Magazine*, at http://www.satmagazine.com/story.php?number=5592572 (Accessed January 2, 2014).
10. "3D Printing and Defence: A Silent Revolution", Institute for Defence Studies and Analyses, at http://www.idsa.in/idsacomments/3DPrintingandDefence_stomar_030114 (Accessed January 3, 2014).
11. "Revitalizing Manufacturing with Next-Gen Production Technology", Lockheed Martin,at http://www.lockheedmartin.com/us/news/features/2013/3dprinting.html (Accessed January 3, 2013).
12. "Lockheed Martin Moves 3D Printing to the Production Line", *Gizmag*, at http://www.gizmag.com/lockheeddigitaltapestry/29332/?utm_source=Gizmag+Subscribers&utm_campaign=99b5bf595c-UA-2235360-4&utm_medium=email&utm_term=0_65b67362bd-99b5bf595c-90303470 (Accessed January 3, 2013).
13. "NASA Plans First 3D Printer Space Launch in 2014", *BBC News*, September 30, 2013, at

http://www.bbc.co.uk/news/technology-24329296 (Accessed January 3, 2014).

14. "New Transistors: An Alternative to Silicon and Better than Graphene", at http://phys.org/news/2011-01-transistors-alternative-silicon-graphene.html accessed January 5, 2014.
15. "Hopping Transport through Defect-Induced Localized States in Molybdenum Disulphide",atwww.nature.com/ncomms/2013/131023/ncomms3642/full/ncomms3642.htm (Accessed January 7, 2014).
16. Roger F. Sebenik et al., "Molybdenum and Molybdenum Compounds", in *Ullmann's Encyclopedia of Chemical Technology 2005*, Wiley-VCH, Weinheim.
17. "Climax Molybdenum", at http://pubs.acs.org/doi/pdf/10.1021/i650563a721 (Accessed January 5, 2014).
18. Researchers in Berkeley Lab's Materials Sciences Division (MSD) with Cornel and Ritsumeikan University.
19. "New Materials: Industrial Innovations", Industrial Innovations, at http://industrial-innov.lbl.gov/II-materials.html (Accessed January 3, 2014).
20. "An Unexpected Discovery Could Yield a Full Spectrum Solar Cell", Berkeley Lab News Center, at http://newscenter.lbl.gov/news-releases/2002/11/18/an-unexpected-discovery-could-yield-a-full-spectrum-solar-cell (Accessed January 7, 2014).
21. Simon Redfern, "New Shape-Shifting Metals Discovered", *BBC*, October 4, 2013, at http://www.bbc.co.uk/news/science-environment-4400101 (Accessed January 3, 2014).
22. http://www.bbc.co.uk/news/science-environment-24400101 (Accessed January 7, 2014).
23. "Introduction to Shape Memory Alloys", at http://www.tinialloy.com/pdf/introductiontosma.pdf (Accessed January 6, 2014).
24. "Windshield Wiper for Mars Dust Developed: Actuator Moved by Materials that Have Shape Memory", *Science Daily*, Universidad Carlos III de Madrid - Oficina de Información Científica, Sep. 24, 2012, at http://www.sciencedaily.com/releases/2012/09/120924101804.htm.
25. Chevrons are the saw-tooth patterns on the trailing edges of some jet engine nozzles that are used for noise reduction. Hot air from the engine core mixes with cooler air blowing through the engine fan, the shaped edges serve to smooth the mixing, which reduces noise creating turbulence.
26. "Superelasticity and Shape Memory Alloys - Applications", DoITPoMS, University of Cambridge, at http://www.doitpoms.ac.uk/tlplib/superelasticity/uses.php (Accessed January 3, 2014).
27. "Geek Answers: How Do Self-Healing Materials Self-Heal? | Science", n.d., at http://www.geek.com/science/geek-answers-how-do-self-healing-materials-self-heal-1577707 (Accessed on January 7, 2014).
28. "Self-healing Materials: Fundamentals, Design Strategies, and Applications", Google Books, at http://books.google.co.in/books?hl=en&lr=&id=4NH64BONX94C&oi=fnd&pg=PR5&dq=self+healing+materials&ots=L_Del6O1X3&sig=8fCfZn6AcSDRKAwXGqWcjtIa2Fw#v=onepage&q=self%20healing%20materials&f=false (Accessed January 5, 2014).
29. "Material Slicker than Teflon Discovered by Accident", *New Scientist*, November 21, 2008, at http://www.newscientist.com/article/dn16102-material-slicker-than-teflon-discovered-by-accident.html#.Usp3u9IW3QU (Accessed January 5, 2014).
30. "New Ultra-Slippery Alloy is Second Hardest Known Material", Gajitz | Neat Gadgets, New Materials & Futuristic Technology, at http://gajitz.com/new-ultra-slippery-alloy-is-second-hardest-known-material/ (Accessed January 5, 2014).
31. "Materials in Ames Laboratory", Success Stories, Ames Laboratory, at https://www.ameslab.gov/news/inquiry/success-stories (Accessed January 7, 2014).
32. http://depts.washington.edu/matseed/mse_resources/Webpage/Ceramics/ceramics.htm, http://astarmathsandphysics.com/a-level-physics-notes/materials/a-level-physics-notes-ceramics.html, http://en.wikipedia.org/wiki/Ceramic_matrix_composite, http://www.ceramtec.com/ceramic-materials/?gclid=CNLhg-WSrb0CFUUF4god8jwAjw and http:/

/chemistry.about.com/od/engineeringglossary/g/advanced-ceramic-definition.htm (Accessed March 25, 2015).

33. Cole Latimer, "Geologists Uncover New Mineral", August 5, 2013, at http://www.miningaustralia.com.au/news/geologists-uncover-new-mineral (Accessed March 26, 2014).
Sarah Zielinski, "Qingsongite", *Science News*, November 16, 2013.

9

Conclusion and Recommendations

'Strategic Materials' are key components of resource geopolitics. The macro study and analysis presented in this work build up a complex picture of the varying levels of vulnerability for different minerals. The notion of strategic material could differ with every country depending on its perceptions, needs and nature of mineral deposits available for its use. Globally, since the World War II era, states have been aware about the importance of various strategic materials. However, the advent of massive industrialisation because of various rapidly developing states has led to a significant increase in the demand of strategic materials and monopoly of a few states in regards to the supply of such materials, and the issue of strategic materials has gained significant importance globally.

Significant amount of fallacies in demand and supply chain in respect of strategic materials indicates that there is a need to lobby for a transparent mechanism globally in order to avoid any domination of interest groups and any possibilities of hoarding. It is also essential to identify how both demand and supply options could be best enunciated to secure state's interest. States need to factor in the reality that the demand is going to increase substantially in the coming days, and no immediate change in supply quantum is expected. Under such a situation, the states could regulate demand by opting for substitutions, recycle of strategic materials, researching on new materials and finding innovative solutions to reduce the dependency on specific strategic materials. It is essential to evolve policies towards 'dematerialisation' (i.e., reduction in the amount of material and energy to service function area) of strategic minerals from national stocks and reserves. Also, states need to ensure surge in supply of minerals. For this purpose, streamlining of export policies needs to be undertaken. It is essential to identify ways to increase production, and additionally, emphasis should be given towards achieving innovations and developments in technologies. Also, significant investments should be made to exploit options like deep sea mining.

Presently, various states have begun to realise the importance of devising a focused strategic minerals policy. They understand that geopolitical balance in respect of global materials distribution is askew. There have been many deferring perceptions of states in regards to export/import policies in this field. In addition, there are increasing economic and environmental pressures on states in regards to use, recycle, purchase, sale and conservation of various energy and mineral materials. There is a necessity to evolve an integrated approach for continuous assessment needs and development of policies to assist decision-makers with unbiased information. Efforts are needed to undertake risk analysis and find problem areas to guard against.

India is emerging as one of the major economies of the world, and it has unfortunately been blamed by major powers for consuming relatively more quantity of strategic materials and is indirectly being held responsible for creating competition in the global materials market. However, it is obvious that world would have to live with the reality of impact of developing economics like China, India, Brazil and Mexico on the global strategic materials market.

Presently, China has monopoly in regards to the global supply of the strategic materials. Moreover, due to an increase in domestic consumption, China's export potential is likely to decrease in future. It is important for states to conduct periodic national assessments to ensure that mineral supplies are sufficient. It is essential to undertake quantitative mineral resource assessment. Also, there is a need for states to undertake a micro assessment within their geographical boundaries about the possibility of undiscovered mineral resources. Undoubtedly, excavation and future processing of minerals to make them useable would be a very costly proposal particularly in comparison to importing the 'ready to use' materials. However, it needs to be appreciated that with the monopoly of single state in this business, it would be incorrect to assume that unhindered and economical supplies would always remain a reality.

For last few decades, various new minerals have been introduced, and various science laboratories have been making concentrated efforts to achieve breakthroughs in various arenas of material sciences. Moreover, few new materials (essentially alloys or as by-products of known minerals) are showing significant amount of potential for revolutionising the field of materials. New materials are expected to support many key business sectors including general manufacturing, construction business and clean technologies and transport industry. Innovation in new materials development could also allow benefits in high-value-added products sector and processes and services sector. It is expected that relevance of strategic materials could increase with the introduction of new materials essentially because most of them would be required as raw materials for new minerals.

Currently, strategic materials exploration and expansion activities are at crossroads. There is an evolving milieu involving multiple stakeholders globally. States have begun to realise the need for strategic materials resource assessment and examining the nature of their dependency on imports. India-specific assessment carried out during the course of this study provided the following information:

- As a developing economy and with ongoing rapid industrialisation, India's need for minerals for multiple industrial sectors is expected to grow manifold. India's need for strategic materials is also growing mainly owning to its investments in nuclear, aerospace and defence sectors which are strategic material intensive industries.
- In case of India, many of the strategic minerals identified and minerals belonging to higher risk bracket are also listed as strategic materials for various other countries. This indicates that presently there are multiple buyers for the same material globally, and this number is expected to grow further. India needs to factor in this proliferation in users while undertaking future planning. Also, there is a need to develop a dynamic mechanism to calculate national stock and mineral reserves of strategic minerals in the country which could be used to as an element for the calculation of projection for the future.
- The assessment carried out in this study indicates that for India cobalt, germanium, molybdenum and tungsten are the strategic minerals in the higher risk bracket. There is a significant amount of import dependence for procurement of these materials. Also, presently India is importing alloys and scrap from many countries as raw material. This is turn is increasing India's import dependence significantly. It has been observed that India has substantial dependence on states like China and Africa in respect of imports of strategic minerals. Particularly, violence-prone states like Democratic Republic of Congo (DRC) with a discredited political system is a cause of concern for India, and there always would be some uncertainty in regards to imports from such states. India's political relationship with China, with an unscrupulous past and not so exultant present, and China's

opaque policies in the arena of mineral exports need to be factored in while ascertaining the 'dependency' factor.

- For India, issues related to export/import policies of strategic minerals should not be restricted as a job of the Commerce Ministry alone. Foreign policy decisions play an important role towards gaining access to relevant minerals and technologies. It is important for India to advance various useful bilateral and multilateral collaborations by keeping present and future requirements of strategic materials in mind. Particularly, there is a need to engage states like Brazil, Japan and the US not only from an import destination point of view but also for undertaking joint projects.
- In general, it has been observed that India's policy of multiple sourcing has helped to avoid resource traps.
- Unfortunately, India is not able to get free access to exhume the mineral deposits within its own country owing to some domestic factors.
- Apart from the management of imports, it is also important for India to factor in various important domestic issues for undertaking mining planning. The issues are both political and environmental in nature. There are various pressure groups within the country which keep a strict watch on various activities which could damage the environment by conducting mining in an unscientific way. It is important for India to link such groups with the existing government network to monitor the environmental challenges arising from mining and take corrective measures. Besides, India's major problem concerning mineral deposits is the problem of Naxalism. It is not restricted to being a law and order problem and has various social dimensions too which require delicate handling.
- There is an interrelationship between the Naxalite conflict and India's mineral production and mining policies. Table 9.1 lists the type of strategic minerals found in the Naxal-affected regions within India.

Table 9.1: Strategic Minerals Found in Naxal-affected Regions in India

Type of strategic material	Region
Beryllium	Jharkhand, Odisha
Fluorite	Chhattisgarh
Tin	West Bengal
Tungsten	Chhattisgarh, Jharkhand
Nickel	Chhattisgarh, Jharkhand
Molybdenum	Jharkhand, MP
Cobalt	Odisha
Gallium	Odisha

Source: Compiled based on chapter VI.

- A healthy solution to the problem of Naxalism could also lead to domestic increase in the production of the strategic minerals. India also needs to guard against illegal mining, and it is important for the state to overcome the political pressures and take appreciate corrective measures. All in all, finding solutions to specific internal problems could lead to an increase in the production of strategic materials and eventually reduce the dependence on imports.
- It is important to encourage research institutions for innovation of new minerals and modification of existing materials and also develop a mechanism to undertake improvements in existing mineral processing and extraction methods. There is a need to establish a dedicated facility for strategic mineral research including finding efficient methods for recycling.
- Rare Earth Element (REE) dependency of various nation-states on China has been one of the most hotly discussed subjects globally. Various states are looking for an alternative to decrease their overdependence on China. For India, this situation could be considered both as challenge and opportunity. India many not be as blessed as China in regards to natural deposits of REE. However, there is a possibility for India to make appropriate investments in this sector particularly by undertaking deep sea mining.
- As per the Government of India, Department of Science & Technology Ministry of Science & Technology Annual Report 2013, the government has promised support to both basic and applied research on Material, Mining and Mineral Engineering. Already 29 new research efforts have been initiated/identified for support, and another 39 are under evaluation. Such measures by the government are highly encouraging. It needs to be ensured that such efforts are sustained and monitored regularly. There is a need for the institutionalisation of material research in Indian universities and encourage private sector to undertake research and development in this sector.

Overall, it has been observed that the 'expanse' of strategic materials has increased manifold during the last couple of years, and for a developing economy like India, it is important to evolve a multidisciplinary architecture for policy formulation on this subject.

Recommendations

Based on the overall assessment of the global strategic materials architecture and pattern of Indian investments being made in such materials following are the few India specific recommendations:

Recommendation 1

There is a need to contextualise strategic materials as an important component of overall national security architecture. A systemic risk analysis needs to be carried out to appreciate various challenges. The process of risk assessment is a dynamic process. There is a need to develop a practice of undertaking requirements assessment and devising risk management strategies for key strategic materials for present and future. The entire domain of undertaking assessments, factoring strategic needs, managing domestic production and deciding on export/import policies would be a complex and multidisciplinary task. Hence, it is recommended that a separate 'Materials Commission' could be constituted.

Recommendation 2

Strategic industries like nuclear, aerospace and defence could be encouraged to undertake various new studies and initiatives to project their needs, shortages (if any), future requirements and current policies of procurements. The domestic private industry associated with various strategic industries could also be constructively engaged by formulating various study groups.

Recommendation 3

There is a need for formation of new policies to address various issues concerning strategic materials. It is important to note that any process of decision-making should not be exclusivity based on economic cost-benefit analysis. In specific cases, export policy should not only factor in the reality that local excavation is costlier than imports. Various strategic considerations needs to be examined before any policymaking.

Recommendation 4

The issue of strategic materials (based on feasibility and interests) in various bilateral and multilateral deliberations with other nations needs to be factored in. Excavation and processing technology is the key for the development of domestic strategic materials industry. Research and development within the country in that respect should be encouraged, and also opportunities for joint collaborations/transfer of technology should be sought.

Recommendation 5

It is essential to factor in India's need for strategic materials while attempting to find solutions to the problem of Naxalism.

Recommendation 6

Detailed supply-chain analyses could be undertaken with major emphasis on weapon-specific supply-chains.

Recommendation 7

Studies should be undertaken to explore the possibilities of devising specific material substitution strategies. Also, private industry should be involved both in mining activities and undertaking research and incentivised for its efforts.

Recommendation 8

Investments should be made in studies on new materials.

APPENDICES

Appendix A

History of Mining and Evolution of Mineral Legislation in India

The earliest and most authentic record of information relating to minerals in India is found in 'Arthasastra', at reatise composed by Kautilya famously known as Chanakya, between 321 and 296 B.C. This treatise gives a comprehensive account of the properties of ores of minerals and metals with the methods of their large scale production and treatment as well as the manufactures of alloys like brass, bronze and also gold and silver alloys with base metals. The records available in Kautilya's 'Arthasashtra' give the earliest stipulations in regulating mining industry as prescribed in the qualifications and responsibilities of the Superintendent of Mines who possesses the knowledge of the science dealing with copper and other minerals, expertise in mineralogy and equipped with mining labourers and necessary instruments. The Arthasashtra also provides for stringent punishment to those persons who carries on mining operations without license or who steals the mineral products. It also provides that the Superintendent of Ocean Mines (Khanyadhyakshah) shall attend to the collection of conch-shells, diamonds, precious stones, pearls, corals and salt and also regulate the commerce in the above commodities. Arthasashtra also provided that both mining and commerce in minerals shall be State monopoly.

In the medieval ages, India had a fairly well developed metallurgical industry. During 1400-1800, individual kingdoms prescribed the controls for mining activity until Mughals established more strict regulatory controls. The first recorded history of mining in India dates back to 1774 when Mr John Summer, Mr S.G. Heatly and Mr. Redfarne were granted permission by Mr. Warren Hastings, the then Governor General of Bengal for mining coal in Pachete and Birbhum. M/s John Taylor & Sons Ltd. Started gold mining in Kolar Gold Fields in the year 1880. The first concrete proposal for the inspection and regulation of mining operations in India came in 1890 from the Secretary of State Lord Cross.

In 1895 Government of India appointed a Committee to frame general rules applicable to mines or groups of mines and to clarify the heads under which legislation was desirable and the provisions which need to be made unde reach head. Finally, the Mines Act was enacted in 1901 and brought in force in the same year. The Mines Act which came in force in 1901 covered all minerals worked up to a depth of over 6 meters and provided for appointment of inspectors, appointment of persons possessing the prescribed qualifications as managers of mines, empowered the Chief Inspector to enter and inspect mines, and to enquire into accidents and prohibit the employment of children. Some additional legal provisions came into being in coming years.

During 1948, the in enactment of the Mines and Minerals (Regulation and Development) Act, 1948, the first legal framework in independent India for the regulation and development of mines came into practice. The Mineral Concession Rule 1949 (MCR 1949) were made for regulating the grant of prospecting licenses and mining leases for minerals other that petroleum and natural gas. The MCR 1949 was the first basic regulatory mechanism initiated for grant of mineral concessions in independent India.

The Mines and Minerals (Regulation and Development) Act (1957), an act concerning the regulation of mining and mineral development in India was passed by the Indian parliament in December 1957. Also, Mineral Conservation and Development Rules were formulated during 1958. Subsequently, various rules, regulations, acts and amendments have been put in place.

In 1986, the Mines & Minerals (Regulation and Development) Act, 1957 was amended and important provision of requirement of Mining Plan before the grant of mining lease was made compulsory. Also, the Mineral Conservation and Development Rules, 1958 were repealed and a new set of Regulation namely 'Mineral Conservation and Development Rules, 1988'. Succeeding appendixes presents important initial and recent legal documents.

Source: http://ibm.gov.in/re port.htm, Accessed on Apr 12, 2014.

Appendix B

(Extracted portion for the act giving information about minor minerals)

Mines and Minerals (Development and Regulation) Act, 1957

(No. 67 of 1957)

An Act to provide for the 1[development and regulation of mines and minerals] under the control of the Union.

BE it enacted by Parliament in the Eighth Year of the Republic of India as follows:

PRELIMINARY

1. **Short title, extent and commencement.**—(1) This Act may be called the Mines and Minerals [(Development and Regulation)] Act, 1957.

(2) It extends to the whole of India.

(3) It shall come into force on such date as the Central Govt. may, by Notification in the Official Gazette, appoint.

2. **Declaration as to the expediency of Union control.**—It is hereby declared that it is expedient in the public interest that the Union should take under its control the regulation of mines and the development of minerals to the extent hereinafter provided.

3. **Definitions.**—In this Act, unless the context otherwise requires:-

(a) "minerals" includes all minerals except mineral oils;
(b) "mineral oils" includes natural gas and petroleum;
(c) "mining lease" means a lease granted for the purpose of undertaking mining operations, and includes a sub-lease granted for such purpose;

(d) "mining operations" means any operations undertaken for the purpose of winning any mineral;

15. Power of State Governments to make rules in respect of minor minerals.—(1) The State Government may, by notification in the Official Gazette, make rules for regulating the grant of quarry leases, mining leases or other mineral concessions in respect of minor minerals and for purposes connected therewith.

(1A) In particular and without prejudice to the generality of the foregoing power, such rules may provide for all or any of the following matters, namely:-

(a) the person by whom and the manner in which, applications for quarry leases, mining leases or other mineral concessions may be made and the fees to be paid therefor;
(b) the time within which, and the form in which, acknowledgement of the receipt of any such applications may be sent;
(c) the matters which may be considered where applications in respect of the same land are received within the same day;
(d) the terms on which, and the conditions subject to which and the authority by which quarry leases, mining leases or other mineral concessions maybe granted or renewed;
(e) the procedure for obtaining quarry leases, mining leases or other mineral concessions;
(f) the facilities to be afforded by holders of quarry leases, mining leases or other mineral concessions to persons deputed by the Government for the purpose of undertaking research or training in matters relating to mining operations;
(g) the fixing and collection of rent, royalty, fees, dead rent, fines or other charges and the time within which and the manner in which these shall be payable;
(h) the manner in which the rights of third parties may be protected (whether by way of payment of compensation or otherwise) in cases where any such party is prejudicially affected by reason of any prospecting or mining operations;
(i) the manner in which the rehabilitation of flora and other vegetation, such as trees, shrubs and the like destroyed by reasons of any quarrying or mining operations shall be made in the same area or in any other area selected by the State Government (whether by way of reimbursement of the cost of rehabilitation or otherwise) by the person holding the quarrying or mining lease;

(j) the manner in which and the conditions subject to which, a quarry lease, mining lease or other mineral concession may be transferred;

(k) the construction, maintenance and use of roads, power transmission lines, tramways, railways, aerial ropeways, pipelines and the making of passage for water for mining purposes on any land comprised in a quarry or mining lease or other mineral concession;

(l) the form of registers to be maintained under this Act;

(m) the reports and statements to be submitted by holders of quarry or mining leases or other mineral concessions and the authority to which such reports and statements shall be submitted;

(n) the period within which and the manner in which and the authority to which applications for revision of any order passed by any authority under these rules may be made, the fees to be paid therefor, and the powers of the revisional authority; and

(o) any other matter which is to be, or may be prescribed.

(2) Until rules are made under sub-section (1), any rules made by a State Government regulating the grant of quarry leases, mining leases or other mineral concessions in respect of minor minerals which are in force immediately before the commencement of this Act shall continue in force.

(3) The holder of a mining lease or any other mineral concession granted under any rule made under subsection (1) shall pay royalty or dead rent, whichever is more in respect of minor minerals removed or consumed by him or by his agent, manager, employee, contractor or sub-lessee at the rate prescribed for the time being in the rules framed by the State Government in respect of minor minerals: Provided that the State Government shall not enhance the rate of royalty or dead rent in respect of any minor mineral for more than once during any period of three years.

Source: http://mines.nic.in/index.aspx?lid=80&level=1&chk=24dfe45y5edf5e3, Accessed on Apr 12, 2014.

Appendix C

Mines and Minerals (Development and Regulation) Act, 1957

(No. 67 of 1957)

As amended up to 10th May, 2012

Since 1957 this act been amended several times in order to cater for various challenges including the environmental concerns. Following is the list of these amendments. In recent times this act was attended on 10th May 2012. This document (number of pages 47) is available on (http://mines.nic.in/index.aspx?level=1&lid=80&lang=1)

LIST OF AMENDING ACTS

1. The Mines and Minerals (Regulation and Development) Amendment Act, 1958 (15 of 1958)
2. The Repealing and Amending Act, 1960 (58 of 1960)
3. The Mines and Minerals (Regulation and Development) Amendment Act, 1972 (56 of 1972)
4. The Repealing and Amending Act, 1978 (38 of 1978)
5. The Mines and Minerals (Regulation and Development) Amendment Act, 1986 (37 of 1986)
6. The Mines and Minerals (Regulation and Development) Amendment Act, 1994 (25 of 1994)
7. The Mines and Minerals (Regulation and Development) Amendment Act, 1999 (38 of 1999)
8. The Mines and Minerals (Regulation and Development) Amendment Act, 2010 (34 of 2010)An Act to provide for the [development and regulation of mines and minerals] under the control of the Union.

Cabinet 30 September, 2011 14:05 IST **Appendix D**

Press Information Bureau
Ministry of Mines, Government of India
Mines and Minerals (Development and Regulation) Bill, 2011 approved

The Union Cabinet has approved the proposal to introduce the Mines and Minerals (Development and Regulation) Bill (MMDR Bill), 2011, in terms of National Mineral Policy, 2008 in Parliament and also to repeal the existing Mines and Minerals (Development and Regulation) Act, 1957.

The new MMDR Bill, 2011, aims to introduce better legislative environment for attracting investment and technology into the mining sector by the following:

- States may call for applications in notified areas of known mineralization for prospecting based on technical knowledge, value addition, end-use proposed ore -linkage etc. and to invite financial bid;
- States may grant of direct mining concessions through bidding based on a prospecting report and feasibility study in notified areas where data of minerals is adequate for the purpose;
- State Government may set up a minimum floor price for competitive bidding;
- Special provisions for allowing mining of small deposits in cluster, where cooperatives can apply;
- National Mining Regulatory Authority for major minerals - State Governments may set up similar Authority at State level for minor minerals;
- Imposition of a Central cess and a State cess, and setting up of Mineral

Funds at National and State Level for capacity creation;
- For the purpose of sharing the benefits of mining with persons or families having occupation, usufruct or traditional rights in mining areas, and for local area infrastructure, creation an amount equal to royalty in case of mineral other than coal, and 26% of net profits, in the case of coal, has been proposed to be credited each year to district Level Mineral Foundation;
- Sustainable and scientific mining through provision for a Sustainable Development Framework;
- Consultation with local community before notifying an area for grant of concession, and for approval of Mine Closure Plans;
- Enhanced penalties for violation of provisions of the Act, including debarment of person convicted of illegal mining for future grants and termination of all mineral concessions held by such person; and
- Establishment of Special Courts at the State level for speedier disposal of the cases of illegal mining.

The new draft MMDR Act would have financial implications in the creation of an independent National Mining Tribunal and National Mining Regulatory Authority at the Central Level, and the expenditure involved in the capacity building of the Indian Bureau of Mines. The funds for this expenditure are likely to be met from levy of cess at the rate of 2.5% on the basis of Customs/Excise Duty.

The new MMDR Act would be implemented immediately after receiving Parliamentary approval and President's assent, and a date of commencement would be notified separately.

The approval will help in developing the country's mining sector to its full potential so as to put the nation's mineral resources to best use for national economic growth, and ensure raw materials security in the long term national interest.

Background

The Government constituted a High Level Committee (HLC) in 2006, which suggested for evolving a mining code adapted to the best international practices, streamlining and simplifying procedures for grant of mineral concessions to reduce delays, etc. Based on the HLC recommendations, the Government had announced National Mineral Policy (NMP) on 13.3.2008. To give effect to the policy directions in NMP, the Government has now evolved a new Mines and Minerals (Development and Regulation) Bill, 2011, after several rounds of consultations with the stakeholders including State

Governments, concerned Ministries and Departments of Central Government, Industry and Civil Society. The MMDR Bill, 2011 was referred to a Group of Ministers (GoM) on 14.6.2010 and which has now, after five rounds of discussion, had recommended the draft Bill to the Cabinet. The GoM in its meeting held on 7th July, 2011 has recommended the draft MMDR Bill, 2011 for introduction in Parliament.

Source: http://pib.nic.in/newsite/erelease.aspx?relid=76352Accessed on Apr 12, 2014

23-August-2013 16:19 IST **Appendix E**

Press Information Bureau
Ministry of Mines, Government of India

The Mines and Minerals (Development and Regulation) Bill 2011 (MMDR Bill) was introduced in the Lok Sabha on 12.12.2011 which was then referred to the Standing Committee on Coal and Steel (Standing Committee) for examination and report on 05.1.2012. The Standing Committee submitted its 36th Report on the MMDR Bill on 07.5.2013. The recommendations made by the Standing Committee on the MMDR Bill are under consideration in the Ministry.

The salient features of the MMDR Bill, inter-alia, are as follows:

(i) It provides for a simple and transparent mechanism with clear and enforceable timelines for grant of mining lease or prospecting licence through competitive bidding in areas of known mineralization, and on the basis of first-in-time in areas where mineralization is not known,

(ii) It enables the mining holders to adopt the advanced and sophisticated technologies for exploration of deep-seated and concealed mineral deposits, especially of metals in short supply through a new concession,

(iii) It enables the Central Government to promote scientific mineral development through Mining Plans and Mine Closure Plans enforced by a central technical agency namely the Indian Bureau of Mines, as well as the Regulatory Authorities and Tribunals,

(iv) It empowers the State Governments to cancel the existing concessions or debar a person from obtaining concessions in future for preventing illegal and irregular mining,

(v) It empowers the Central and State Government to levy and collect cess,

(vi) Establishment of the Mineral Funds at National and State level for funding activities pertaining to capacity building of regulatory bodies like Indian Bureau of Mines and for research and development issues in the mining areas,

(vii) It provides for reservation of mineral bearing areas for the purpose of conservation of minerals,

(viii) It enables the registered co-operatives for obtaining mineral concessions on small deposits in order to encourage tribals and small miners to enter into mining activities,

(ix) It empowers the Central Government to institutionalize a statutory mechanism for ensuring sustainable mining with adequate concerns for environment and socio-economic issues in the mining areas, through a National Sustainable Development Framework,

(x) It provides for establishment of the National Mining Regulatory Authority which consists of a Chairperson and not more than nine members to advise Government on rates of royalty, dead rent, benefit sharing with District Mineral Foundation, quality standards, and also conduct investigation and launch prosecution in cases of large scale illegal mining,

(xi) It provides for establishment of the State Mining Regulatory Authority consisting of such persons as may be prescribed by the State Government to exercise the powers and functions in respect of minor minerals,

(xii) It provides for establishment of a National Mining Tribunal and State Mining Tribunals to exercise jurisdiction, powers and authority conferred on it under the proposed legislation,

(xiii) It empowers the State Governments to constitute Special Courts for purpose of providing speedy trial of the offences relating to illegal mining, and

(xiv) It empowers the Central Government to intervene in the cases of illegal mining where the concerned State Government fails to take action against illegal mining,

(xv) It provides for stringent punishments for contravention of provisions of the proposed legislation.

The Ministry has sought comments of various Central Ministries/ Departments, and of all State Governments & Union Territories on the Report of the Standing Committee on the MMDR Bill.

This information was given by the Minister of Mines, Shri Dinsha Patel in a written reply to a question in Lok Sabha today.

Source: http://pib.nic.in/newsite/PrintRelease.aspx?relid=98580. Accessed on Apr 12, 2014.

Index